D0806175

EXTRAMARITAL RELATIONS

GERHARD NEUBECK, editor of this book, is President of the American Association of Marriage Counselors and acting head of the Minnesota Family Study Center at the University of Minnesota in Minneapolis. He conducts a postdoctoral program on marriage counseling, as well as a private practice in marriage counseling.

EXTRAMARITAL RELATIONS

edited by

GERHARD NEUBECK

A SPECTRUM BOOK

Prentice-Hall, Inc., *Englewood Cliffs, N.J.*

We gratefully acknowledge permission to use the following materials reprinted in this book:
"On Marriage" by Thomas Flatman. In William Cole, ed., *Fireside Book of Humorous Poetry* (New York: Simon & Schuster, Inc., 1959), p. 405. Copyright © 1959 by William Cole. Reprinted by permission of Simon & Schuster.
Excerpts from *The Autobiography of Bertrand Russell* (Boston: Atlantic, Little, Brown and Co., 1967), pp. 10, 33. Copyright © 1967 by George Allen and Unwin, Ltd. Reprinted by permission of Atlantic, Little, Brown and Co. and George Allen and Unwin, Ltd.
The quotation from Dr. Joseph Fletcher is from a debate on the new morality printed in *Commonweal* (Volume 83, No. 14 [January 14, 1966], p. 431) and is reprinted by permission of the publisher.
The epigraph is a quotation by Erik H. Erikson from *Identity, Youth and Crisis* (New York: W. W. Norton and Company, Inc., 1968).

 C–13-298166-1; P–13-298158-0. *Library of Congress Catalog Card Number* 70–90973. Printed in the United States of America.

Current printing (last number):
10 9 8 7 6 5 4 3 2 1

Prentice-Hall International, Inc. (*London*)
Prentice-Hall of Australia, Pty. Ltd. (*Sydney*)
Prentice-Hall of Canada, Ltd. (*Toronto*)
Prentice-Hall of India Private Limited (*New Delhi*)
Prentice-Hall of Japan, Inc. (*Tokyo*)

This book is dedicated to my intramarital friends, Ruth, Ralph, Eva, and Peter, and to my many extramarital ones, secretaries, students, and colleagues. Pat Norling, my girl Friday for this special project, deserves particular mention, and so does George Coy of Prentice-Hall who kept after me. Thanks to all of you.

CONTRIBUTORS

STEPHEN E. BELTZ is a behavioral psychologist and Executive Director of the Center for Behavior Modification, Inc., in Philadelphia, Pennsylvania. He received his PhD at Pennsylvania State University. Dr. Beltz is happily married with five children, all by the same wife! His main interests are the applications of behavioral principles to everyday life.

WILLIAM GRAHAM COLE has been President of Lake Forest College since 1960. He received the BA and PhD degrees from Columbia University and the BD from Union Theological Seminary, and has served on the faculties of Western Reserve University, Smith College, and Williams College. He is the author of *Sex in Christianity and Psychoanalysis* and *Sex and Love in the Bible* and is the Founding Director of the Sex Information and Education Council.

JOHN F. CUBER is Professor of Sociology at The Ohio State University. He received his PhD at the University of Michigan and has taught at Sioux Falls College, Marietta College, and Kent State University. Dr. Cuber wrote the first book on marriage counseling published in the United States, *Marriage Counseling Practice,* and is the author of numerous articles in professional journals. His most recent book (with Peggy B. Harroff) is *The Significant Americans: A Study of Sexual Behavior Among the Affluent.*

ALBERT ELLIS is Executive Director of the Institute of Advanced Study in Rational Psychotherapy and practices individual psychotherapy, marriage and family therapy, group therapy, and marathon encounter therapy at its Consultation Center. He is the author of over 250 articles and many books, including *Sex Without Guilt, A Guide to Rational Living,* the *Art and Science of Love,* and *Reason and Emotion in Psychotherapy.*

YOON HOUGH KIM is Assistant Professor of Sociology at East Carolina University, N.C. He received a law degree in his native country, Korea, and received the MA and PhD degrees from the University of Minnesota. He is the author of the forthcoming research monograph, "The Community of the Blind."

HYMAN RODMAN is a Sociologist at the Merrill-Palmer Institute and Member of the Board of Directors of the National Council on Family Relations. He received his BA and MA at McGill University and his PhD at Harvard University and has taught at Harvard, Boston, and Wayne State universities. Since 1960, he has been engaged in research on lower-class family organization and values.

CONSTANTINA SAFILIOS-ROTHSCHILD is Senior Research Associate at the Merrill-Palmer Institute, Research Association at the Harvard Center for Population Studies, and Adjunct Professor at the Department of Sociology, Wayne State University. A Greek citizen and a permanent resident of the United States, she has conducted comparative family studies in America and Greece. She has served as associate editor of the *Journal of Marriage and the Family,* has published many articles on family fertility, mental illness, and social stratification, and is preparing a textbook of comparative family sociology.

VERA M. SCHLETZER is Associate Professor of Psychology and Director of Counseling at the University of Minnesota. She received her BA at Ohio University and her MA and PhD degrees at the University of Minnesota. She has published numerous articles in professional journals.

ROBERT N. WHITEHURST is Associate Professor of Sociology at Indiana University in Fort Wayne, Indiana. He received his BA at Butler University and his MS and PhD degrees at Purdue University and has taught at Bowling Green State University. Dr. Whitehurst is a reserve officer in the Naval Air Force.

CONTENTS

Part Three: Cause or Effect? *127*

"Fidelity without a sense of diversity can become an obsession and a bore; diversity without a sense of fidelity, an empty relativism."

—Erik H. Erikson

EXTRAMARITAL RELATIONS

Part One

WE ARE HUMAN

Extramarital relations have existed as long as has marriage itself. There are references to it in the laws and taboos of many lands and cultures. Strangely enough, there are only a handful of studies or books about this subject, even though people talk about it a great deal and there are many references to infidelity in popular articles. This volume has been put together to fill a definite void. Authors from many fields have contributed their ideas. There are research studies, theoretical formulations, and case histories.

In areas where there is a great deal of opinion and feeling, I hope to help the reader to study the human phenomenon of extramarital relations in a more comprehensive way. This book is not meant to be a "how-to" or a "how-not-to" compendium, however. Subjectivity is not totally avoided; polemics are.

Anthropological studies have shown us where other cultures stand in regard to monogamy and extramarital relations. The Kinsey studies, summarized here by Yoon Hough Kim, give us evidence of the contemporary American extramarital scene. But what is evident from these studies, and openly displayed in everyday public behavior, is denied in our public acknowledgments.

The second chapter is a reprint of an earlier published paper of mine and is designed to introduce the reader to conceptualizations about extramarital relations. Following a lead by Kurt Lewin, I tried to view marriage as a group situation, and this led me to understand more precisely how difficult monogamous marriages can be.

This is further illustrated by the rich interchange among various professionals who really let themselves go in the chapter entitled "Two Clinicians and a Sociologist." Here clinical and personal insight blend with theoretical concepts and open the way to further explorations for the reader who wants to be more subjective.

Our ethnic heritage is described by William Graham Cole. We are, after all, the latest in a long line of cultures influenced by the Judeo-Christian tradition, and Cole has traced this moral tradition.

Gerhard Neubeck

PERSPECTIVES

TYPICAL SITUATIONS

Mr. and Mrs. L are in their middle forties and for twenty years have had a relatively successful marriage. At a national sales meeting Mr. L attends a party, flirts and is flirted with, and ends up with a single woman in her room and spends the night.

The D's, also in their forties, have a rather stormy marriage although the marriage has survived. Mr. D has a relationship with another woman he met through his business affairs; this relationship has lasted for about four years. The other woman has an apartment, and Mr. D visits her regularly.

Mr. F, happily married, has a tremendous social life. He flirts with a great many women, and on one occasion at a social dance he has an erection. He and his dancing partner talk about this erotic experience, but no further sexual advances are made.

Mr. and Mrs. S, who have a humdrum life together, are on vacation. At poolside in a motel in the far West they become acquainted with another couple. The two couples spend two hours together swimming and drinking. During this time, Mrs. S and the other husband appear to be attracted to each other, but nothing comes of this except for some attempts they make to grab each other in the pool.

Before going to sleep, Mr. P fantasizes of seducing his secretary, who began working the first time that day. Mr. P has been married in a routine sort of way for twenty years, and has had these fantasies about his secretaries off and on, but has never made a pass at any of the girls up to this point.

Mrs. K dreams of escaping to a desert island with her fantasy lover, whom she conjures up every night before going to sleep. She is fifty, has been divorced once, and is now married to a man whom she does not love but with whom she has a rather successful marriage in terms of day-to-day life.

In a metropolitan area a young lawyer and his wife, deep in their cups with another young married couple in their late twenties, decide, on the spur of the moment, that they want to experiment. After some checking out among all four, the couples switch partners. The morning after, nothing is said and no further switches are arranged for.

Mrs. V, in her late twenties, a personnel worker in a large industrial firm, is carried off her feet by a company executive. She accepts his invitation for a drink after work and the evening ends up as an adventure in a motel room. Mrs. V, afraid of pregnancy, begins using birth control pills. The company executive is married and he makes no further attempts to continue the relationship.

A couple in their late thirties have three children. He is a self-employed accountant. On the surface, their marriage appears to be successful, but they both feel a lack of satisfaction. He is on the church board. During the meetings he becomes enamored of a woman on the board. After one meeting they have coffee together. They continue to meet for coffee for four years. There is no attempt at converting this relationship into a sexual one, but the need for each other is great. The wife discovers the relationship and breaks it up.

We have names for all this: extramarital relations, infidelity, adultery, unfaithfulness, affairs. Women and men, men and women. The eternal attraction between the sexes, the basic desire of the one for the other. Since the beginning of time there have been pairings and rules declaring which pairings were proper, which improper. But always—he and she, she and he.

But the he's and she's do not necessarily remain the same. That is the theme of this book. If anything is true, then it is true that next to the eternal polar bond, there is the eternal triangle, a third party, a new man or a new woman who appears on the horizon, comes closer and closer, and then become a new twosome, another him for her, a new her for him. Accidentally, deliberately, planned—what does it matter? Male and female He made. Mother and sons, father and daughters, virgins and roués, young and old, the never-ending stream of human beings attracted to and by human beings of the opposite sex.

THE HUMAN CONDITION

This book is concerned with extramarital heterosexual relationships. Since marriage has been and still is the norm, the term "extramarital" is, of course, quite legitimate. But as Hy Rodman, in his chapter on West Indian patterns points out, and the anthropological literature in general reflects as well, marriage is a flexible arrangement and it exists in a variety of forms, all of which have their own version of what extramarital means. Polygamy is a form of marriage, obviously, but from another point of view relations with a second wife are perceived as an extramarital affair. What is this extramarital system like? That is the question which needs to be answered in order to determine the character of the relationship with a third party.

The human condition implies a continuous searching for love and attention, occasionally sublimated and diverted, but often rawly sought and passionately set into motion. The marital condition, as we will see through these pages (at least in its monogamous form), leaves much to be desired in providing love as a steady diet; so if love is seen as just around the corner of another establishment (so often erroneously), it is grabbed. That is the human condition.

But, as Erich Fromm has so definitely said, love is more than making love. Yet making love has achieved, at least in recent years, a quality of its own, apart from the deeper commitments that the Frommian concepts seem to imply. The pleasantness of a short-term relationship within the bonds of mutual care seems to be accepted in our culture today, to a certain degree, as a valid human encounter. An example is the reply to a question I put to a woman:

> You ask me what it takes for me to do it with a man not my husband. The answer, of course, is complicated, but actually all of the deliberations have gone on before. Once the scene is set, I seem to be single minded, and nothing seems to interfere any more. I am eager to be with this guy and his crotch, so I hasten to get skin to skin and to have him in me. That is the fun I am looking for. Nothing else counts. Now if you ask me if I am looking for it, that's another matter. I am not usually, but since we get to talk in the neighborhood, we started to experiment, and since we are agreeable, well, that's it. Now why are we agreeable? Perhaps this came more for intellectual reasons. We are in a way experimental minded, but also, of course, we are adventurous, and so it went. Of course, I have to like the guy to a certain degree, but maybe even that isn't important. But I don't know. If I didn't like him, we wouldn't have made the arrangements in the first place. But I think once the stage is set, that is, we are in the same room together

> for the purpose of going to bed, then nothing matters, like I said before. I go completely into heat. That is the best way I can describe it.

Therefore, when it involves a non-spouse and can be accepted or tolerated by a spouse, sexual relations can enlarge the realm of human experience. This acceptance and tolerance, of course, is still to come. The majority of the population, when confronted with what they believe is a breach of the mores, will probably feel and act with hostility. The question of tolerance may be related not only to the wish to be the *only* loved one, but, more importantly, to be the qualitatively *best* one to have around. We want love and when it is not forthcoming, when constant exposure has eroded interest in one another, then a new partner brings new moods, new opportunities to reveal oneself, and obviously presents a new way of love. A new partner presents a change in a person's life who is hungry for change. The trouble with permanence is that people change over time as well, and a husband or wife who does not work at providing answers for new needs obviously runs the risk of others' providing answers to the needs of their spouse. In his chapter, Beltz describes a number of couples whose longings led them to personal complications and consequent destruction of the existing marriage. Their personalities, however, seem to have led them relentlessly into self-defeating behavior, not only on the sexual level but also on the marital. Marriage could not offer them a solution, but neither could extramarital affairs. They feel doomed. Perhaps many of us are doomed. Is there no solution to the quest for love on a permanent basis?

Robert Blood and others have talked about disenchantment, and the term "seven-year itch" is well understood. But to go to a third party for love when love is not present or available or possible in a current marital relationship is only one of the motives.

Human nature has still another pattern to offer: rules beg to be broken. So the taboo on outside relationships offers a challenge. "Why observe it?" says the rebel, and the flaunting of the taboo becomes a project, regardless of the person involved. A momentum is begun based on some *idée fixe,* a compulsion, and the person to whom one relates (with whom one "sleeps") is only a tool in the realization of an idea.

A SWEEPING PANORAMA

Attraction to people other than spouses is universal. As a psychologist, I know of individual differences and understand that some of us are more attracted to outsiders than others, but the phenomenon is a global one and one doesn't have to look very far to discover this theme, even if it is not present in oneself.

The fantasy of the child seeking his mother in the arms of a man not his father (believe in the Oedipus complex or not) to the works of fiction culminating in the 1968 John Updike novel, *Couples,* from the mate-swapping clubs of today to the polygamous patterns of yesteryears' Mormons.

These experiences have been recorded across the human horizon, from Sexton's beautiful poem in *The New Yorker* of February 3, 1968, "For a Lover Returning to His Wife," to Thomas Flatman's poem (3) called, "On Marriage":

> How happy a thing were a wedding,
> And a bedding,
> If a man might purchase a wife
> For twelvemonth and a day;
> But to live with her all a man's life,
> For ever and for aye,
> Till she grow as gray as a cat,
> Good faith, Mr. Parson, excuse me from that!

Reality: the humanitarian and scientific convictions that produced the events set down in Bertrand Russell's *Autobiography*:

> They obtained for my brother a tutor of some scientific ability—so at least I judge from a reference to his work in William James's *Psychology*. He was a Darwinian and was engaged in studying the instincts of chickens, which, to facilitate his studies, were allowed to work havoc in every room in the house, including the drawingroom. He himself was in an advanced stage of consumption and died not very long after my father. Apparently upon grounds of pure theory, my father and mother decided that although he ought to remain childless on account of his tuberculosis, it was unfair to expect him to be celibate. My mother, therefore, allowed him to live with her, though I know of no evidence that she allowed any pleasure from doing so. This arrangement subsisted for a very short time, as it began after my birth and I was only two years old when my mother died. (7, p. 10)

On another occasion Russell speaks about his mother's mother and says,

> Since I reached adolescence she began to try to counteract what she considered namby-pamby in my upbringing. She would say that nobody can say nothing against me, but I always say that it is not so

> hard to break the seventh commandment as the sixth, because at any rate it requires the consent of the other party. (7, p. 33)

Speaking of tolerance, what other than a humanitarian/scientific intellectualism made it possible for Russell's father to enter into this arrangement?

Since its invention the novel has shown the side of life that science has only recently begun to analyze, and this is not the place to evaluate the many attempts that writers have made to picture complex relations among three people. A recent attempt by the French writer Georges Simenon in *The Confessional* has added one dimension: when a young son discovers his mother's infidelity he is given a larger understanding about this matter by his father. As far as tolerance is concerned, perhaps the suggestion here is that, as an extramarital affair becomes known throughout the family, tolerance is needed by the other members as well as by the spouse. I mentioned Updike's book earlier. He has attempted, of course, to show the pan-sexuality of a modern suburban community and its futile attempts to discover meaning within this. Despite Updike's beautifully professional writing, we do not gain insight into either motivation or resolution, but we do obtain a realistic picture of what it takes for couples to "get together."

The extramarital experience has been reflected in stories and jokes. One of these is the well-known story of the psychiatrist who goes to a convention in another town and sends his wife a card. She reads it and sends him a card saying, "Dear, your Freudian slip is showing." When he returns home he confronts her and asks her what she meant. His wife shows him the card he had sent her, which reads, "Dear, having a wonderful time, wish you were her." Another story bearing on this point concerns a group of film people in the 1940's, among them the then most beautiful woman in the world. As the story goes, the talk came around to fantasizing oneself on a desert island with someone other than one's spouse, and the woman is said to have revealed that her dream was to be on a desert island with her favorite obstetrician.

In this cursory review of extramarital relations throughout the total culture, psychiatry is next. There are many points of view that reflect various theoretical positions within that field. Psychoanalysis, represented by Leon Saul's recent work, *Fidelity and Infidelity* (8), in which continuous monogamous marriage is seen as a healthy way of life and in which lack of achievement of such a marriage is related to intra- and interpersonal disturbances. Fidelity is the normal, good way of life; infidelity a sick way of life. People like O. Spurgeon English in "The Affair" in the journal *Voices* (5), and Titus P. Bellville (1), writing in *Medical Aspects of Human Sexuality*, however, do not take this point of view. English sees the possibility of an extramarital relationship fulfilling deep personal needs. Bellville takes the point of view that infidelity is not only based on abnormalities or deviate sexual desires, but that it may be a search for new forms of human endeavor.

Sociologists have seen the area of sexual relations as a field for studying contrasting cultural norms, and have made many contributions to this area. Christensen (2), for instance, compared American and Scandinavian sex norms and was one of the first to discover the more liberal leanings of the Scandinavians, a discovery that has been confirmed since his first studies appeared. *The American Annals of Political and Social Science* devoted their March, 1968, issue to sex and the contemporary American scene, and some reference to extramarital coitus was included. However, it was really a rather curious effort to put extramarital coitus into the category of sexual deviance, neglecting the view that the cause of extramarital relationships may be marriage itself. Anthropologists have studied this area more than any other group, and a chapter in this book is a review of anthropological points of view. More in line with our overview here, Margaret Mead, in the Summer, 1967, issue of *Daedalus* suggests, "Up to the present, the events of malfunctioning of existing social forms has been ineffective in raising questions about our emphasis on the exclusive dependence on a single mate. (With its implications of serial monogamy). . . ." So Margaret Mead is obviously aware of the difficulty of the monogamous system.

The earnest attempts of researchers to see extramarital relations as a human phenomenon as well as that of novelists to see extramarital relationships as a human experience seem quite proper. That such earnest attempts should be critically reviewed by moralists is to be expected. A recent example of this sort of criticism is a pamphlet by Frank M. Darrow, "Sex Ethics for Survival," a polemic in which history is quoted in a fortuitous fashion and the death of cultures is related to the liberalization of marital norms (4). Darrow claims that "In each society where sexual opportunity was reduced to a minimum, society began to display great energy." His logic and evidence leave much to be desired.

CONCLUSION

The theme is everywhere, and it has existed since there has been marriage. This book, with its research and theory, discussion and deliberation, is only a limited attempt to bring the issues up to date. This collection will be out of date as soon as it is published. But it should serve the function of taking the problem seriously. As with other issues, we have reached a time where we need no longer be afraid to discuss a controversial phenomenon. This fear to be improper, I believe, is a major reason why extensive research on extramarital relations has not been attempted before.

This book gives a description of extramarital patterns, not a prescription for or a proscription against them. Albert Ellis comes closer than any other contributor to this volume to making actual recommendations.

The "attraction is a constant" theme is stressed. But it is also strongly suggested that extramarital relations are sought when the marriage has left needs unfulfilled, and that extramarital relations do not necessarily lead to the breakup of a marriage. All in all, it has been my intention to talk less about the statistical frequencies of extramarital relations than to stress the nature and character of this phenomenon itself.

Again, attraction is a constant, and marriage is difficult. Jerome Weidman in his book, *My Daughter Iris,* says, "Human beings do not obtain possession of each other when they marry. All they obtain is the right to work at the job of holding on to each other."

The difficulties of marriage can also be illustrated by an analogy: marriage is not unlike an automobile. One chooses a model, sometimes with care, often impulsively. Once one gets the car one better take care of it, wash it and polish it once in awhile, clean the carburetor, and for God's sake, watch the differential. Lubrication is a must, and tire changes are necessary at certain intervals. Proper acceleration is only possible if the points are in good shape. And one gets better mileage by using "super." And even with all this attention, a new model may seem more attractive, and a trade-in may be in order. Drive carefully.

We should not underestimate that together with affinities in marriage also go hostilities generated by the conflict of the wanting to be together and having to be together. Love and hate, as we know, are not as far apart as rational definition would have it.

References

1. Bellville, Titus P. "A Psychiatrist Looks at Infidelity," *Medical Aspects of Human Sexuality*, 3, No. 4 (Winter 1967), 9–14.
2. Christensen, Harold T. "Scandinavia and American Sex Norms," *The Journal of Social Issues,* 22 (No. 2), 60–75, 1966.
3. Cole, William (Ed.). *The Fireside Book of Humorous Poetry.* New York: Simon and Schuster, Inc., 1959.

4. DARROW, FRANK M. *Sex Ethics for Survival.* Hanford, California: Scott Printing, 1968.
5. ENGLISH, O. SPURGEON. "Values in Psychotherapy: The Affair," *Voices,* 3, No. 4), 9–14, 1967.
6. OTTO, HERBERT A., and JOHN MANN. *Ways of Growth; Approaches to Expanding Awareness.* New York: Grossman Publishers, 1968.
7. RUSSELL, BERTRAND. *The Autobiography of Bertrand Russell.* Boston: Atlantic Press Book, Little, Brown and Co., 1967.
8. SAUL, LEON. *Fidelity and Infidelity, and What Makes or Breaks a Marriage.* Philadelphia: J. B. Lippincott Co., 1967.

Gerhard Neubeck

THE DIMENSIONS OF THE "EXTRA" IN EXTRAMARITAL RELATIONS

IMPLICIT AND EXPLICIT GROUND RULES

Anyone who writes about marriage must deal with the problem of ground rules. Men and women who have agreed to live together in that relationship we have called marriage are bound by such ground rules, be they implicit or explicit. The evolution of these ground rules is well known, and they have remained relatively stable for centuries. Though often questioned, in recent years more serious doubts about such ground rules have been raised. Experiments engaged in by married men and women showed that transgressions of ground rules did not necessarily end up in the destruction of the marriage. The writer has previously suggested in other research (7, 8) that the problem of ground rules be investigated further.

One must start with the assumption that whatever ground rules exist are subject to local cultural as well as overall sociological/psychological deviation. The ground rules, of course, have been shaped and refined by religious institutions, and in almost all societies are codified by governmental authority. Again, interpretation of the rules will differ from person to person, from couple to couple. Variation within the marital pair—for whatever reason, be it culture or sex-linked—is a problem which will be discussed later. As Foote (2) suggests, marital dynamics may also vary according to developmental phases of the marriage.

It is certainly difficult to extrapolate from this complex set of rules (which for the individual before he or she is married exists in the

"The Dimensions of the 'Extra' in Extramarital Relations," by Gerhard Neubeck. From Hirsch L. Silverman, *Marital Counseling: Psychology, Ideology, Science*, 1967. Reprinted by permission of Charles C Thomas, Publisher, Springfield, Illinois.

abstract) a set of personal, marital expectations. Yet, individuals do grow up with personal goals to be fulfilled through marriage, goals which will determine to a large degree the interpretation they will make of the ground rules and the decisions they are going to make to live by them or violate them.

We know, of course, that, with rare exceptions, ground rules are hardly ever specifically discussed before marriage, but are nevertheless *assumed* to be the same for both spouses. Rarely is there an explicit agreement ahead of the marriage ceremony. Jokes, cartoons and commentaries about the violation of ground rules by some one person occasionally give people an opportunity to think about the rules, but only infrequently is this a serious and weighty consideration. Only when a ground rule has been violated does the consideration become critical. For most persons the rules agreed to during the marriage ceremony or in discussions of the rules with the clergy in premarital instruction are taken for granted. I doubt that many individuals really internalize the meaning of these rules at this, the so-promising stage of marital union.

This is not to say that in the fantasy life of individuals ground rules are not dealt with. To whom one is married forever and ever or what other heroes may appear on the scene may indeed occupy the dream world of our lovers. But after all *this* kind of world is not for real. One thing is certain, though; ground rules have never included the realm of fantasy; ground rules govern behavior. (It also follows that there are no external penalties for transgression of rules when transgressions take place in fantasy.)

In today's world the problem of ground rules receives a great deal of attention. Stage and television, films, novels, real-life events of the neighbor next door present us with frequent examples of how the rules work or fail to work. Occasionally this leads to an actual challenge of the validity of the rules, though the discussion is usually fainthearted and abortive; it is taboo territory except for iconoclasts writing in offbeat journals. The only serious attempt that I know, one which received a good deal of public attention, was Albee's *Who's Afraid of Virginia Woolf?* But the problem of ground rules does deserve our attention.

WHAT ARE THE GROUND RULES?

1. Individuals enter marriage on a voluntary basis.
2. Marriage is a permanent relationship.
3. In monogamous marriage one man is married to one woman.

While partners marry voluntarily, these marriages take place in a culture which places high value on marriage and in which an ever-increasing number of the population does marry. While marriage is assumed to be permanent, divorces are permitted in a majority of cultures, and the contract, "till death us do part," remains unfulfillable. The third rule, in which marriage is regarded as an exclusive relationship—the seventh commandment—implies that marital parties are assumed to be sufficient unto each other in the areas of human functioning, to the marked exclusion of outsiders (4). It is this third rule on which this paper's attention is focused.

Jackson has commented also on what he calls the "Achilles paradox." Though a voluntary act to begin with, marriage continues on the basis of "having to want to stay together." As Torbett and I have pointed out earlier (8), "We must examine how this voluntary relationship, this regulated coming together, fulfills the expectations of meeting needs for both of the participants, the spouses." Winch and his associates (9) investigated this problem, and a host of others have since addressed themselves to the question of complementary needs. Torbett and I asked the question: "How well does *marriage* do the job of meeting the expectations of the spouses?" The term "efficiency" was then introduced, which Webster defines as: "Serving to effect the purpose, or producing intended or expected results." We went on: "How effectively is marriage working for those who enter it? . . . Effectiveness in marriage can only take place when both spouses behave toward each other in certain ways. Marital effectiveness is a product of the effectiveness of both spouses. The institution of marriage can only be effective when both spouses behave in these certain ways." We further claimed that "effectiveness can only be produced if, when one partner expresses a need for a certain satisfaction from the other, this other assumes the obligation to meet that need." This is Jackson's Achilles paradox. The obligation to meet a spouse's need starts out as a "means to an end." But as behavior it develops quickly into an "end in itself," and possibly into a need. If I assume an obligation to meet my spouse's need for closeness—however that is felt—and come close, I have also met my need for wanting to please. My behavior is means and end at one and the same time. Obligation and need-fulfillment are so closely linked that it is probably impossible to distinguish between them in most marital situations.

MARRIAGE AS A GROUP SITUATION

Significance

The environment in which the needs of marital partners can be met mutually can best be described by referring to the marriage situation as a group situation. The work of Lewin (1940) has been helpful in conceptualizing marriage as a group, and, more recently, Levinger has used this concept. Lewin's essay, "The Background of Conflict in Marriage," dates to 1940 and was published in his book, *Resolving Social Conflicts* (6). He begins this essay by saying: "Marriage is a group situation, and, as such, shows the general characteristics of group life." Levinger (5), in a piece called "Marital Cohesiveness and Dissolution: An Integrative Review," declares that "the marriage pair is a two-person group." I am borrowing this concept from Lewin and Levinger to describe further the environment for which the ground rules are operative.

Lewin declares that married group life has greater significance than ordinary group life since "marriage is very closely related to the vital problems in the central layer of the person, to his values, fantasies, social and economic status. Unlike other groups, marriage deals not merely with one of the aspects of the person, but with his entire physical and social existence." Lewin further describes the adaptation of the individual to the group. He declares that "belonging to a certain group does not mean that the individual must be in accord in every respect with the goals, regulations and the style of living and thinking of the group. The individual has, to a certain degree, his own personal goals." It can be readily seen, however, that in a two-person group, deviation from group goals may be much more catastrophic than in a group in which there are greater opportunities for a pooling of personal goals. Deviation in a group of two obviously has greater consequences than deviation in a group of six or twelve. Lewin himself says later on that, "because of the small number of members in the group, every move of one member will, relatively speaking, deeply affect the other members, and the state of the group. In other words, the smallness of the group makes its members very interdependent."

Social Distance

Another aspect of the marital situation as a group situation is the variation in social distance. Lewin says: ". . . willingness to marry is considered as a symptom of desire for the least social distance." What is said here, then, it seems, is that the willingness to marry itself is an admission of the willingness to lose a degree of privacy and accept permanent proximity. It obviously follows that privacy is restricted in marriage. Levinger also quotes the work of Festinger, Schachter and Back when he refers to their definition of group cohesiveness as "the total field of forces which act on members to remain in the group." So, with the lack of privacy and the quest for permanent proximity, cohesiveness is established which in itself, then, is a constant reinforcer of the maintenance of the group situation, i.e., the marriage situation.

Free Movement

Closely related to this is Lewin's reference to the amount of space of free movement of a person. He goes on to say: ". . . too small a space of movement generally leads to a high state of tension." This confinement to the small space of the two-person married group quite likely leads to the seeking of less-confining situations, though again this may be dependent on how much free movement is required by an individual.

Jealousy

Lewin, in his 1940 analysis of the marriage group situation, is not afraid to suggest some ideas about jealousy. His explanation of jealousy is based partly on the feeling that one's property is taken away. Lewin suggests that a great amount of overlapping exists: "from the tendency of love to be all inclusive, this feeling may be easily aroused if the relation between two persons is very close." He goes on to say that "the intimate relation of one partner to a third person not only makes the second partner 'lose' the first one, but the second partner will have, in addition, the feeling that something of his own intimate life is thrown open to a third person." By permitting his marriage partner to enter his intimate life he did not mean to throw it open to the public. The relation of the partner to the third person is felt as a "breach in the barrier between one's intimate life and the public."

If I understand Lewin correctly, he suggests that, whatever the marriage environment furnishes in line with need satisfactions, the environment itself is confining and will force group members to make certain kinds of sacrifices in order for these needs to be met. The sacrifice includes not only a lack of freedom but also the sharing of property, in this case the properties of one's spouse, and the giving up of relationships with a variety of other peripherally related individuals.

Abstraction and Reality

Again, it must be emphasized that the degree of deprivation and the degree of frustration are highly individualized and can be measured only on an individual basis in line with the kinds of conditioning and building up of expectations that we have described earlier as a function of early upbringing and learning. The hypothesis that suggests itself, however, is quite clear. The greater the need for freedom, the more confining the marriage environment might be, and the subsequent wish to escape from it; the greater the need for the possession of property and subsequent unwillingness to share property, the greater the jealousy and willingness to be faithful on one's own part. It must be understood, however, that these are highly abstract expectations and that they may be discarded in the wake of impulses that are triggered by tempting situations. We also know that the double standard is applied here, so that faithfulness is expected more of women than of men. Again I would think, however, that this is a result of the ability to control superego functions in regard to impulse stimuli (7).

Marriages Have Developmental Phases

Lewin, in his essay, contributes an idea that has not been developed by anyone else until recently. He spoke of marriage as a group in the making. This refers to what is now called the life cycle of a marriage (though he did not lay down any rules in the essay which would describe in more detail the various cycles such as early marriage, marriage in the thirties, and later marriages). He suggests, however, that in the young marriage, "the situation is not clear in regard to the balance between one's own needs and those of the partner. That leaves typical conflicts, but at the same time allows greater flexibility for their solution."

OBLIGATIONS AND ROUTINES

I discussed earlier some aspects of the voluntary *versus* the obligatory responsibilities between marital partners. The hopes from premarital days that "hubby" will do all those nice things develops quickly into an expectation that hubby has a duty to do them. But there is more that takes place than a change in expectations: Need-meeting behaviors become routinized. They become routine duties. It is from this shift from the voluntary "wanting to" to the obligatory routinizing that we can explain the feelings voiced that "our marriage has gone stale." The "fun" has gone out of the relationship. "Fun" depends in this case on more spontaneous actions, actions decided on when and how the mood strikes one rather than when one is "scheduled" to perform these acts. With such "fun" missing it is likely that relationships are sought which by the very fact that they are outside of the marriage promise voluntary and spontaneous responses. This may be similar to or accompanied by a need for "playfulness," to which I will refer shortly.

OVEREXPOSURE AND VARIETY

Other dynamics of the marital situation can be viewed as overexposure, with subsequent satiation. Since marriage is expected to extend over the total life span, exposure will be constant, and there is no escaping from the presence of the other person with whom one "lives together." This permanent togetherness results in quantitative and qualitative exposure that may lead to satiation, since there is only a finite number of personality aspects available. These traits or characteristics may be exhausted, though occasionally they can be altered enough to serve as a new challenge. When the scenery remains constant, however, after a while one may have seen enough, and new scenery looks desirable. On the other hand, it may not be impossible that, in some cases, marriage partners who seek escape avenues from the steady, taken-for-granted confrontations with their mates, once recognizing this need, can develop within their marriage such conditions that would offer them new glimpses at each other under new circumstances and in different environments, with new horizons from what life was like before. But even such attempts are governed by the limitations within the very nature of personality and personality interaction; there is only a certain degree of variability. When needs for variability are not met sufficiently, a new person with a new set of characteristics will seem attractive. Not only is the grass greener on the other side, it is also a different kind of grass.

Closely connected with this is the feeling of boredom. If all the "tunes" upon the instrument of our personalities have been played, and even the variations have been exhausted, and even when, after having given the instrument a rest, a taking up of the old exercises and the playing of the well-known tunes has brought temporary satisfactions, will they not soon yield to the resignation that it is "the same old thing, all over again"? Bored, one turns away from an instrument that offers no new discoveries and turns to one that does offer them.

PLAYFULNESS

Playfulness itself, implying lack of seriousness and, to a degree, lack of responsibility, is in many ways incompatible with married life. Individuals with psychopathic personalities do not fit into the restricted space of marriage. Because marriage calls for responsibilities and seriousness, the playful personality cannot find enough opportunity for play and will look for such opportunities where they can be found. Outside of those persons who are outright psychopaths, however, there are many whose playfulness is not socially destructive. For them marriage can become a playground where games of many varieties can be played. To what degree such couples can build into their life together experiences which momentarily have a minimum amount of seriousness and responsibility, such as "evenings out," vacations (depending upon the age of the children and other phases of the marriage) or conduct that includes a certain degree of playfulness, will be the result of a shared system of values that regards playfulness as not only legitimate but even wholesome. Traits such as flirtatiousness may also be related to the kind of game-playing mentioned above. If flirtation, according to the dictionary, means "making love without meaning it," it is obviously not possible to flirt with a spouse. A spouse is not a candidate for consummation; spouses have already consummated. Reintroducing elements of courtship into one's life can only be accomplished by the courting of someone new.

With such courting may also go a degree of anxiety, a non-crippling type, which a person needs to sustain an emotional momentum. Such anxiety-provoking moments are hard to find in a relationship with a mate of long standing, and newcomers will seem attractive. This anxiety will then be fostered by situations which make one live more dangerously, live with ambiguity, live in a vacuum rather than in the well-defined, well-circumscribed, as well as predictable, marital environment. Only those marital situations which open themselves up to experimentation among spouses will bring enough security to prevent experimenting on the "outside" for the experimentally minded person.

SEXUALITY

There is no special reason why sexual needs should not be seen in a vein similar to that of other marital dynamics. That it has received and maintained a special loading, however, is clearly traceable to the taboos surrounding sexual conduct. These are likely to remain with us, and will, therefore, give the sexual area an aura that it really does not warrant. Let us look at the phenomenon of sexuality in greater detail since it does have a complexity all its own.

A good deal of recent writing has attempted to see sexual appetite as related to an exclusively physiological base, an appetite for both spouse or other-than-spouse partner. Other writers and researchers, notably Ford and Beach (3), produced evidence that sexual response is a physiological/social/psychological phenomenon, and extramarital sex activity should be seen in this context. (Even enormous sexual appetite, let us say a few standard deviations away from the Kinsey norms, cannot be understood simply as mere physiological drive.)

Sexual relations with "outsiders" can then be seen against the background of the earlier discussion. The relative importance of sexual expression will leave the individual to concentrate on that aspect of the "outside" relationship rather than on another. Sexual relations may become inevitable, not necessarily because one "lusts" sexually after the "outsider," but because one believes sex belongs in the relationship. This is true in light of the fact that sex carries with it a symbolic function. So, while sexual activity serves basic physiological needs, the psychological ones are not far behind. Our culture makes manifold uses of sexual stimuli, and it is easy to fall for the "sex thing" even if sexuality is not what is primarily wanted. Sex is "in," and one better have it. This is not to say that there are not perhaps a great many individuals who are naturally and simply desirous of sex partners who may be other people's spouses. And again, in fantasy such pairings are often imagined and consummated. Men, more so than women, are given to fantasy couplings. By the mere fact that we are men and women, attraction is a constant. Our ground rules of long standing forbid us to go further than fantasy, but the rules are often broken, and some cultures do not include rules that forbid sexual enjoyment of other people's mates. A few more primitive cultures actually encourage it. Unfortunately, there are also a set of individuals, notably the psychopaths already mentioned, whose emotional and sexual impulses are not governable by either internal or external controls. The objects of their impulsivity are seldom aware that they are simply utilized for essentially exploitative purposes, sexual ones in this case, though there is probably a good deal of mutual exploitation as well.

In the sexual area, temptation has greater significance than in others because we value sex so greatly today. But Oscar Wilde's bon mot, "I can resist everything but temptation," really points to what is regarded as the "right opportunity." Opportunities which bring one together alone with a nonspouse are almost expected to produce an extramarital sexual involvement. Partial opportunities of this sort are built into our social life. Party ritual calls for a degree of flirtation. There are seductive moves, first tentative "dares," then more pronounced invitations that end up in full-fledged sexual episodes. Our culture, while explicitly puritanical, promotes social affairs which are, in fact, institutionalizing men-women opportunities. There is, for example, the case of social dancing, where close bodily contact is "allowed," leading not infrequently to sexual relations as a matter of course.

The "seven-year itch" phenomenon or the middle-age adventure refers to a yet different aspect of extramarital activity. Linked to the age of the marriage, it is implied that, periodically, sexual appetites arise which have as their target a person outside the marriage. But, since we have assumed earlier that this sexual appetite really encompasses a variety of other motivations, these "itchings" should then be understood as the arising of new needs over the life span of the marriage which, if not met by the spouse—and a good deal of testing may go on with the partner inside the marriage first—are pursued in outside relationships.

CAN MARRIAGE MEET ALL THE NEEDS?

In an earlier comment I discussed one of the corollaries to the ground rules of marriage, namely, that marriage is an exclusive relationship in which mates are expected to be sufficient unto each other to such a degree that satisfaction given by or sought of third parties is not included. That marriage should serve all the needs of the spouses is built into our marital expectations, yet anyone who examines this proposition realistically is struck with its impossibility. Marital lives are not conducted in isolation, and husbands and wives are in contact with numerous other people during each twenty-four-hour day. So, as a matter of course, spouses will experience satisfactions from a great many other men and women. The quantity and quality of these satisfactions will determine to what degree they are tolerated by the spouse, though the tolerance level of the spouse is at least as much of a determinant.

TOLERATION OF "OUTSIDE" SATISFACTIONS

We also know that marriage cannot serve to meet all of the needs of both spouses at all times. Many marriage partners define at least implicitly—certainly discretely—what area of satisfactions they will leave to outsiders, and they are not only *not* disturbed that outsiders serve in this capacity, but probably relieved that they themselves are not called upon to have to address themselves to each and every need or whim of their mates. In this sense the extramarital relationship becomes a supplement to the marriage relationship. The "extra" no longer refers to the geographical outside, but to something additional. Again, the degree of tolerance depends upon what these satisfactions are like, how and when and how often they take place, and what meaning is read into them. Meaning obviously is a function of individual taste and value system, or is connected with psychological mechanisms such as projection. The trouble over meaning usually arises from lack of understanding or from not having made one's point of view more explicit. To some degree, feelings of jealousy can be explained in this way, and clarification of meaning may enable spouses to be more tolerant about involvements with outsiders. In fact, some relationships of this kind are acceptable to everyone, perhaps even taken for granted. A co-worker of the other sex with whom one shares many hours during the day (thereby having available opportunities for personal communication) is commonplace in today's world of work where men and women work side by side. And on a social level we assume that friendships extended to other couples will include intimacies on a verbal or even affectional level between different-sex friends. For housebound wives, however, outside relationships become immediately suspect, while for men these bonds, office and work linked as they are, have a more neutral quality. In a study by Babchuk and Bates (1) called "The Primary Relations of Middle-Class Couples: A Study in Male Dominance," a hypothesis was tested that "the husband will initiate a greater number of mutual primary friendships shared by the couple than will his wife." While the nature of that study is not primary to my investigation here, dealing as the study does with male dominance, it is of interest to see that, in the case of their couples, both the husband and the wife acquired friends with whom they both shared intimate confidences.

It is possible, then, to maintain relationships with both spouses of another pair, and even though it has been usually assumed that there will be less of a "threat" when both partners share these confidences, it seems from the Babchuk and Bates study that, in successful marriages, different degrees of intimacy between spouses and outsiders, in this case members of friendship pairs, are maintainable. Side by side with a substantial and satisfactory level of communication between mates can go a sharing of "intimacies" with outsiders.

So, with meaning understood by both spouses, and under an umbrella of an acceptance that marriage for them is not an all-inclusive relationship, it is feasible to have outsiders taking care of needs which cannot be met within. But does this include sexual needs as well? Faithfulness is ordinarily seen as faithfulness in the flesh, and transgressions of sexual nature have always been seen as the most crucial kind. So, to allow sexual relations between one's mate and an outsider seems to call for more than an intellectual willingness. The momentousness of sex—however artificially fanned by the culture—produces emotional roadblocks which cannot, so it seems, be overcome by realizations that parallel those mentioned earlier, that is, to see sexual relations simply as an area of general needs and to deal with them in line with a point of view that sees marriage as a not-all-inclusive relationship. Sexual relationships outside of marriage are not tolerable by such individuals as if they were just another unshared area, since guilt is great and they are unable to tolerate the burden inflicted upon them by religious and cultural mores. Persons must either experience relatively little guilt or a high degree of guilt tolerance to participate in extramarital sexual affairs.

To tolerate any kind of outside involvement—and probably sexual involvement more than any other—an ability to compartmentalize is of vital importance. To separate out one personal relationship from another seems absolutely necessary if these outside experiences are going to result in anywhere near meaningful satisfactions.

FAITHFULNESS AND LOYALTY

I have discussed at some length the tendencies of marital partners to seek satisfactions outside of their marital bonds, and I have tried to delineate the dimensions of these extramarital relations, trace their motives, and suggest mechanisms by which they can be tolerated by spouses. Concomitant with this behavior, however, are forces of contrary nature. While it is, perhaps, not possible to separate out ideas fed to us by our superegos, spurring us to behave "morally" and be trustworthy, there are in most of us substantial ingredients of conservatism. We want change, but we also want to preserve; we like the new, but we cherish the old as well; we desire thrill and excitement, but calmness is also welcome; ambiguity seems interesting, but lack of it feels so secure; we may be bored, but familiarity also breeds content. But, most of all, human beings have an affectionate nature which makes for loyalty and a continuing concern for the welfare of the other (spouse). A momentum built up during years of intimate marital contact is not only the result of "having to stay together," but stems also from innumerable reinforced mutual need satisfactions which "pay off" over and over again. And, last but not least, there are those husbands and wives who simply want to do right, for whom virtue has its own reward.

The mechanism of marriage as a means to regulate the relations between the sexes has limitations and imperfections which need constant repair and readjustment. To fit one's expectations into the confines of the marital scheme and the limitations imposed on it by its very nature is never easy. That so many spouses are able to make use of the mechanism of marriage and make such good use of it is a tribute to the invention itself. One should not only deplore failures, as demonstrated in divorces, but should also applaud the successes of those who over time provide each other with pleasure and are able to conduct their joint affairs effectively. At the same time, it is now clear that marriage can work out successfully for both of the spouses even when it is not an all-inclusive relationship, when either in reality or in fantasy there are other persons who share one's life.

References

1. BABCHUK, NICHOLAS, and BATES, ALAN P. "The Primary Relations of Middle-class Couples: A Study in Male Dominance." In William J. Goode (Ed.), *Readings on the Family and Society.* Englewood Cliffs, N.J.: Prentice-Hall, 1964.
2. FOOTE, NELSON N. "Matching of Husband and Wife in Phases of Development." In Marvin B. Sussman, *Sourcebook in Marriage and the Family,* 2nd Edition. Boston: Houghton Mifflin, 1963.
3. FORD, CLELLAN S., and BEACH, FRANK A. *Patterns of Sexual Behavior.* New York: Harper and Row, 1951.
4. JACKSON, DON D. "Family Rules: The Marital *Quid Pro Quo.*" Unpublished paper delivered at Conference on Family Process and Psychopathology, Eastern Pennsylvania Psychiatric Institute, Philadelphia, Pennsylvania, October 9, 1964.
5. LEVINGER, GEORGE. "Marital Cohesiveness and Dissolution: An Integrative Review," *Journal of Marriage and the Family,* 27 (No. 1): 19–28, 1965.
6. LEWIN, KURT. *Resolving Social Conflicts.* New York: Harper and Row, 1948.
7. NEUBECK, GERHARD, and SCHLETZER, VERA M. A Study of Extramarital relationships. *Marriage and Family Living, 24* (No. 3), 279–281, 1962.
8. NEUBECK, GERHARD, and TORBETT, DAVID. "Dynamics of Marital Effectiveness." Part of a paper delivered at the Groves Conference, 1962, in Baltimore, Maryland.
9. WINCH, ROBERT F. *Mate-Selection.* New York: Harper and Row, 1958.

Gerhard Neubeck

TWO CLINICIANS AND A SOCIOLOGIST

On April 18 to 20, 1966, at the Annual Groves Conference on Marriage and the Family (an interdisciplinary meeting bringing together sociologists, psychologists, social workers, psychiatrists, and others interested in family relations) a seminar in adulterous sexual behavior was held. The Chairman was Gerhard Neubeck. His consultants were Jessie Bernard, Ph.D., formerly of the Department of Sociology of Pennsylvania State University and now a private consultant and writer residing in Washington, D.C., and Wardell Pomeroy, Ph.D., formerly of the Institute of Sex Research at Indiana University and a member of the Kinsey team, now in private practice as a psychotherapist and marriage counselor in New York City. Other members participating in the discussion are not identified, and although the following discussion has been transcribed from a tape, it has been edited to fit the dimension of this book.

NEUBECK: The thing that binds us here today is that we are interested in extramarital relations. Let's see how interested we are in this. Have all of you got some paper with you that you can write on? If you don't, will you avail yourself of that, please. I can give you some paper; do you have a pencil with you? Good. You all have paper and pencil now, is that right? We will kind of make the rounds.

We're going to start this off. I'm going to show you a number of the cards of the Thematic Apperception Test. I'm going to show you one of the pictures now and give you some instructions, and I want you to do certain kinds of writing. This is Card 13. Can you all see that? A room with a man and a woman. The woman is on the bed, her breasts are half exposed, and the man stands there as we see him, with his head kind of bowed. Now I want you to do the following: Will the women in the room please identify yourselves with the woman, and the men in the room please identify yourselves with the man. This scene that you are identifying yourselves with is about five minutes or so after these two people, not married to each other, have had sexual intercourse.

SEMINAR MEMBER: Are they married to each other?

NEUBECK: They are married, but not to each other. She is lying there as you saw and he is standing there as you saw. You are they. You are either the woman or the man. I would like you to put down your reactions to this as you would have reacted if you were in this situation. Whatever occurs to you, whatever thoughts you have, not restricting any of your fantasies, thoughts, reactions. You do not need to put your name on this. . . . Don't put your name on this, please. We will give you about five to ten minutes to do this now. Don't be too pressured to write down immediately. You can think about it if you want to or you can do whatever you please, but identify yourself with this man or this woman. Reactions, fantasies . . . it is five minutes after this intercourse has taken place. You are the man or the woman. We are kind of arbitrary about this part of it. You are the man or the woman.

(Pomeroy and Bernard are sorting out responses at this point.)

NEUBECK: All right. Obviously there is nothing mysterious about this. As it must have occurred to you that what we tried to do is to bring you as close as possible to an experience of extramarital intercourse so that you will be able to identify yourself with the situation to some degree. You might later on want to talk about the values of such an experience and to what degree this has actually been a quasi extramarital experience. But for the time being, let that be enough of an explanation. We want you to get involved in this personally rather than academically. We will try to get as many facets into this topic as possible, so statistics will be cited sooner or later. But we hope you are all properly motivated now. A little anxious, perhaps shivering, guilty; we will see in a moment. I want to now read a sample of your responses, and between Jessie and Wardell and myself try to see if from this sample we can start conceptualizing a bit. Categorizing, conceptualizing, identifying, and analyzing to make sense out of this experience. Here's a response: "I have a headache and feel ashamed and guilty."

POMEROY: Shame and guilt come up very, very commonly.

BERNARD: I am trying to find out if this is a man or a woman.

NEUBECK: It is a male. Our instructions probably were not good enough, some people felt threatened because they are using the third person rather than I. But here's a female response: "Relaxed, fulfilled, and without apparent guilt. Perhaps the husband is an unsatisfying sexual partner and I am justified in seeking relief with another sexual partner. My pose may also reflect an attempt to withdraw from the reality of the situation."

POMEROY: Here's one. A man who says, "Wow!" Evidently this is his first adulterous act. He can't believe that he has done this and he is ashamed of himself. This shame and guilt. He said "Wow." I should think this meant that it has a big emotional impact.

SEMINAR MEMBER: What's wrong with okay?

POMEROY: Well I don't think he was reflecting that this was okay. He just says "Wow."

NEUBECK: Fulfillment was not as great as he had anticipated. Here's another: "The relationship with my wife has been permanently altered because of the episode."

BERNARD: Does he begrudge that?

NEUBECK: Well, I think it is more neutral than that. It is a new experience. But he goes on, "How did I get here in the first place? What can I do not to have to repeat the performance?" Interesting, the term performance here as against experience. Now maybe it is used the same way, but performance to me indicates something a little different than simple experience.

POMEROY: About to *perform* you mean?

NEUBECK: No, I think it is more of a role than a real personal experience. Performance is much more neutral, much more objective. "My relationship with my wife" is the key here.

POMEROY: Affecting marriage.

BERNARD: Is this a different person talking?

NEUBECK: No, this is the same person.

POMEROY: All right, this is a male, Jessie. It says, "Feelings seem to be a mixture of remorse, guilt, regret." Both in regard to himself, over the extramarital sex, and what he feels he has done to both the girl in the picture and his wife. Obviously there is little or no joy, only the expression of pain of several varieties. He also has a questioning attitude; for example, "What are the consequences now? How will I be able to deceive my wife after this . . . about this, deceive my wife about this? What will I do now with this girl? And what did I do to this woman?"

BERNARD: Should we stop now and analyze these?

NEUBECK: I would like a couple of more, please. I have a female. "I'm ashamed as well as exhausted. I have helped him feel guilty, helped him betray his wife. Neither of us has been satisfied, just tortured. We feel repugnance rather than affection. I'm not thinking of my husband, but of my lover. If only it could have been in less sordid surroundings."

POMEROY: One more female, Jessie. "Woman feels happy, fulfilled, herself. More pleasurable sensation than conscious of anything else. This is pleasure."

BERNARD: Yeah?

POMEROY: "Delightful, quiet and quieted, a loved response. Not too conscious of anything else at the moment. No particular awareness of what the man is doing, only that he is near in the room."

NEUBECK: As interesting as it might be to pick out further comments, I think this sample will probably suffice for the time being, and perhaps the next step is here to see what you yourself want to say about this. What are your reactions, your comments, your interpretations?

BERNARD: The first thing that jumps out at you is how much guiltier the men feel.

POMEROY: Isn't that interesting?

SEMINAR MEMBER: I would like to suggest that there is a reaction to the man's pose.

NEUBECK: If you'll pardon the pun, the card was stacked. There's no doubt about that, but I think that no matter what the exact nature of the picture would have been, it would not have been essentially different. I think you have a variety of responses such as you got here in a more positive, less sordid picture. Jessie pointed out here the real strong suggestions of guilt for the man.

We have all the time in the world, so as we look at these things now we can immediately go into a discussion on any of these points. So what about guilt? Do you want to dismiss it and go onto the next or do you want to talk about it?

SEMINAR MEMBER: With this picture guilt is written all over it.

NEUBECK: That only would explain that the guilt has been so prominent, but it would not explain why other people were not able to see different kinds of responses over and above the guilt.

SEMINAR MEMBER: Was this a casual pickup, I wonder?

NEUBECK: That's right. We know nothing at all about this. This is another variable then. At what age does this occur? Is this a one-night stand, or is this a continuous experience? So we start to classify these things. Do you want to record these things?

SEMINAR MEMBER: But isn't it possible that all these feelings of guilt that all of us feel are universal?

NEUBECK: Well, you are taking this very serious now, the picture, and I wish you wouldn't any more. We used this as a point of departure to get you involved. Let's get away from the picture and the hands and postures and these kinds of things.

SEMINAR MEMBER: I was struck by the fact that only the males feel guilty.

POMEROY: And this may be a function of the picture itself. I went through a very quick reading of these responses by the males and I don't find any that didn't have some aspect of guilt, although there were many other positive things.

NEUBECK: Let me make a very bold interpretation, then. You don't think that guilt is one of these very important variables any longer; under certain circumstances you believe the superego problem, the guilt problem we have been faced with for centuries, no longer is the essential issue. Is that what you are saying?

SEMINAR MEMBER: No, I didn't suggest that.

NEUBECK: So superego is still here?

BERNARD: May I read something from my materials?

NEUBECK: Go ahead.

BERNARD: There is still at least lip service for the ancient proscription of adultery. On a television program, January 23 of this year, 88% of a national sample reported as believing that adultery was wrong for women, and about the same number, 86%, that it was wrong for men as well. If the wife was cold, 26% more men than women it was reported, consider it acceptable. The *it* all depends upon a point of view which has also found advocacy in the so-called situational ethics among theological thinkers. Thus Joseph Fletcher, professor in the Episcopal Theological School, Cambridge, Massachusetts, in a debate in the Catholic magazine, *Commonweal,* has this to say: "There is nothing against extramarital sex as such, and in some cases it is good. . . . The Christian criteria for sex relationships are positive. Sex is a matter of certain ideals of relationships. These ideals are based upon a certain belief about God, Christ, the church, who man is, and destiny. Therefore, if people do not embrace that, and most don't, there is no reason that they should live by it, and most do not. It is time we faced up to this. If true happiness means a marital monopoly, then let those who believe in it recommend it by reason and example. Nothing is gained by condemning the unbeliever. Indeed, to condemn him is more unjust, unmoral than a sexual escapade."

POMEROY: I think this is very good that you brought this up and I have feelings along this line, too. I raised the point in a slightly different way; that it is possible to be "unfaithful" without extramarital intercourse in a variety of ways. It is also possible to have extramarital intercourse without being unfaithful, but this word, "adultery," which was the word you used and the word we used in our title, is even more confusing because it is really a legal term. This confuses the issue also.

SEMINAR MEMBER: In addition to that, I think we have what we call permissive or permissible extramarital affairs.

POMEROY: That's right. From a legal standpoint it wouldn't make any difference. Adultery is just extramarital intercourse.

SEMINAR MEMBER: Extramarital intercourse is not adultery or infidelity?

NEUBECK: No, that's not what he said. He said it may be adultery, it may be extramarital relations, but it may not be infidelity. Why don't you elaborate on that a little bit?

POMEROY: Well, this is one example. With the permission, knowledge, and encouragement of the spouse, it wouldn't be infidelity, although people may disagree with this. This could be extramarital intercourse without being unfaithful. It depends on how you . . .

SEMINAR MEMBER: But that's sick!

POMEROY: Somebody suggested this is sick, and I wonder if you would elaborate about this and just why you feel it is.

SEMINAR MEMBER: Well, it isn't done.

POMEROY: Are you equating sickness and unacceptability? In other words, it is sick then in that it is deviant from our culture?

SEMINAR MEMBER: Or is not really acceptable in terms of ethics?

POMEROY: But do you think this has to be unacceptable to the person giving his consent?

SEMINAR MEMBER: They shouldn't.

NEUBECK: Well, now we are getting to the sticky territory.

POMEROY: Again, let's keep it out of the sexual in another example for a second.

NEUBECK: Only for a second.

POMEROY: Only for a second. Here's a man who enjoys some particular activity. Let's say playing tennis. His wife despises tennis and doesn't want to get involved, but she is happy to have her husband play tennis with another man or woman, as the case may be, and he does this openly and with her knowledge. Does the sexual context of the extramarital intercourse give this something special or different than you would get under the tennis example?

SEMINAR MEMBER: I don't get it.

POMEROY: She herself doesn't like it, but doesn't want to get involved, but she is happy for her husband.

SEMINAR MEMBER: She has no involvement?

POMEROY: Does she have another involvement in the extramarital? What is the involvement—in the extramarital part—in the marital part?

NEUBECK: Let's go slow. Let's, for a moment, look at this piece of behavior in more detail. Here you have a tennis match between two people, and there are a set of ground rules between them;

they are involved in an activity which expends energy, one will get some joy from winning, the other some sorrow by losing, but they are having fun, they are having a good time batting the ball back and forth. There is some congeniality in doing this together, even though there will be a loser and a winner. They are outdoors, and I suppose we could describe this episode of behavior in many ways, but it is some form of social interaction. Now if you look at sexual intercourse in the same minute episodic way, then it is also an example of social relationship with sexual contact added, in which there is some emotional quality, whatever this emotional quality may be. They are indoors, there is also a time limit, and there are certain kinds of rules —ground rules of the game they are following—and there is some communication, and then it is done with. Now, how do these two differ, if they differ?

SEMINAR MEMBER: No commitment.

POMEROY: Yes, but would you say that this isn't universal, that there are some people who don't have this personal commitment to be sexual?

NEUBECK: I think what we are really saying is that there is for most of us a commitment. It varies in intensity and degree. Life itself makes it either possible for us to stick by this commitment and I think, in my own paper at least, I tried to delineate some of the difficulties as to why it is so tough to stick by the commitment because there are all these other problems, such as free movement, jealousy, obligation, overexposure, and variety. I don't want to go over the paper, but I do want to refer you to it. These conditions of life and the ideal of marriage itself seemingly make it difficult for us to stick by these commitments in the same way that one enters into the commitments.

POMEROY: I would like to tell you of an experience I had that might throw some confusion on the subject. A few years ago I knew a person who was involved in a wife swapping club. I told him I was interested in the whole phenomenon and I had the privilege of meeting with a group of wife swappers at a natural wife swapping occasion. I felt very privileged that they would let me come in and do this. There were six couples: one college professor, two high school teachers, one truant officer and his wife, and an engineer and his wife, and another couple. Upper-class group. They met in a very nice home about 8:00. All came in and immediately disrobed. The whole group took off their clothes. They sat around in the living room, and I was free to talk to them singly or in groups. The conversation was not ribald at all; it was calm conversation, essentially nonsexual conversation. One of the men would say to the lady next to him, "Would you care to come in the other room?" She would accept. They would retire to the other room and would stay, I timed anywhere from twenty minutes to maybe as long as forty-five minutes, but usually about half an hour. No comments were made as they left. No comments as they returned. They would return to the group, and a little while later, would leave with another partner. So in the course of the evening each man would tend to see five other women; never his wife—that could be done at some other time. Then they would put on their clothes and go home and that was the evening. In talking with these people, and I interviewed all of them individually as well as getting this group flavor, they were reporting consistently a happy marriage. Almost all of them had children; they ranged in age from about thirty to forty-five. They had responsible jobs and expressed concern that their children not learn of this. The children didn't know of this activity. The couples involved would usually do it once a week or once every two weeks, and they wanted to sort of separate out this sexual activity from their marriage. It wasn't a fact that there were no affairs. Affairs in terms of seeing these people outside of this relationship was taboo. There was absolutely no sexual activity going on in the living room with the other people there. In this sense, this was all private. They all felt that this was something beneficial in their marriage. They were happy they were doing it. They certainly reported no feelings of guilt on a conscious level. They appeared certainly not to have them. One couple said they only joined the group two months ago, and prior to that both of them were having a great deal of extramarital intercourse, with recriminations, with fights over the activity of the spouse, until they joined the group. When they were able to do this openly with each other, all recriminations seemed to stop. They thought it was a very healthy thing in their marriage to do it. These people obviously had a totally different idea of what a commitment was or what part sex had in marriage, but I was sort of struck by the fact that they seemed to be making this type of adjustment seemingly comfortably. I couldn't get any other pathologies, if you want to call this pathology.

BERNARD: I would like to ask a question. Was every woman assured that she would be asked, and would every woman have to accept a man?

POMEROY: No, and they didn't have to. All of these women were highly responsive women—orgasms of two to twenty per session. The males in one evening, if they had five partners, they weren't able to perform five times; a good many of them would retire to the room and perhaps have petting or cunnilingus or fellatio or what not and there didn't seem to be any anxiety that I could bring out that they had to perform.

BERNARD: Were there any wallflowers?

POMEROY: There were no wallflowers.

BERNARD: And would you have to pass any test to get in? Suppose somebody came in that you wouldn't be caught dead with?

POMEROY: No test, and that happened on occasion. They told of one couple that they didn't like. The other people didn't like them, and they weren't asked back. They would do sort of like you would invite people to a bridge party, and if you didn't like them, you wouldn't ask them back.

BERNARD: By the time they came everyone had accepted them.

POMEROY: Yeah, they were willing to put up with this one time.

SEMINAR MEMBER: Were these good marriages?

POMEROY: Well, I think I can remember. It was a rather dramatic thing for me to be in on this, so I think I can remember. The engineer —it was his second wife. He had suggested it to the first wife, and she had not wanted to, but there were many other problems in this marriage as well as that. I also knew the first wife and interviewed her. The one couple I told you about. There was another couple that also gave a history long back; they had been doing this for many years. Long back they had a very poor marriage until they got involved in it. The other three couples were all first marriages, to my memory.

SEMINAR MEMBER: The women were "normal"?

POMEROY: Oh, there was no question about it. These were very highly responsive women.

SEMINAR MEMBER: And the men?

POMEROY: I felt that they were not particularly highly sexed, but they didn't have difficulty with impotence, they didn't have low sex rates. They were also, of course, all of them having intercourse with their wives at home as well as this. So they weren't very low themselves.

SEMINAR MEMBER: What about contraception?

POMEROY: Most of the women, as I recall, were using diaphragms.

SEMINAR MEMBER: Social games, then.

POMEROY: Yeah, it was sort of like playing bridge.

SEMINAR MEMBER: You said there were no feelings of guilt.

SEMINAR MEMBER: But you said they didn't want their children to know about this?

POMEROY: Right, right.

SEMINAR MEMBER: Why didn't they want their kids to know?

POMEROY: Well, I don't know if I talked to every single one about this. But the ones I did talk to about it said that they felt that their children couldn't understand what was going on, or that they might tell other people and get them into social difficulties as a result of it.

SEMINAR MEMBER: That could be guilt.

POMEROY: Perhaps, but even one's income you very often don't tell your children until you feel they are old enough to know what this means. They were sort of taking this position.

NEUBECK: We are not examining whether this is a way of the future. We are examining the quality of this type of experience as against another one. Let us examine who these people are, what kind of behavior they are involved in, without the usual types of prejudices. Is this a slice of life or is it not? And what does it mean? What kind of person does it take to participate in it? That is the question.

SEMINAR MEMBER: Motivation.

POMEROY: They were certainly interested in the variety of partners.

SEMINAR MEMBER: Where are we?

NEUBECK: I remind you, I'm a little pedantic in this, because I feel some responsibility in keeping this in line. I called on Wardell because he tried to see what the difference between tennis and sexual intercourse is, and I think we are still at that point. I, frankly, am not satisfied as yet, to understand some of the deeper implications of the difference.

SEMINAR MEMBER: Go back to commitments.

NEUBECK: What is the commitment, and how does the commitment change, if it does, over time?

POMEROY: May I just say one thing myself? Someone brought up the fact that she didn't think we should spend too much time on wife swapping, and I agree with her. I didn't bring this up to be concerned with wife swappers, really. There aren't very many in the country. The reason I was bringing it up was to try to show an example of a group of people who did look on sex pretty much like tennis. It was sort of a bridge game, and it was fun, too. All I'm trying to point out is that I think we can do this in a different way. I'm not trying to say what is right or wrong, but as far as I could determine, these people, from other criteria, had a good marriage, in the sense of responsibility, raising children, having good jobs, being happy, and so on. I was just using this as an example.

NEUBECK: But how does this affect the quality of the relationship? You are suggesting that with this kind of motivation, having intercourse with a person to whom you are not married, this is like tennis, this is something mechanical, a utilitarian kind of bodily exercise. How does this relate to the question of tennis?

BERNARD: I would like to ask if *this* is true. You know in the Victorian period, they tried to downgrade the importance of sex. You can't build a marriage on it, and you shouldn't think it's too important, and go ahead with the other aspects of marriage. And there has been a return to that, but in a different way. The Victorians tried to downgrade sex by inhibiting it, and this kind of thing, the tennis type of sex, downgrades sex. . . .

POMEROY: Yes, but you're defining sex in your own terms there. They are using a different term. They are saying this isn't Victorian, this is sex all over the place.

BERNARD: I'm talking about the evaluation of it in terms of marriage. You're talking about their having very good marriages, but, you know, the sexual part is not all that important.

POMEROY: Well, they still have marital intercourse.

BERNARD: Yes, but so did the Victorians.

POMEROY: I'm not sure it's the same difference.

BERNARD: I want you to see a point now. You want us to see it in respect to tennis. Now I would like you to see that the function it performs is almost identical. Quite aside from what people say or think about it, it has the same sociological reason, the same function as downgrading sex. They just do it a different way.

POMEROY: Well, is that downgrading it?

BERNARD: Well, that's what you're telling us. The marriage is very good. They have a good, solid, substantial life.

POMEROY: Including good marital intercourse, which they have regularly, and enjoy and have orgasm. This is something over and beyond it.

BERNARD: Are you sure that it is all that good, that they have to go and have . . .

POMEROY: Yes, you see, now you are . . . that is exactly the point. I take it there are very few wife swappers in the room, and I think it is very difficult for you to understand that there is a possible different kind of way of looking at sex.

NEUBECK: I would like to refer you back to what I said in my paper about the overexposure and variety. It seems to me that you can conceptualize it in this way. Since marriage goes on over time, over two, three, or four decades of actual sexual potency, are we expecting people to behave in similar fashion or with some variety within this context? This is the essential problem. Of course, variety is not distributed equally among the population in the first place. Some people want more variety than others. But the fact is that some may have such need for variety that marriage cannot meet, no matter how much we work on it, no matter how compatible the partners are. Our need for variety calls for substantial experiences with different people, even if it's only in the head to begin with. Now again, without generalizing, this need exists in some people, and some people will meet it by fantasizing, either with their own wives, or by masturbation, because the superego is so great that they cannot make themselves take advantage of other men or other women. Most people, however, seem to be able to meet their needs for variety primarily within marriage. But I think that is just one of the "givens" you have, different needs for variety over time.

BERNARD: It's just sort of remotely related, but if the intercourse is just sort of a casual play episode, that is one thing. But if it is a serious relationship, then it is another. There is no way of knowing from the kinds of data Kinsey and Wardell supply what the nature of the relationship was. If we assume that length of the relationship is some sort of index, the one-third or 35% of the women who had carried on adulterous relationships for four years or more must have included many of the 41% who had had only one partner. Kinsey and his associates tell us only that a smaller proportion of the females in the sample had ever developed regular and long-time relationships with males who were not their husbands, and I wonder if such relationships might not be considered polyandrous rather than adulterous. The significance is surely different than sexual play adultery. There must have been overriding reasons why the partners did not marry.

POMEROY: I think this is another issue. If you will just let me do this off the top of my head, because we didn't count cases in this research. I'm quite sure that we found that the men and women (it worked both ways) who had affairs in which there was emotional interaction, or love or whatever you want to call it, between extramarital partners, on an average had more difficulty in their marriage than the persons who were interested in a variety of experiences outside the marriage. This created a bigger problem for them. But, again, this was not universal. There were some people, as Cuber found, who were able to do this very well. It might be a selective factor, rather than cause and effect. This is a possibility, but I don't think it is true.

NEUBECK: I would like to do a very bold thing. I am shaky in doing this, but let me try. I am now in Kansas City, I am happily married, for a period of over twenty-five years. I have grown-up children. My sexual relations with my wife are very fine. Qualitatively and quantitatively we are in good shape. I am at loose ends tonight in Kansas City, and I am sitting at some coffee shop or some bar, and I am making the acquaintance of a girl who is sexually very attractive to me. I proposition her. She is not a commercial prostitute, she is not a call girl seemingly. We go to her apartment. The language we have straightened out. We both know that we are interested. I am interested, and she obviously wants to accommodate me. There is no commercial transaction involved. I have intercourse with her, a woman that I have never seen before. I have the usual reactions that a man has. I could, of course, be anxious and impotent, but I am not. Our skins contact, there is communication. We have talked about ourselves to some degree, about what we are doing with each other, for each other, and so on. I like her—she smells good, she looks good, she talks well. She moves well, she is responsive to me, she appreciates me. I appreciate her. There is affection, there is no love, as far as I can make out. She is appetizing—Well, let your fantasy go as I did mine now. I have now had extramarital intercourse. This has been a sexual and a human relationship. Does this differ from tennis?

SEMINAR MEMBER: Yes.

NEUBECK: All right, it differs from tennis in what respect?

SEMINAR MEMBER: What were your reasons?

NEUBECK: My need for variety is great. I'm putting myself in that category. I'm getting older, don't forget. I figured this one out to give you an example of what may not be a typical extramarital experience, in order to get at the quality of this relationship.

SEMINAR MEMBER: Why not pick a person from your acquaintances?

NEUBECK: Yes, it would be very different. With such a person I would have an entry of some sort of affectionate or intellectual relationship, whereas with this girl I would not.

POMEROY: I would say that this is quite different from playing tennis. What you said and I think the reason I would say this is because of the way you told the story. You had to give all this build-up. If you had said, "Well, tonight I met a babe and we went home and did it, and it was quite an experience, I enjoyed it." I think this would be much more telling it.

SEMINAR MEMBER: Then it is like tennis with one exception.

NEUBECK: Yes, I think your point is probably true. In other words, the real difference is the touching of the genitals. Is that right?

SEMINAR MEMBER: Well, I think you can make all kinds of distinctions. And I agree with the guilt and I agreed with the essential aspects of a tactile relationship, but I didn't ask this facetiously if the real difference in the long run wasn't in the genital distinction. When it comes to genital play or genital contact, this is different in quality from any other kind of contact.

SEMINAR MEMBER: Let's consider consequences.

NEUBECK: By consequences, are you again talking about the practical consequences, or the consequences of whatever I read into this act that I have to live with?

SEMINAR MEMBER: Well, I'm thinking in terms of the possible consequences if your wife found out about this, consequences if this led to a continuing relationship with this woman, say if you fell in love with her. Consequences if your community found out about it, what about your job, what about your public life there.

NEUBECK: Don't think I haven't thought about that. I acknowledge all of that. I still don't think that you are talking to the point, however. If you take the episode itself, for a moment. I know this is isolating it from reality, but the actual episode of this game, whatever it is, tennis or some other exercise, and again the genital contact.

SEMINAR MEMBER: And there is a lot of this, I bet.

NEUBECK: This is the problem. You don't have enough data to really know. According to Cuber, there may be, in a nonclinical population, people who do not turn up in our agencies and in our offices. There may be a vast population who are involved in this type of relationship, and succeed in it. Yes, why don't we get the statistics at this point?

SEMINAR MEMBER: But you don't live in isolation.

BERNARD: Yes, as a sociologist, I can't think of anything outside of the social context. The social context is as much a part of this game as the game itself. These are what Wardell and Kinsey found.*

[the following day]

POMEROY: Well, I think that I have sort of misunderstood some of the things which were said before, and I think we have clarified this in our private conversations, and if you want me to, I will repeat it.

NEUBECK: Will you share that with us?

POMEROY: All right, then you come in. The wife swapping—somebody said why wasn't it husband swapping. Obviously, it was both. There is no reason why we call it wife swapping.

NEUBECK: Jessie could tell us about that.

POMEROY: All right. What I was trying to do was to give an illustration of how different people handle sex in marriage, and in this case, outside of marriage. And in my way of looking at these people, it seemed to me that they were handling it, although in a totally different way, not necessarily a "wrong" way or a destructive way, or in a way that was interfering with their lives. It was just different. And what I was hoping that the group would accept was that people can be different in many different ways. This is one example. They can do it in other ways. And I sort of got the feeling that the objection to this was in terms of that there were certain commitments in marriage which they had which precluded the possibility of this, but evidently you weren't saying this at all.

SEMINAR MEMBER: I was saying there may be different commitments.

POMEROY: I think this is exactly the point. If we look at some statis-

* Here followed a report of the Kinsey data which are discussed in this book, in the article by Yoon Hough Kim.

tics . . . if we take 50% of the males who had extramarital intercourse, and of that 50%, 61% said that, as far as they could determine, it hadn't affected their marriage.

SEMINAR MEMBER: But that does make a difference.

POMEROY: But isn't the difference only in degree, not in kind?

SEMINAR MEMBER: I think it is a difference in kind. It is a difference in the time between a long-term love arrangement that may have a great deal more worth than the marriage that actually exists between the two people. . . .

SEMINAR MEMBER: I think Gerry's idea of compartmentalization ought to be primary.

POMEROY: I agree with this except it seems to me that there is a great deal of compartmentalization in a great many of the 61% of the 50% too. And I don't quite see your differentiation of this in kind rather than in degree. I see this in terms of there being all sorts of ways for people to adjust to extramarital intercourse, including guilt.

SEMINAR MEMBER: What is important to me is not just the way they have extramarital intercourse, but how, and what this means to them.

BERNARD: Yes. I can't conceive of the point of view of genital sex in a vacuum. I mean, I can get the point that adultery per se is possible and all that, but it is so different. Genital contact, in and of itself, without any adhesive, is something very difficult . . . maybe it is the sex difference.

NEUBECK: I beg to differ. Let me tell you about my experience. I want to give you the feedback. I was successful in my enterprises. We . . . I had a good time. The experience was as aesthetically pleasing as I had hoped it would be. The commitment was for. . . . The contract that we had, although we obviously didn't make a contract, was for mutual pleasure. I made sure there wouldn't be a pregnancy involved. As far as I could find out, I don't know whether she was married or not, by the way, but she had a ring on, so I thought that she was. . . .

Well, I told people what I was planning to do. So, here I enjoyed myself and I hope that I gave pleasure to the other person.

BERNARD: I don't see the relevance to the point we are trying to make. You would have genital contact with a streetwalker, right?

NEUBECK: No.

BERNARD: You would have had orgasm with a prostitute, right? What would be the difference? You know, looking for this . . . finding this. . . .

NEUBECK: I want certain kinds of conditions for my extramarital relationships.

BERNARD: Oh!

NEUBECK: I told you about that.

BERNARD: This is the point we are trying to make.

NEUBECK: Yes, but what's the point? What are the conditions? This is what I am trying to get you to say.

SEMINAR MEMBER: Well, the conditions are whatever the person who is having the extramarital relationship at that point of time feels is his or her particular need. They may live to be very glad about it, they may live to regret it terribly, or they may be quite in between about it. But what is important is the feeling of the two people and the results on the people.

BERNARD: Why is it that a girl who can make a man feel that he has given her a great deal of pleasure is worth more than the streetwalker that takes them in in ten minutes and then out? Why is it? This costs more. This is worth more. It has more value. This is what men are willing to pay for, if they can afford it. You know, in Japan, a geisha girl doesn't even have to go to bed. She gives them all this other, and it is worth it.

SEMINAR MEMBER: The next thing is, what is important to an adulterous relationship which is really the relationship talked about in *The Significant Americans*? Whether it is two or three times and then they separate, or whether it is something carried on over a period of years?

POMEROY: But this is for the individual, for Gerry Neubeck. Another man could have taken a completely reverse situation and said, "I couldn't possibly have tolerated this sort of a situation, it is too much like my marital intercourse. All I want is a pickup and a screw. And this is what is meaningful to me."

SEMINAR MEMBER: That is what I am asking. What is meaningful to the individual? What is more important to him? It may not be something that he will want to have as a permanent thing, or it may be.

BERNARD: And I would like to add that in this club you were talking about, if they were gagged and blindfolded, and didn't have any social contacts with the bodies in bed next to them, I bet it wouldn't last three weeks.

POMEROY: I would think you are right. I would agree.

NEUBECK: Let me shift this about forty-five to sixty degrees over. I think you can perhaps more readily identify with this kind of situation than the one I played up before. Now, all of us as professionals have lots of friends, and many of these are colleagues, collaborators and co-authors, have relationships with people of the other sex. Some of us have pretty intimate relationships in terms of both duration, commitment, how often we see each other, how much we reveal about ourselves in the wake of the professional relationship, so you perhaps often develop friendship. Now, if you can picture it, some of you have friends like this, I am sure. All right. Now, the next step is that this develops into an erotic relationship and the two of you do go to bed together to have intercourse. This is what you are saying: What makes the relationship that I described before different now that you have had intercourse? Is it a fair question?

SEMINAR MEMBER: What is the difference between, say this relationship and with . . .

NEUBECK: No. The way I would like to see this is what happens, what is the difference in the relationship before the intercourse and now with the sex involved. This is what I am looking at.

SEMINAR MEMBER: But it all began in what?

NEUBECK: Now, could we look at them one at a time? So this is the question before the house. What changes, if anything, because of the intercourse?

BERNARD: Well, the relationship between the man and the woman can take any one of several directions according to, you know, the kind of people they are. Now, it can be a much better relationship. They understand one another, they have really quarried one another. Or it can cause the most violent revulsion. It can break up the relationship. Sometimes girls make the point, college girls, that after they have had sex relations, then the relationship is off. If they had built up to it, it might have prospered.

NEUBECK: For the sake then, at this point of really pinpointing it, let us assume that the relationship continued happily after this.

BERNARD: You are answering the question, then.

NEUBECK: Am I? This is what I would like to hear some more opinion on: If the question is really answered, because you are assuming—you are saying then that the relationship is really substantially not different.

BERNARD: Oh, it is different, but you are saying . . . .

NEUBECK: How is it different? This is what I would like to find out. How is it different? Because of the genital contact?

SEMINAR MEMBER: Well, for one thing, you know each other better.

BERNARD: You are either disappointed or . . . .

NEUBECK: No, you have expanded the area of knowledge because you have included sexual knowledge.

SEMINAR MEMBER: This expanded knowledge of the other person has continued to be a satisfying . . . . That is the reason for it to be continued. Now, if it were a disappointment over the other relationship. . . .

NEUBECK: Yes, all right. I will keep that out for the time being. So, one is the expansion of knowledge.

BERNARD: You are moving everything out except an improvement of the relationship.

NEUBECK: No, I am really not interested at the moment in improvement or non-improvement. This is the dichotomy I want to get away from. I say, what is different?

SEMINAR MEMBER: To the idea mentioned by someone that in the very vital sense that intercourse does something to a person that can never be obliterated, and they become, as a result of this, a part of this other person, whether this takes place with a prostitute, a colleague . . . that can never be changed and this is different from when you shake hands, or when you cooperate on the court.

NEUBECK: This is exactly the question that I am raising. Is this a proposition that you would agree with?

BERNARD: It is interesting that all of the men picture this adulterous relationship as so glamorous and successful, and you have all delighted the women. You don't know how many of them were terribly disappointed.

NEUBECK: I am going to be pigheaded, you may think I am pedantic, and maybe I am, but I am still, and I am going to shift it again a little bit. All right. While before my relationship, or whatever, with this particular colleague, as intimate as it was, with great emotional impact, self-revelation, thinking about the past, you have come about as close to this person as you would to any friend. This relationship has existed for a while. It is irrevocably changed by the fact of genital contact. It can never be the same because you have had this genital contact. There is something new in the relationship that is indelibly a part of it.

BERNARD: So what? I don't understand what you are driving at. It seems to me that the points that the men think are so terribly important, and that we have to discuss, you know, don't seem that important at all.

SEMINAR MEMBER: This seems, however, to be of tremendous importance. But adultery in any form or one form or another is the sin that is so greatly condemned just because you break the rules.

POMEROY: Right!

BERNARD: I don't think it can be indelible just as any relationship can be indelible. But I don't think it is necessarily all that critical.

NEUBECK: See, I am raising the question, Jessie. This is exactly the point where I think we have disagreement. Here is where most people make a point. They will let other people relate themselves to each other in the way that I have described, but they will set the limit at the genital contact because that is so terrifically, and substantially, different. Are you saying now that it is or it isn't?

BERNARD: That it isn't.

NEUBECK: Now here two of you are in disagreement. Now Jessie really clarifies her position. She does not believe that its gets altered at that moment.

BERNARD: It gets altered.

NEUBECK: It gets altered, but not necessarily in the extreme.

SEMINAR MEMBER: Well, if I understand the question at this point, I am in absolute disagreement. I believe it becomes tremendously altered. I think that . . .

BERNARD: Now, wait a minute. Supposing I can see where a man and a woman had fallen in love with each other and kissed, but it was a really meaningful relationship. This I can see would alter the relationship indelibly. But if these people who have known each other for a long time and, in the process, go to bed together, and they are not in love with each other . . . right? Wasn't that one of the specifications? Yes.

NEUBECK: Well, this is a matter of definition.

BERNARD: Well, that makes the difference. But I had the notion that it was just a sort of casual thing and I can see how it . . . you know.

NEUBECK: Now these people are friends—however that differs from love I leave . . . I can't discuss that here.

SEMINAR MEMBER: The thing is, there must be people who work closely with other people, who are terribly intimate, must have contemplated this business of going to bed with somebody whom they have met, or enjoyed, or just liked at some time or another.

NEUBECK: I am glad that is a "given." I am glad you are mentioning this, because that is a "given" for most of us.

SEMINAR MEMBER: Well, here we are. Now why is it that also, for a number of us anyway, and I think for most of us, to do this, to step over the genital line, means or would mean something that is quite different? There is something special which lets some people go on to the next stage, but which holds some of us back, but most of us are aware that is a way that surrounds us.

SEMINAR MEMBER: I think that here the question of culture is a very important point. In view of the experiences I had during the German Mardi Gras, which is a religious festival. This is a period of total freedom. Whether you are married or not married, here anyone has the freedom to take another partner. And this is encouraged.

NEUBECK: It is a Catholic population.

POMEROY: Yes, it seems it is cultural, because you can get the opposite feeling in that you can have my body, but my soul is my own. There they feel that this is not the "all." It depends on the cultural framework.

NEUBECK: How about women, Jessie?

BERNARD: I think women are changing very, very greatly in this respect. It used to be in our culture, that women did not have sex relations until the relationship was a real thing to them. This was an ultimate thing, and they could not be casual about it. I think we are evolving or developing a type of woman who can be casual about it. One of my major sources is Helen Gurley Brown, who describes the "matinee." According to her, it is a purely playful relationship which uses the lunch hour and an apartment. The basic rule for such a relationship is: never become serious. The hazards, beyond that of being found out, for, of course, it must be secret, is that one partner or the other might become bored or might fall in love and become serious. Either eventuality is fatal to the relationship. In fact, to forestall the likelihood of the relationship becoming serious, one of the conditions of success for the "matinee" is that one or both partners be happily married.

Well, this is the kind of thing which most women in the past would never have been able to engage in. But it seems to me that a new kind of woman is emerging, or an old kind is re-emerging on the scene, and one of the distinguishing characteristics of this woman is that she can be casual about sex. In the past, as I said, she could not. And in the past, therefore, husbands were justified in feeling alarmed if they found out that their wives were engaged in sexual relations with another man. Because otherwise, if it hadn't been a deep relationship, she wouldn't have done so. But for the women today this is no longer true. They can be as casual about sexual relations in or out of marriage as men. They can accept sex at some point without conflict. Even a regular extramarital relationship does not faze them or in fact interfere with their marriage. So that I think if you are talking about extramarital sex as related to women, you have to recognize that great changes are apparently in process, and this is true apparently also in France, and I have a lovely little quote about Mary Ann . . . and this is about Mary Ann: "The only time I ever saw Mary Ann really hysterical was when she found out that while she was spending evenings with her lover of that season, her husband had been calling on the wife of the concierge downstairs.

> "Imagine," she screamed, "that woman is nobody. I shall divorce him." "But how about your own affair?" "That is absolutely different, Madam." This time, however, Mary Ann was all smiles. She looked ready to purr. "I have a new young friend, Madam. He is a young man, so charming. He is twenty-one, about to become twenty-two." "But don't you feel a little like you were robbing the cradle, Mary Ann?" "No, Madam, because it is a trend. All my friends have young friends nowadays. The oldest I have heard of is twenty-seven, and that is

already getting old. It is this way," Mary Ann said, "We are making money nowadays. We have good jobs and we don't need what your musical comedies call 'sugar daddies.' We can pick and choose; and after all, why not have someone who is young, easy, and amusing. Young friends are much more generous. My little pet gave me this." She pointed to a new mink coat hanging on a peg. "And he is looking for a nice little apartment where we can meet. There are so many handsome, eager, virile, and appreciative young men in Paris, why should any of us put up again with men who are older and more tired."

NEUBECK: There are a number of loose odds and ends that I think we ought to discuss. I personally would like us to make some projections into the future, some soothsaying, some prediction of where we are going. But I would also like us to end up with this tolerance problem. Mainly, what does it take to be able to live within this new trend, if there is any such new trend. So don't let's get lost all over the place. Let us be a little economic about it. We only have an hour. I hope I am not riding herd on you too much.

BERNARD: This was just a question about the guilt feeling, that maybe the double standard has boomeranged against men. The double standard which allowed them to be the aggressors always gave women the ego protection, "I was wronged. I wasn't guilty because I was had." So that he, therefore, has to bear the entire brunt of the guilt feeling where any is called for.

POMEROY: While we are talking about guilt, I would like to spend just a few minutes on a very poignant story which seems to me to illustrate this. I was taking the history of an older woman who had been wracked by guilt. She was a missionary, she and her husband were in Africa, she was happily married without a flicker of erotic response—no orgasm in the marriage. She came home on a year's sabbatical. She was returning. She was going up the Nile. She and the captain were the only two white people on the boat. One night the captain unexpectedly grabbed her, according to this history, and kissed her passionately. She was horrified and upset, and retired to her cabin and stayed there for the rest of the trip. But for the first time in her life, she was sexually aroused. She returned to her husband and for the first time in her life, she started to have orgasm with him, and for ten years they had a much better sexual adjustment. She came in and gave the history. She, of course, had never told anybody this, including her husband, but she was terribly wracked by guilt by this event. I attempted to say, "What a wonderful thing happened to you. Wasn't it great that you had this experience so that you are now more responsive?" She had never looked at it this way. She had looked on it as a dirty, terrible thing that had happened to her on the boat. I am just giving this story to try to give another example of the effect that guilt can have on people. It was really hurting what I thought was a very good sexual adjustment in the marriage. But it had seemed sullied, muddied, and affected by her own guilt feelings over this.

NEUBECK: So the double bind in this case really worked to her disadvantage.

POMEROY: Yes.

POMEROY: I still disagree with Jessie that this is institutionalized in any way in our culture. It is under all the . . . .

BERNARD: Technically speaking, it is. I mean, well, Wardell, using your own knowledge to make a point . . . did he say it in a group or just in private conversation that if he were making generalizations on the basis of his clients and patients, then he has one picture and would draw one set of generalizations about extramarital relations. But in terms of his survey . . . .

POMEROY: I don't see how this applies.

BERNARD: Well, it is going on all the time.

POMEROY: Right.

BERNARD: Extramarital relations are going on all the time, no one calls the police, no one does anything about it. We just don't want to have it called to our attention. As long as no one is flagrant about it, as long as no one is neglecting the children, we don't want to be bothered.

SEMINAR MEMBER: We do do something about it.

POMEROY: Yes, we have seminars on it.

SEMINAR MEMBER: We point a finger at them.

BERNARD: Do you mean that two-thirds of the men are having fingers pointed at them? And one-third of the women who are forty or over are having fingers pointed at them?

POMEROY: No, but they are concerned about society's disapproval of this.

BERNARD: Well, the norm is, not to be flagrant about it. It is being flagrant that violates the rule.

POMEROY: The point I am making is that they are pointing their own fingers at themselves because they feel that this is not approved and there is no way of doing this in our culture.

BERNARD: Are the people you interviewed in your survey feeling this way?

POMEROY: About roughly half of the ones who are having extramarital intercourse have feelings against it—no, a third, I would say.

NEUBECK: I want to go a step further than that. I think this superimposed guilt, even if society is not pointing a finger at me, has a result. I think it makes sex pretty lousy. We have been talking about sexual experiences as if they were all of one kind. And it is one thing to have an orgasm, it is another thing to have another kind of orgasm. And I think that guilt certainly, and guilt as we have defined it, now ranges from one end of the continuum where one has guilt feelings about one specific person to the other end of the continuum where it is a vague anxiety, unconscious superego pangs, so you have that whole compact of guilt, that this usually makes for pretty lousy relations in and out of bed, of course. But certainly as a sexual act. Let me wave my own flag in the area of sex. I think that in order for a sexual act to be a good, effective, successful sexual act, it is part and parcel of a total relationship. I am not talking about love in some identical way. But I am talking about the total context of the social and emotional realms in which you live, in which you develop a set of behaviors which are going to pay off for you. So now I will wave my real flag. I don't believe that genital contact in and by itself is purely genital contact. I just don't believe that. Except for the psychopath. The psychopath who is unable to put himself in this perspective or is having a variety of feelings, including the social kinds, he can do it over and over again with anybody. And, of course, they are lousy bets for marriage, anyway.

To go back to where I started, I think that this compact feeling of discomfort, guilt, anxiety, you name it, really results in very lousy sexual payoffs.

BERNARD: This is the point I was making, that women are changing. I think the difference isn't so great for men.

SEMINAR MEMBER: A feeling about one's spouse, a feeling about oneself, a feeling about the kind of world you want. I think it is a kind of total integrity which says this way even though I don't think that any of us will reach such a narrow line, where we can comfortably say.

SEMINAR MEMBER: But it is a very basic factor that no man can make two total commitments at the same time.

NEUBECK: Oh, but that is not a basic fact.

SEMINAR MEMBER: It is a logical fact.

NEUBECK: No, but I think we do this. . . .

POMEROY: Of course, the question is whether extramarital intercourse has a total commitment.

SEMINAR MEMBER: I think there is still a need to differentiate here, differentiate between this thing we set up as adultery and extramarital affairs. And I think that there is quite a distinction here. When we think of adultery, what do we think about?

SEMINAR MEMBER: It is a dirty world.

BERNARD: By definition it is bad.

SEMINAR MEMBER: It has a negative connotation, and I think here is a good reason for it. I don't think it is there for no reason. I mean, there is a good reason. On the other hand, I think "extramarital" has an entirely different meaning to it, and it is a different sort of thing. I can relate it, I think, to somebody's example in Germany; and we can do the same in Scandinavia. And I think we have extramarital affairs. I don't think they are defined as adultery in that culture. Do you agree with what I'm saying? And I think we need to make that distinction here, that there is quite a decided difference, and if we look at it and try to decide between these two things . . . .

SEMINAR MEMBER: From what you say here, society or culture makes the difference in adultery and extramarital relations.

SEMINAR MEMBER: Yes, certainly this is one big factor.

POMEROY: And that our culture is changing.

SEMINAR MEMBER: How would you define adultery?

SEMINAR MEMBER: My definition of adultery, and this may be all wet, is a dishonest relationship, and I think this is where the guilt lies. In other words, it is breaking off a relationship with another person, breaking a commitment, whatever you want to call it.

NEUBECK: So this would be quite different from where people give each other mutual permission to do these things.

SEMINAR MEMBER: In other words, I need to use the example we have used: the club—the kind of examples where permission is granted which is similar to the fun in Germany where permission is granted at Mardi Gras time, or the Scandinavian mores.

NEUBECK: This will lead us back to the question of tolerance, because then both parties are aware of what is going on. Your point of some spiritual entity that prevents you from taking the final sexual step is kind of a conglomeration of a number of things that you call life style, personality, values—a whole compact.

SEMINAR MEMBER: I don't like to use the word "spiritual." For me it has other connotations.

NEUBECK: It may or may not have a spiritual component as well. Some people probably will call all of this spiritual. After all, we are not clear on that. For you this is the most important factor. I would once more say to you, I think that for many people who cannot define it as specifically as you can, it is simply fear of the unknown, that would prevent them from taking this final step, that they are going out into an ocean. And they don't know really will their skill in swimming carry them across?

SEMINAR MEMBER: That might be fine, but there is also the lure of the unknown.

POMEROY: If you will allow me to project into the future. . . . This would be my guess as to what I think is going to happen. I think that we would have a lot of change from the 1920's. And I think that after that a lot of gradual increase in premarital intercourse at the upper levels for females, there has been a gradual increase in extramarital intercourse for both male and female. And I see now a continuation of this gradual, not sudden change or revolution, so that now we have one-half and two-thirds, it may gradually be 40 per cent and 80 per cent.

SEMINAR MEMBER: What will it do to us?

POMEROY: What will it do to us? To the family in terms of children or to your . . . .

NEUBECK: I will let our sociologist here speak on that. Again, I think you ought to realize that he is only talking about a slight increase in percentage of something that is here now. I think most of us would agree that American family life, despite all the disastrous future people predict for it, is doing pretty well. If we are not too idealistic about marriage and family life to begin with, and as professionals we shouldn't be, then it appears that the family is doing its job about as well as can be expected in this . . . .

BERNARD: Divorce is not going up . . . I don't know how long this will take . . . .

NEUBECK: Take as long as you like.

BERNARD: Let me make a long running start. I don't think that all trends necessarily increase; you know there are cyclical things, too. For example, Restoration England was extremely profligate, and then came Victorian times which were very puritanical. So it does not follow that a trend will automatically continue in the same direction, and I think I see the beginning of a change in one trend which has had sort of equivocal or ambivalent results, and that has to do with female sexuality. The bodies of women are much more susceptible to cultural control. If you were going to trace male sexuality from Adam on, you would find, just taking ejaculation as your index, it has varied, but within very small limits. Modern men, if they don't have to work too hard, still have about the same number of ejaculations as would Adam.

POMEROY: Oh, I don't agree with that.

BERNARD: It is in your book, practically.

POMEROY: On the contrary, for other cultures there is a tremendous increase.

BERNARD: I asked you this once before. If they don't have to work so hard . . . .

POMEROY: You think Adam was working? You are taking . . . .

NEUBECK: Without slighting ejaculation here, would you accept the proposition that the variety for men is certainly much more limited? That we can accept.

BERNARD: In the case of women, however, their bodies are extremely susceptible to cultural control. In the fifteenth century they were . . . you know, they frightened men. They were so aggressive, and it was taken for granted that they were much more sexually active than men (and the satires on women and Chaucer's wife of Bath, if you remember her). Well, then there was a change, and in the nineteenth century women were not supposed to be responsive. And who ever talked about female orgasm? Most women didn't even know what it meant. Only loose women even responded sexually. Women were proud of being frigid. Well, then, about the turn of the century we have this movement back until orgasm became compulsive. They just had to have orgasm. And I think I see a change going on. Ethel Nash has a lovely story about Master's works now. Where girls used to come to counselors to find out if they were getting the right kind of orgasm, now they don't have to worry about that, now they worry about whether they are having the right kind of rash. But in other words, orgasm became almost a compulsive thing. Many women have been happily married, and many women even in Victorian times were happily married, never having had an orgasm. Since it was never expected, they didn't know what they were missing, they weren't unhappy about it. But in the twentieth century, not only must a woman be responsive, not only must she have orgasm, but a specific kind of orgasm . . . you know climbing the hill, and seeing sunsets, and all that sort of thing. If she didn't, she wasn't 100% woman, or he wasn't 100% man. I think this period of compulsive orgasm may be waning and women won't feel they have to make a career of finding the man . . . . And that, by the way, was also blamed on men, because they were responsible, so here were the poor men going around with guilt because they weren't producing the proper orgasm in women, and the women blaming them for it, which I think was a sick thing that maybe we had to go through, but I think perhaps the time may be coming when we can be more relaxed about it. Many women can be happily married, if their husbands love them, they are responsive, they get pleasure by giving their husbands pleasure. They don't feel all that awful if they don't have orgasm. I think it will be much better when they don't have to. When they can be relaxed about it, if they have it, okay, if they don't, okay. It isn't the whole thing. Provided they have a good relationship. I think this is what is important to a woman. They want to feel secure, they want to feel loved, they want to feel that they are important, that they are women. Most of all, they want to be made to feel that they are women, and it doesn't have to be only this insistence on a certain kind of orgasm. So, for the future, and maybe I am sort of projecting my own wishes, I would forecast a time when both men and women can be more relaxed about sex, in or out of marriage. And I think this more relaxed attitude would be a good thing.

POMEROY: Do you see this as a wave of the future? I mean, you were talking about where this was going.

NEUBECK: I am not pushing this, I am saying that this is what I see as a possibility of happening. I don't know the answers, what the payoffs are. We really haven't studied this enough.

But there is enough evidence on the other side as well. As we have discussed here, we have discussed these cases of people who seem to be operating within a different kind of framework. So, in terms of evidence, there is evidence on a variety of sides. I think there are two or three, in fact, or even three or four, not just two. But don't let's get involved in a controversy which we cannot possibly hope to solve. I would rather go in the direction that I asked you before, to end up with. Namely, that is the tolerance angle, if in fact we do have patterns emerging of this sort.

SEMINAR MEMBER: I would like to call your attention to what this man had to say here. I think we are missing a point. Aren't we saying that this has to be an all-or-nothing proposition for everybody? And I think this is a big mistake to think this way. I think what is emerging from experience is that some marriages are going to be of this type, whether we like it or not. This does not mean that all marriages have to be of this type. But we are getting to the point where this may be eventually permissible, for people to have various kinds of monogamous marriages, call them semi-monogamous or whatever you want.

NEUBECK: I think you clarified that very neatly. Let us go on that assumption.

SEMINAR MEMBER: In the tolerance area, I would like to try what a friend of mine calls the "symbiotic suburban syndrome." He says that in different marriages there are multiple relationships. For example, there are serial monogamous marriages, if that makes sense, where the original father is supporting the children from the first marriage where there is a second marriage of both partners, where another original is still supporting his children. You get into the third marriage where the first father is still supporting the children. What you get is these people do not move away, they stay in the same church, they take the children to church. The mother takes them, the father picks them up. Instead they feel highly moral, not immoral, because they made the choice and decided to divorce and then to remarry and to stay within the norms of society. Instead of seeming to break up the family, the family stays together, but the parent of one is not the biological. . . .

NEUBECK: Which goes on the principle that marriage cannot possibly fulfill all of the needs of all of the people all of the time. And therefore one gives up one's rights to the other person in certain kinds of areas. That is what we are really saying.

When we get into this question of tolerance there was a question that it seems that women have always had to be more tolerant of the extramarital behavior of their men. Is there a difference now coming up that men have to develop a tolerance toward the extramarital behavior of their wives? Would you care to say something about that? Because this is the other side of that coin, and perhaps much more painful.

POMEROY: It is curious that we have two words in the English language—correct me if I am wrong—for a wife stepping out on her husband. He is "cuckolded." But then there is another, if he knows what she is doing and accepts it, he is "withholded," which is worse than being cuckolded because he knows about it, and doesn't do anything. But there is no word in the other direction, as far as I know.

NEUBECK: You can personalize this again. What would it take for me as my wife's husband to compartmentalize myself so that I could tolerate her experiences outside of our marriage.

BERNARD: From the point of view of competitive concerns, extramarital sex relations are considerably more threatening than premarital. If a girl who has had premarital relations and marries a man, he can assume that, everything considered, he was the best sexual partner. At least he had something that compensated for whatever he may have lacked. But in the extramarital sex relations, he has no such reassurances. He is competing with a partner or partners, who, for all he knows, may be better performers than he. And if the difference is great enough to warrant her wanting a divorce, he knows clearly he has lost. Women have long since known the anguish of this humiliation, of knowing that they were less attractive sexually than the other woman. It is one of the hardest defeats in the world to take. It may be ineffable. Women learn to forgive, rarely to forget. In the past, acceptance of this type of defeat has been almost impossible for men to swallow. The law has been lenient if a man resorted to violence, even assault and murder. But apparently a change has been taking place in this respect.

NEUBECK: This I feel is a much more difficult proposition. At the moment anyway, certainly as a next step. But it is an extremely important point. This may be a future position. We have various sociological evidence how in various societies people have worked it out. And it is not only the Mormon culture, but other cultures, too, in which these things have been tried. But as much as we can learn from the past, it seems to me that we do live in the twentieth century. We do live in a modern society in which the ground rules may be quite different. Now if there are natural "givens," and if there are physiological "givens," may there not be some human "givens" in general that cannot be violated? My answer to him was that I did not think so, that there was enough evidence of that. This was essentially my answer to you, Jessie.

BERNARD: Well, I think there are, but I don't want to start a whole new train of thought here. I think there are certain "givens."

NEUBECK: Well, I think so too, and on a note of no closure which we predicted . . . . I won't even attempt a summary because I think we can all see the funneling of our thoughts and ideas. I have been greatly impressed both with your willingness to talk about yourselves, your intellectual honesty, and I hope this will pay off for you. Thank you, Jessie and Wardell, and everybody.

William Graham Cole

RELIGIOUS ATTITUDES TOWARD EXTRAMARITAL INTERCOURSE

The conventional language of both professionals and amateurs in psychology has traditionally divided sexual relations into three temporal categories: premarital, marital, and extramarital. This ignores the fact that a very considerable number of individuals never marry, but do, nonetheless, engage in sexual activity. From this standpoint, then, there are only two kinds of sex: that which takes place within marriage and that which occurs outside the bonds of matrimony. One cannot ignore the significant differences in sexual contacts experienced in a context of total freedom from commitment—legally, emotionally, or religiously—and those which have long been called adulterous, but the term premarital should properly be reserved for relations seen in hindsight from the later status of wedlock. At the time they occur, no one can guarantee that the individuals involved will subsequently marry anyone.

Our present concern is with those activities carried on by married persons with individuals other than the spouse. Historically, the great religious traditions of the world have frowned upon such activities with considerable severity, though there have been many variations in the definition of marriage and in the penalties prescribed for those who violate its restrictive taboos. Polygamous cultures have, on the whole, taken a rather tolerant view of concubinage. The question arises, however, whether such relationships are, strictly speaking, extramarital, since the concubine is taken into the home, or harem, and the male assumes full responsibility for her welfare. When Abraham's wife, Sarah, proved barren, it was she who urged him to bed with her handmaiden, Hagar, in order to provide the continuation of Abraham's seed. Jacob's two wives, Leah and Rachel, used their handmaidens in their rivalry for the affections of their husband, the four women producing among them the twelve sons of the patriarch. In none of these marriages does the Bible adopt a pejorative tone. Even Lot's incest with his two daughters is reported without censure.

What is most striking about the religious traditions of the West is the double standard that is consistently encountered. In historic Judaism, Christianity, and Islam alike, the restrictions placed upon women do not apply to men, and the punishments for violations of those restrictions differ dramatically. Both the Hebrew and the Muslim codes of law were the products of nomadic cultures evolving at a time when progeny was highly desirable, for economic and military purposes. If the female is capable of producing offspring every nine months at the maximum, while the male can sire an indefinite number of babies, polygamy was naturally the result. The woman in ancient Canaan and in pre-Muslim Arabia was essentially a chattel, belonging first to her father whose will was originally absolute, embracing the power of life and death, and then to her husband, who early possessed the same rights as the father. The power of both husband and father generally came to be limited by law. Coitus on the part of an unmarried daughter made her damaged goods, rendering it impossible for her father to marry her off and collect the bride price from her husband. Deuteronomy 22:13–21 spells out the primitive rite of displaying the "tokens of virginity," apparently the bloodstained garments and bedclothes of the bride, soiled by the rupture of the hymen. If the "tokens" were lacking, the young woman was to be stoned to death! No such limitations were placed upon the man, either before or after marriage. He could not rape a betrothed girl on penalty of death; to rape or seduce an unpromised maiden brought the penalty of paying the bridal price to the father, and, if the latter demanded it, marriage. But it was in almost every case the father's rights that were of primary concern. There was no law forbidding the male to have coitus with a female not under the protection of some man, either father or husband. Adultery was understood, not as the sexual relations of a married man, but rather as the violation of another man's wife or as any sexual act of a married woman with anyone other than her husband. So long as the male avoided offending another male, he was free to act, with few restraints.

If he was detected in an adulterous act with another man's wife, he shared with her the fate of capital punishment. In this respect, at least, a single standard prevailed. But again, it was as a punishment for his crime against the husband, not against the woman as such. This sprang from the Hebrew's great concern for the continuation of his family line. A barren woman could be divorced easily, and the most elaborate arrangements were made to assure offspring. If a man died childless, leaving a still nubile widow behind, it was the solemn duty of his nearest male relative to take her to wife, to beget a baby, and to raise it as the seed of the deceased. The story of Onan and the Book of Ruth both illustrate the institution of the so-called Levirate marriage, from the Latin *levir,* meaning brother-in-law.

The early Hebrews had only the haziest notions of any life beyond death, and to continue beyond one's own limited existence depended, therefore, upon offspring. There was never any question about the maternal parentage of a child; only its paternity was a matter of speculation, and therefore, the virtuous fidelity of the Hebrew wife was zealously and jealously guarded. There was even a religious ritual prescribed for a husband who suspected his wife of adultery, described in gruesome detail in Numbers 5:11–31. This was evidently a variant of the earlier Babylonian ordeal by water, when a philanderer who could not swim had best exercise extreme caution! As time went on, some of the primitive harshness was gradually softened. Actual witnesses to adultery were required, and to bear false testimony was to suffer death, which was the fate of the frustrated elders who accused Susannah.

Mohammed, after an opaque experience with his favorite wife, Ayesha, demanded the evidence of four witnesses and replaced the death penalty with flogging. Both the guilty male and the unfaithful wife were to receive one hundred lashes. But anyone making an accusation of adultery and unable to substantiate the charge with four witnesses was to receive eighty lashes. Islam, strongly influenced, especially in the Prophet's early career by the Old Testament, has not, until very recent times, followed the gradual transition, which took place in Judaism, from polygamy to monogamy. Mohammed, in a rather obscure passage in the Koran, seemed to have provided license for the faithful male to take four wives. He, himself, married fourteen times and left nine widows behind him. But four and one were his favorite, mystical numbers, and the scholars of the Koran were entirely consistent in setting the legal limit on wives at four, although no restrictions were placed upon the number of concubines a man might have, if he could afford to keep them and was willing to endure the inevitable rivalries and hostilities within his household. Like the Hebrew, however, the Muslim guarded the fidelity of his wives with fanatical zeal, ultimately veiling them and shutting them away in harems protected by eunuchs. No such limitations were placed upon his sexual activity. He was required to be faithful, neither to any one wife nor to all of them together. Extramarital relations for him were entirely open. He was enjoined from violating another man's wife, but, as with the early Hebrews, any woman not under male protection was fair game.

In Israel after the Babylonian exile, the egalitarian concerns of the prophets were codified into law at many points, and post-exilic

Judaism considerably modified the double standard governing sexual relations. Polygamy gradually withered away, partly because of economic factors. It requires impressive financial resources to support multiple wives and their offspring. In both Hebrew and Muslim circles, extra wives served as much as status symbols as outlets for erotic impulses. The contemporary suburbanite displays his growing affluence by buying a second car. In polygamous cultures, the same conspicuous consumption is manifested by taking another wife. So Solomon's collection of three hundred wives and seven hundred concubines was flaunted, not as a commentary on his sexual prowess, but as a symbol of his fabulous wealth. In Muslim lands, polygamy has almost always been limited to the rich and the powerful. The ordinary man could not afford more than one wife at a time, and now that the economic circumstances of most countries where Islam is the official faith are rendering polygamy less and less feasible, parents are seeking monogamous marriages for their daughters. And the theologians are adapting the Koran to the changing scene, pointing out that the Prophet granted permission for a man to take a second, third, or fourth wife, *providing* he treated them equally with the first. That, say the scholars, is clearly impossible, so by implication the Koran enjoins monogamy.

This is not the first time that theology has adapted to changing economic vicissitudes, and something of the same process seems to have occurred in Judaism after the exile. It is against the background of the heightened ethical awareness, the strong emphasis on inner motivation, and the broadening egalitarianism, all developed in the Judaism of the first century B.C., that the New Testament pronouncements must be seen. By the time of Jesus, the Jewish woman had achieved a far greater level of equality than her ancestors had enjoyed under the old law. The Pharisees, a much-maligned and misunderstood group, had broadened and deepened the law by a process of interpretation, later codified in the Talmud. Adultery was seen as sexual infidelity on the part of either husband or wife with any other person. Indeed, Jesus' famous words about a man's lusting in his heart after another woman already constituting adultery (Matthew 5:27–28), is echoed or foreshadowed in the sayings of the rabbis. A faithful monogamy until death was clearly the ideal, though the practice obviously fell somewhat short of that, as has always been the case with Christians.

Jesus sought to internalize the law and thereby transcend it. His emphasis was not so much on the outward act as on the inner motivation. And he made no distinctions between males and females. He went behind the law, in his words about divorce, to the divine purpose of creation (Mark 10:2–12; Matthew 19:1–9; Luke 16:18). In this context, we find the saying, "Whoever divorces his wife and marries another commits adultery against her; and if she divorces her husband and marries another, she commits adultery." Thus, even a divorce sanctioned by the civil authority, or in Jesus' time, by the religious leaders of Judaism, does not grant liberty for a married man or woman to have sexual relations even with a legal second spouse. This has been the historic foundation for the traditional Roman Catholic position that a second marriage, contracted while the original partner is still alive, constitutes an adulterous union.

The Pauline Epistles, and the other New Testament writings, which are relatively sparse on the subject of sex in general, follow the line taken by Jesus. The strictures against sexual irregularities of any kind, outside the marriage bond, are sharp and harsh, with strong condemnations of prostitution. Paul even goes so far as to say that "He who joins himself to a prostitute becomes one body with her." The somewhat negative (I have in another context called it dualistic[1]), questionable attitude toward sexuality in general, however, forms a striking contrast to the spirit of Jesus, who taught no asceticism and regarded the sins of pride, arrogance, malice, envy, and so on, as far more serious than those of the flesh. It is curious that Paul could so well understand his Master's mind at the core and yet miss the point on the periphery. In Romans 13:8–10, he could write, "He who loves his neighbor has fulfilled the law. The Commandments, 'You shall not commit adultery, you shall not kill, you shall not steal, you shall not covet,' and any other Commandments are summed up in this sentence, 'You shall love your neighbor as yourself.' Love does no wrong to a neighbor; therefore, love is the fulfilling of the law." This is pure Jesus, plain and undefiled, penetrating to the heart, to the inner motive, concentrating attention there, rather than on the outer act. Yet, elsewhere, Paul could scald and blast transgressors with a fervor worthy of Jonathan Edwards. And this is particularly true with respect to sexual deviations.

Paul was, like Jesus, primarily and essentially a Jew, who did not see life split into a realm of pure spirit opposed to an unclean and evil material world, where the body and its impulses were suspect and spurious. But, unlike Jesus, he was a Jew of the Dispersion and, therefore, not unaffected by the dualism that was the predominant mood of the later Hellenistic Age. His clear preference for celibacy was doubtless motivated primarily by his apocalyptic expectations, but one cannot escape the overtones, at least, of an inchoate asceticism

[1] *Sex in Christianity and Psychoanalysis* (New York: Oxford University Press, 1955).

concerning sex. He was a realist and, therefore, made allowance for marital coitus as a preferable alternative to being consumed with passion (I Corinthians 7:9). But any sort of extramarital relations were for him a special kind of anathema. The only exception he made to lifelong fidelity in a monogamous marriage was in the so-called "Pauline privilege," which was centuries later to be taken up by the reformers. If a Christian was married to an unbeliever, and the pagan's spouse chose not to remain in the union, then the church member was free to marry again, this time within the household of faith. But even here Paul was careful to hedge his counsel, confessing that this was his own opinion, not the word from the Lord. (I Corinthians 7:12–16)

All of this, both Jesus' absolute stand on divorce, coupled with his counsel of perfection on inner lust, and Paul's sternly moralistic view of sex were taken up and codified by a Church which very rapidly, as the first century drew to a close, lost its roots in Jewish soil and became primarily a Gentile, Hellenistic community. The dualism which dominated the time, in theory if not in practice, was resisted by the Church at many crucial points in its theology. Against the Gnostics, it retained the doctrine of Creation, regarding the material world as essentially good; it insisted that the Incarnation was a fact, that the Divine Word had indeed "become flesh," fully uniting very God with very Man; it clung to the real human life and the genuine human death of Jesus. But its stubborn refusal to capitulate to Hellenistic spiritualism in theology was not matched by a like intransigence in sexual ethics, where celibacy rapidly became the ideal, with monogamous marriage as a concession to human weakness. The old double standard reasserted itself with respect to extramarital relations. The same code of rigid sexual purity applied both to men and women, except in this one area. Basil of Caesarea, in Epistle 199, reluctantly conceded that the sexual relations of a married man with an unmarried woman are not, technically speaking, adultery. A wife whose husband had so behaved should forgive and forget, but any married woman guilty of infidelity was to be put away as "polluted." Basil agreed that "the requirement is not easy, but custom has so directed."

By the time of Augustine in the fourth century, the only legitimate usage of sex, even within marriage, was for the privilege of procreation and to quiet the lust of the spouse. Any other sexual activity constituted a grave sin. Yet curiously, Augustine found it necessary to admit that prostitution was an institution with certain positive uses. "Remove prostitution from human affairs," he wrote, "and you pollute all things with lust." Thomas Aquinas took a similar view. "Although God is omnipotent and supremely good, nevertheless he allows certain evils to take place in the universe, which he might prevent, lest without them greater goods might be forfeited, or greater evils ensue. Accordingly, in human government also, those who are in authority rightly tolerate certain evils lest certain goods be lost or certain greater evils be incurred." Prostitution he viewed as like the sewer in a palace, in the absence of which the whole place would be filled with pollution. In the absence of prostitution the world would be filled with sodomy. Aquinas, therefore, agreed with Augustine that "The earthly city has made the use of harlots a lawful immorality."

This is not to say that either Aquinas or Augustine countenanced Christians' consorting with prostitutes. By scripture and tradition adultery remained a grave sin in the sight of God. Yet even for the Church member, Aquinas found the female guilty of three sins in extramarital relations, while the male commits only two. The adulterous wife was unfaithful to God, committed an offense against her husband by making him uncertain whether her children were actually his, and bore the offspring of another man. The husband wronged his own children by his union with another woman, and he hindered the good of another's progeny. Why he was not also unfaithful to God was never made clear by the angelic doctor. Adultery was for him a "natural" sin, unlike bestiality, sodomy, and masturbation, which were contrary to nature. Nonetheless, it was, save only for the rape of a married woman, the gravest of such transgressions, serious enough in matter to be regarded as a "mortal" sin if carried out deliberately and with full knowledge.

The Reformation generally rejected clerical celibacy and took a somewhat more realistic, if no less positive view of sex, but the attitude of Luther toward extramarital relations was as rigorous and as uncompromising as were the traditions of Rome. Luther, confronted with the practical problem of monarchs' seeking divorce in order to marry more sexually responsive wives, found no way to evade the clear scriptural prohibition of divorce and suggested that the Bible permitted polygamy. But this represented a second marriage and not extramarital relations. Calvin hated adultery with a deadly passion. It was, for him, worse than fornication because by it the sanctity of marriage is violated and "a spurious and illegitimate offspring is derived." He approved the death penalty provided by the Old Testament law, although he was never able to get such a statute on the books of Geneva, where the sentence was nine days imprisonment on bread and water, together with a fine. To those who pointed at the example of Jesus' forgiving the woman taken in adultery, Calvin responded that the Lord was content to exercise his unique office, which did not include the responsibilities of the magistrate. No judge could possibly follow Jesus' example without gross abuse of his office. So heinous a crime did Calvin find adultery that he believed it to sever the marriage bond, rendering the wronged spouse free to marry again.

Luther, likewise, allowed remarriage of divorced persons who were either innocent victims of adultery by the partner, or who were bound to a sexually unresponsive spouse. His famous remark, "If the wife refuse, let the maid come," raised eyebrows all over Europe. But he was not suggesting that a man could make a mistress of his maid, only that he was within his right to marry again if his first wife refused to render "the conjugal debt." So, essentially, the Reformation took as dim a view of extramarital relations as did the Roman Catholic Church. In the Anglican tradition, the Bishop's book condemned all coitus as being "of itself and in its own nature damnable," but rendered pure and clean within marriage by the power of the Word of God and the sacrament of matrimony. Without that cleansing action, of course, all sex was evil. The King's book contented itself with the simple statement that coitus is unlawful unless sanctioned by wedlock. This position has been uniformly held by both the Christian and Jewish ecclesiastical authorities until very recent times.

One of the early moderns to take issue with the traditional religious posture was John MacMurray, the British philosopher and theologian. In a book published in 1936, *Reason and Emotion,* MacMurray included a chapter, "The Virtue of Chastity," which he defined as emotional sincerity. He rejected the traditional ethical approach of Christendom as owing more to Stoicism than to the New Testament. The whole of Western morality, according to MacMurray, has been built on principle, "a universal judgment upon which we base our conduct," a "rule defining how we ought to behave," applied to particular situations, either positively or negatively. Behind the principle lies the Stoic concept of *will,* which presupposes a conflict between reason and emotion. The proper conduct of life is to rule the passions by the mind, acting rationally whether one really wants to or not. This was the basis of Roman law, which profoundly influenced all European institution. Even Kant—the greatest European moralist—built his entire moral structure on the difference between acting on impulse or desire and acting on duty or will. In sexual ethics, this has meant that all judgments have been made on external, intellectual principles, regarding all sex outside of marriage as evil and sinful, and any sex within marriage as altogether proper and good.

Against this external, intellectual morality, MacMurray set what he regarded as the essence of Jesus' teaching—an ethics based upon emotional sincerity. "What Jesus did was to substitute an inner and emotional basis of behavior for an external and intellectual one." MacMurray likened emotional integrity to intellectual honesty. To pretend to feel otherwise than one, in fact, does is the equivalent of telling a lie. Sexual relations that spring from mere erotic attraction to another are immoral, both within marriage and outside of it. This is to use and exploit another human being. But sexual intercourse based on genuine love, on sincere mutuality, requires no other justification to validate it, not even marriage. MacMurray carefully defined his terms in an effort to render rationalization difficult, if not impossible, circumscribing his concept of love so as to exclude sentimentality and mere physical arousal. But he was persuaded that real love, understood in the Christian sense of *agape*, made sex pure and fulfilling for both persons without regard to their marital status. He knew that his position was dangerous to conventional morality and that it would arouse much anxiety and hostility, but he felt compelled to assert it. To the question whether his viewpoint might prevent people from having intercourse outside marriage, he could only plead ignorance. And he denied that such a consideration was of prime importance. "Compared with the importance of personal reality, of chastity, it is a point of no significance."

MacMurray was an early pioneer into a territory now well explored and named "situation" or "contextual" ethics. Dietrich Bonhoeffer, a German pastor who began his ministry as an absolutist operating on principles, found, under the Nazi tyranny, that it was his Christian duty to violate the command against murder and became involved in the plot to assassinate Hitler. In prison, he worked out his new system of Christian ethics, based upon the conviction that "the question of the good is posed and is decided in the midst of each definite, yet unconcluded, unique and transient situation of our lives, in the midst of our living relationships with men, things, institutions, and powers—in other words, in the midst of our historical existence." No abstract principle, rule, or law, could be trusted to direct conduct, because it cannot take account of the infinite variety of persons and contact contexts. "Principles," said Bonhoeffer, "are only tools in God's hands, soon to be thrown away as unserviceable." Rudolph Bultmann, the great German New Testament scholar, was led by his Biblical studies to the same position, seeing Paul no less than Jesus as substituting the rule of love for the rule of law. Both Augustine and Luther had said, "Love God and do as you please," following Paul's lead in the passage from Romans quoted earlier (13:8–10). Neither the Apostle nor the Bishop of Hippo, nor the German reformer, however, had had the courage to take this insight to its logical and natural conclusion. This is precisely what the contemporary contextualists or situationists are trying to do.

Paul Lehman, Professor of Christian Ethics at New York's Union Theological Seminary, has taken considerable account of what he refers to as "boundary situations," encounters between human beings which lie outside the walls and fences constructed by a conventional morality. The ordinary rules of the game of life, the distillations of man's collective experience, are applicable and useful in most of life's circumstances, to be followed in the majority of cases. But these must never remain absolutes, binding in every situation; for occasions do arise when Christian law demands their violation out of a general concern for persons. Thus, Bonhoeffer felt compelled to kill Hitler as an act of Christian conscience. The wife in the play, *Tea and Sympathy,* violated all the canons of proper morality by giving herself sexually to the young school lad, her husband's pupil, but, so say the contextualists, hers was an act of genuine love, reassuring the young man about his shaky masculinity.

Paul Tillich and Martin Buber were both, in their way, believers in situational ethics, and there is a growing number of members of this particular school of thought in both Christian and Jewish circles. Thus, we see that the traditional Western religious taboo against any and all forms of extramarital intercourse is, in our time, undergoing considerable modification. It should be emphasized that this is not a mere theological rationalization of Hugh Hefner's permissiveness. None of the religious contextualists would go that far. Some of them, the more conservative, would argue that only the most unusual and extreme circumstances would justify extramarital coitus. And all of them would agree that mere erotic arousal and mutual attraction are insufficient grounds for tumbling into bed with someone other than one's marriage partner. There must be, first of all, genuine Christian love, an outgoing, sacrificial concern for the other's welfare. There must be an absence of any selfish exploitation or abuse of another person, and the act must be totally mutual, expressing in the flesh a union of two personalities.

The most popular presentation of the case has been made by Joseph Fletcher, Professor of Social Ethics at the Episcopal Theology School in Cambridge, Massachusetts, in his book, *Situation Ethics.* He sets this forth in a series of four presuppositions and six propositions. The presuppositions are: pragmatism, relativism, positivism, and personalism. By pragmatism, he means simply that all ethics must be concerned with what *works.* Abstract, metaphysical theories are of no value if they cannot be applied to concrete, actual problems. Relativism means that no human creation, intellectual, moral, or even theological, can be absolutized, "the faith once for all delivered to the saints." Changing occasions dictate changing responses and man must recognize his finitude and limitations. Positivism is the position that recognized that life is primarily decision-making based on commitment to some value, which is nondemonstrable by reason. The Christian operates out of the context of his *positive* faith, which he cannot prove; but then neither can the hedonist or any other advocate of a system of values. Personalism implies the centrality of persons as over against things, abstractions, rules, and laws. God is personal and calls upon men as persons to act in response to the needs of persons.

The six propositions are, briefly: (1) Only one "thing" is intrinsically good, love, nothing else. (2) The ruling norm of Christian decision is love, nothing else. (3) Love and justice are the same, for justice is love distributed, nothing else. (4) Love wills the neighbor's good, whether we like him or not. (5) Only the end justifies the means, nothing else. (6) Love's decisions are made situationally, not prescriptively. On this basis, of course, Fletcher parts company with all traditional sexual ethics which are based on law and abstract principle. But this is not to say that he would easily condone extramarital coitus. There are very carefully defined preconditions for its justification.

The contextualists remain in a minority of Western religious leaders, the majority of whom continue faithful to the traditional taboos. But there has been widespread affect by the new morality within the larger ecclesiastical circles. The British Quakers recently published an official statement on sex ethics which was by no means absolutist, and countless pastors and rabbis, in their personal counseling, if not in their official utterances, are less rigid and more permissive in their attitudes toward actual persons caught in adulterous relationships. Critics of situation ethics argue that it cannot provide a foundation for any social order, however useful it may be for individuals. They also insist that, while love may on occasion demand a jumping of the normal boundaries, these occasions are very rare, indeed, and cannot form the basis for a useful morality for most persons in most of their rather prosaic experiences.

For the majority of the religious West, then, extramarital coitus remains, as always, a sin. A small but articulate and growing group can see exceptions to the rule, justifying what is *de jure* adultery as *de facto* an act of genuine, unselfish Christian love. Which position will prevail in days to come is anybody's guess!

Yoon Hough Kim

THE KINSEY FINDINGS

Whatever may be said in criticism, it seems fair to say that the two reports provided by Alfred C. Kinsey and his associates, *Sexual Behavior in the Human Male* and *Sexual Behavior in the Human Female,* which are under review in the present paper, have contributed to an understanding of human sexual behavior, in and out of marriage, more than any other single work done in this country. There are certain methodological and other inadequacies in their studies, among which the most critical one, in this writer's opinion, is their group sampling design, which seriously restricts the generalizations made through the studies, but almost all critics[1] agree that the Kinsey studies made a monumental contribution to our knowledge of sexual behavior, which had long been kept in darkness.

The Kinsey data were collected from 5,300 males and 5,940 females,[2] who were not probability samples of any existing populations. They over-represented the college-educated, the young, Protestants, urbanites, and certain regions of the country, whereas some groups, such as Negroes, were not included at all. The data, therefore, may well be only a body of isolated data, as informative and interesting as they are, and this must be remembered in regard to all aspects of the Kinsey findings.

[1] The Kinsey study has been subjected to a thorough review in the professional literature. For a review of these reviews, see Erdman Palmore, "Published Reactions to the Kinsey Report," *Social Forces,* 31 (December, 1952), pp. 165–72.

[2] All together, 8,603 male histories and 7,789 female histories were collected, but for various reasons most of the statistical summaries in the two volumes were calculated from 5,300 males and 5,940 females.

INCIDENCES AND FREQUENCIES

When the first volume of the Kinsey Report appeared in 1948, many statistics presented in the report, including those on extramarital intercourse, shocked the public. Of extramarital intercourse, the authors reported that by the age of forty, 26% of married women and 50% of married men in their samples had had this experience. (3, p. 437) These are accumulative incidences.

Even these figures are probably underestimating the reality, according to the authors, because respondents most likely have covered up this experience more than any others. They wrote, "Consequently, the incidence and frequency figures which are given here must represent the absolute minimum, and it is not at all improbable that the actuality may lie 10 to 20% above the figures now given." (2, p. 585)

The active incidence of extramarital intercourse, the number of married people in the sample who were having this experience in any particular five-year period, was, of course, lower than the accumulative incidences. For the men, it was highest among the sixteen to twenty age group, where it reached 35%, and declined thereafter, and for the women, it reached the maximum of 17% among the thirty-six to forty age group, and was lower among the other age groups. (3, p. 437)

Extramarital intercourse, however, is usually a sporadic experience and seldom develops into regular and long lasting relationships. The median frequencies were 0.4 times per week for the sixteen to twenty age groups among the males and forty-one to forty-five among the females, and less in the other age groups of both sexes. In terms of the percentage of the total sexual outlet, extramarital intercourse accounted for less than 10% in the male groups and less than 14% in the female groups. (3, p. 437)

Most of the extramarital activities were experienced with other married persons. For the men, prostitutes supplied something between 8% and 15% of all extramarital intercourse, and most other intercourse was had with companions. (2, p. 588) For the females, the authors reported that the extramarital partners had been, for the most part, married males, but not a few of the unmarried males had had their premarital intercourse with married females, some of whom were the aggressors in starting the relationships. (3, p. 425)

Some 41% of the females in the active sample, those in the sample who had had the experience of extramarital intercourse, had confined their relations to a single partner; another 40% to two to five persons; leaving 19% more promiscuous. The number of partners involved was, of course, related to the length of time over which extramarital activities had been carried on. Some 42% of the females in the active sample had carried on the activities for one year or less; 23% for two to three years; and 35% for four years or more, including 10% who had carried on their relationships for more than ten years. (3, pp. 425–26) No corresponding figures were available for the men in the samples.

There were also not a few married men and women in the sample who had accepted extramarital petting, often with accompanying orgasm, but refused to accept extramarital coitus. The record on this was incomplete, but based on the data collected from 1,090 married women on whom information on this point was available, the authors reported that about 16% had engaged in extramarital petting, although they had never allowed extramarital coitus. (3, p. 427)

RELATED FACTORS

Kinsey and his associates assumed, rather arbitrarily, that human sexual behavior is significantly affected by twelve biological and social factors, including sex, racial-cultural backgrounds, marital status, age, age at adolescence, educational level, occupational level, occupational class of parent, rural-urban background, religious background, religious adherence, and geographic origin. Among these factors, the most important was sex, which was the reason why they divided their work into two volumes; one on the male and the other on the female. Certainly, sex differences showed up in all the areas of sexual behavior they investigated. Some examples of such differences in extramarital activities have already been presented above.

The authors, however, have not always been consistent in explaining these sex differences. It is not always clear whether the authors treated sex as a biological factor or as a socio-cultural factor. For example, when they wrote that "the human male's interest in maintaining his property rights in his female mate, his objection to his wife's extramarital coitus, and her lesser objection to his extramarital activity, are mammalian heritages," (3, p. 412) sex was obviously treated as a biological factor and the whole argument implied a strong biological determinism. On the other hand, they introduced abundant anthropological data which suggest that much of the group differences, including sex differences, in human sexual behavior are the result of different social training and social roles people play. "Most societies," they wrote, "permit or condone extramarital coitus for the male if he is reasonably circumspect about it, and if he does not carry it to extremes which would break up his home, lead to any neglect of his family, outrage his in-laws, stir up public scandal, or start difficulties with the husbands or other relatives of the women with whom he has his extramarital relationships." (3, p. 414) Further, the authors argued in Part III of the Female volume, which dealt with comparisons of the male and the female, that the two sexes do not differ in regard to any of the important elements recognized in physiology. In their own words, "We have already observed that the anatomy and physiology of sexual response and orgasm (Chapters 14 and 15) do not show differences between the sexes that might account for the differences in their sexual responses." (3, p. 688) It seems that this weakens considerably their earlier argument of mammalian heritages.

Furthermore, there is evidence in their writings for changes in patterns of sexual behavior, particularly those among females; they are influenced by social changes such as emancipation or increased knowledge of contraception. In summary, in spite of Kinsey's and his associates' intended or alleged implications of biological determinism, the evidence they presented leaves much room for social and cultural explanations of the sex differences observed in human sexual behavior, including extramarital activities.

Age was another important factor related to different patterns of extramarital activities, as well as of other types of sexual behavior. As has been pointed out previously, age made a difference not only in accumulative incidences of extramarital intercourse, which, of course, were higher among older people, male or female, than younger people, but also in active incidences, which were highest in the youngest group of sixteen to twenty for the males and in the age group thirty-six to forty for the females. The peak for extramarital coitus corresponded roughly to the peak of the growth of sex drive in each sex, a fact that once again implies a biological determinism. Kinsey and his associates, however, also presented some possible social and cultural explanations for the differences. They wrote, for example, "The younger married females had not so often engaged in extramarital coitus, partly because they were still very much interested in their husbands and partly because the young husbands were particularly jealous of their marital rights. Moreover, at that age both the male and the female were more often concerned over the morality of sexual relationships." (3, p. 417)

Educational level was also an important factor in the analysis of extramarital sexual behavior. The relationship between educational level and extramarital intercourse, however, was quite different in the two sexes. For the men in the sample, the authors noted a rather striking interaction effect between educational level and age of extramarital coitus, which made the whole discussion somewhat complicated. Low level males, they observed, generally started extramarital intercourse early in their marriages, often as carry-overs from their premarital relations, and gave it up as they settled down in their own marriages, while high level males generally had most restrained premarital relations only to lose that restraint later in their marriages. They wrote, "In short, lower level males take thirty-five to forty years to arrive at the marital ideals which the upper level begins with; or, to put it with equal accuracy, upper level males take thirty-five to forty years to arrive at the sexual freedom which the lower level accepts in its teens." (2, p. 355)

Lower level males who were married in the late teens have given a record of extramarital intercourse in 45% of the cases, while not more than 27% are actively involved by the age of forty and not more than 19% by the age of fifty. On the other hand, college males of the active sample showed 15% to 20% of the youngest group and 27% by the age of fifty involved in extramarital intercourse. Similarly, the highest frequencies of extramarital intercourse were found among the younger males of lower educational levels, but the frequencies dropped rather steadily with advanced age. Again, this trend was reversed among college-educated males. (2, p. 587)

Educational level was naturally related to occupational level. The authors, however, did not have sufficient data for any detailed analysis of extramarital activities of the males in the sample by occupational level. Within these limits, they observed that "married males of occupational classes 2 and 3 (the laborers and semi-skilled workmen) have 16.7 times as much extramarital intercourse during their late teens as males of occupational class 7 (the future professional group)." (2, p. 588)

For the females in the sample, no significant overall relationship has been found between educational level and extramarital experience. Some 31% of the females in the college sample, as against 24% of those whose education did not go beyond high school, had had extramarital experience. The differences were not significant. Nor did the average frequencies of extramarital intercourse seem to have been related to any significant degree to educational background of the females in the sample. Occupational levels of the females were only somewhat significantly related to incidences of extramarital intercourse when they passed the age of twenty-five; those from upper white collar and professional homes engaged in it more than those from lower classes. But the average frequencies of extramarital intercourse did not vary according to occupational classes. (3, pp. 421–22) The authors did not try to explain these statistical relationships.

Extramarital sexual activities were also influenced by religion, and Kinsey and his associates brought out a very interesting point here; that the differences between religiously devout males and religiously inactive males of the same faith were much greater than the differences between two equally devout groups of different faiths. The active incidence and the frequency of extramarital intercourse were highest among the inactive groups and lowest among the most devout groups. This was true of the Protestant, Jewish, and Catholic groups included in the male samples. The same variation, however, was not found in the female samples. (2, p. 589; 3, p. 424)

Although the authors made some efforts (particularly in Chapter 13 of the Male volume) to account for the above statistical relationships between religious background and sexual outlet, largely relying on historical data, much of this interesting observation remained unexplained.

In their Female volume, Kinsey and his associates wrote that among the 514 females who had extramarital coitus, over 68% had also had premarital coitus, while only 50% of all the married females in the sample had had premarital coitus. In other words, "29% of the females with histories of premarital coitus had had extramarital coitus by the time they contributed their histories to this study, but only 13% of those who had not had premarital coital experience." (3, p. 427) This relationship between premarital coitus and extramarital coitus was strengthened when age was controlled for in the sample.

The authors admitted that there could have been a selective factor in that those who were inclined to accept premarital coitus may have been the ones who were more inclined to accept extramarital coitus, but at the same time they suggested a possible causal relationship between them, pointing out that it is possible that those who had had premarital coitus had persuaded themselves that extramarital coitus is also acceptable.

On the other hand, the experience of premarital intercourse was not related to promiscuity of the females involved, measured by the number of different partners in the extramarital intercourse. No corresponding data have been presented about the males in the sample.

For the females, the authors also found a relationship between their decades of birth and extramarital experience. Both the accumulative and active incidences of extramarital intercourse have been markedly different in different generations. They observed, for example, "The accumulative incidences of extramarital coitus among the females in the sample who were born before 1900 had reached 22% by forty years of age. The incidences among the females who were born in the first decade after 1900 had reached 30% by the same age. The later generations seem to be maintaining that level of incidence." (3, p. 422)

There were, however, no consistent differences in terms of frequencies of extramarital intercourse among these different generations.

Based upon this evidence, the authors concluded that the increase in extramarital coitus, as in other sexual activities which became more prevalent after World War II, lay in the number of females involved, but not necessarily in the frequencies with which the average female had had experience. (3, p. 423) No corresponding data have been presented for the males.

For the males, the authors pointed out that extramarital intercourse occurred more frequently among the males who were living in cities or towns and less frequently in rural populations. (2, p. 588) No corresponding relationships, however, have been reported for the females.

SOCIAL SIGNIFICANCE

Based upon rather fragmentary data, Kinsey and his associates ventured to appraise the social significance of extramarital relations. In their Female volume, which presented this appraisal more systematically than the corresponding section of the Male volume, the authors first suggested the following psychological and social reasons for extramarital relations: variation of sexual experience, social status through the socio-sexual contacts, accommodation to a respected friend, retaliation for the spouse's extramarital activity, assertion of independence, new emotional satisfaction, and spouse's encouragement. (3, pp. 431–35)

In terms of orgasm, they reported that 24% of the females in the active sample had not reached orgasm in their extramarital coitus as often as in their marital coitus; 34% had reached it with about equal frequency; and 42% had it more frequently in extramarital coitus than in marital coitus. The more frequent orgasm in extramarital relations was suggested to have been caused by the male's more extensive courting, sex play, and coital techniques in extramarital intercourse than in marital intercourse. (3, p. 432)

The fact that there was a "not inconsiderable group of cases in the sample in which the husbands had encouraged their wives to engage in extramarital activities" must indicate that there was a drastic change in the traditional sexual union between husband and wife. In the Kinsey samples, some 40% of the females who had had extramarital coitus believed that their husbands knew it and 9% believed that their husbands suspected it. And of those cases in which the husbands either knew it or suspected, some 42% did not have serious difficulty because of it. The authors stated that "adding these cases in which there had been no difficulty to the cases in which the husbands did not know of the extramarital relationships, it is a total of 71% for whom no difficulty had yet developed." (3, p. 434) Kinsey and his associates thereupon challenge the assertion that extramarital relationships will inevitably do damage to a marriage by further stating that sometimes sexual adjustments with the spouse had improved as a result of the female's extramarital experience.

Extramarital intercourse, on the other hand, had figured as a factor in the divorces of a fair number of the males and females in the sample. The authors reported that there were 907 persons, males and females, who had had extramarital experience and whose marriages had been terminated by divorce. Further they wrote, "We have the subjects' judgments of the significance of their extramarital coitus in 415 cases. In nearly two-thirds (61%) of these cases, the subject did not believe that his or her extramarital activity had been any factor in leading to that divorce . . . Some 14% of the females and 18% of the males believed that their extramarital experience had been prime factors in the disruption of the marriage, and something between 21% and 25% more believed that it had been a contributing factor." (3, p. 435)

They further suggested in the Male volume that there were differences at different social levels in their attitudes toward extramarital activities of their spouses. They observed that a considerable portion of the extramarital intercourse at lower levels was experienced without much interference with the affection between husband and wife or with the stability of the marriage, while it was less often accepted in middle-class groups. At higher levels, extramarital intercourse much less often caused difficulty than at lower levels, because it was very seldom known beyond the two persons involved in the relationship. On the other hand, there were exceptional cases at higher levels in which extramarital sexual relations were frankly accepted by the other spouse, which was unknown at other levels.

In terms of sex differences, there was evidence to suggest that wives were generally more tolerant of their husbands' extramarital relations than the latter of the former's extramarital relations when these relations were known to the other spouses. Of the 263 cases about which information on this item was available, 51% of the males, as against 27% of the females in the group, reported that their spouses' extramarital relations had been prime factors in their divorces. On the other hand, 17% of the males, as against 24% of the females, believed that their spouses' extramarital relations had been minor factors in their divorces. (3, p. 436)

The authors concluded their discussion of extramarital relations in the Female volume by pointing out the dilemma between the mammalian heritage of human beings and the social necessity of maintaining a stable marriage. According to them, "it is not likely to be resolved until man moves more completely away from his mammalian ancestry." (3, p. 436)

In general, the authors' discussion of the social significance of extramarital relations has been more subjective than their discussions of other aspects of the problem, and no doubt more specific data must be made available before there can be any overall social explanation of variations in extramarital relations.

It is almost three decades since Kinsey and his associates began their work on human sexual behavior, and no doubt many changes have occurred in this area of human life during the past years. Unfortunately, there have not been enough scientific investigations in recent years to reveal these changes, and no one really knows how extramarital sexual activities are distributed among the various groups now. Much less is known about extramarital relations in other societies. In terms of trends, more and more Asians, for example, seem to accept the monogamous sexual code, if not the practice, which suggests a possible decline of open practice of extramarital sexual relations, whereas more and more married Americans seem to condone such relations, often quite openly, as was suggested by John Cuber. (1) Anyway, it is high time that someone did another "Kinsey-style" study of American males and females, if not the human male and female, as Kinsey and his associates pretentiously titled their original studies.

References

1. Cuber, John F., and Harroff, Peggy B. *The Significant Americans: A Study of Sexual Behavior Among the Affluent.* New York: Appleton-Century-Crofts, Inc., 1965.
2. Kinsey, Alfred C., *et al. Sexual Behavior in the Human Male.* Philadelphia: W. B. Saunders Co., 1948.
3. Kinsey, Alfred C., *et al. Sexual Behavior in the Human Female.* Philadelphia: W. B. Saunders Co., 1953.

Part Two

THE SCENE ELSEWHERE

The universality of the institution of marriage is matched only by the universality of transgressions against it. Longitudinally through the ages and horizontally through most cultures and societies, there have been rules for the maintenance of a system (be it monogamous or polygamous) and proscriptions against the breaking of the rules. "The grass has been greener on the other side," regardless of where the turf is located—Africa or Europe, Asia or America, in cold climates and in warm ones, among the white, the black, and the yellow races.

There are extramarital relations on every continent and regardless of language. Adultery persists in the face of powerful taboos and the most consistent religious dogma. The human needs and sexual impulses of all races seem to say throughout history that they will not be confined to an institution that narrows them, even though the institution, in an overall way, has proved to be eminently workable.

In this part of the book, there are studies that pertain to a current European as well as American setting, and a broad review of a number of societies, not necessarily of our own age.

The contemporary Greek patterns described by Dina Safilios-Rothschild in a country where divorce is not socially acceptable are vastly different from the Caribbean ones, where marriage itself as an institution is ill defined. Fidelity to what is the question. Greece seems geographically and culturally far removed from us, but echoes of the Caribbean dynamics can be heard in the subcultures in the United States today. If we want to understand the black families in today's Chicago, Los Angeles, and New York, we can learn something from Rodman's observations of the Caribbean "paradise." In my chapter on other societies, I come to the conclusion that "as long as there is marriage as a monogamous system, there will be a concomitant system of clandestine relationships, sometimes rivaling and competing with, sometimes nestling next to, the basic marriage."

Constantina Safilios-Rothschild

ATTITUDES OF GREEK SPOUSES TOWARD MARITAL INFIDELITY*

The ideal family values in the United States preclude marital infidelity: as soon as a husband or wife finds out that the spouse is unfaithful there is no alternative but divorce. Because fidelity is considered a necessary condition for the maintenance of a marriage, the investigation of whether or not transgression of the fidelity rule actually brings about its dissolution has been grossly neglected.[1] Family sociologists avoid treating the subject except as a pathological phenomenon enacted by neurotic, "sick" people. And this despite the statistics presented by Kinsey, according to which by age forty about half of all married males have had sexual intercourse with women other than their spouses and 26% of married women have had intercourse with men other than their husbands (6, 7); Neubeck's and Schletzer's findings according to which marital infidelity (sexual or emotional) is related neither to unsatisfactory or weak marital relationships nor to neurotic inclinations or personalities (8); and Cuber and Harroff's data indicating that extramarital relationships are quite frequent in the upper-middle class and may be tolerated with different degrees of acceptance (3).

Ideal norms prevailing in a society do not necessarily correspond to

* Twelve tables originally included in this essay have been deleted because of space limitations. They can be obtained directly from the author.

[1] The only cross-cultural study available on attitudes toward marital infidelity is that of Christensen conducted in Denmark, the midwestern United States, and the "Mormon Country" of intermountain United States (2). Unfortunately, his subjects were unmarried students and they were asked only whether they approved or disapproved of sexual infidelity after marriage, and under what circumstances would they approve of such behavior. The question, of course, remains regarding the extent to which married people are willing to tolerate the extramarital relations of their spouses even when they theoretically disapprove of these relations.

the attitudes held by individuals who have to accommodate themselves to the realities of life. They may believe in the ideal norms but find it unrealistic or unfeasible to put them into practice, molding their own attitudes according to their life experiences and particular personality needs. The reactions of married people to their spouse's infidelity may vary widely due to a variety of circumstances related to the conditions under which the infidelity took place, the type of marital relationship, the presence or absence of children, and economic factors. Depending upon the combination of operating circumstances, spouses may either act in accordance with the ideal social norm concerning marital fidelity or they may more or less tolerate the spousal deviance.

The investigation of those circumstances influencing the spouses' reactions to (hypothetical)[2] marital infidelity within the Greek culture takes on a special interest since the sexual double standard is still quite prevalent in Greece. According to traditional moral norms, the breach of fidelity on the part of the man, while not necessarily expected or desirable, is not considered to be a particularly serious misdeed. Furthermore, a husband's infidelity does not reflect unfavorably upon the wife since such behavior is considered to be "normal" and attributable to the "polygamous nature" of men and not to the wife's faults or inadequacies. A betrayed wife usually has complete social acceptance and, in addition, is considered a suffering martyr because of her husband's wrongdoings. Thus, the culturally prescribed reaction is passive tolerance. However, it is known that at least some urban Greek wives use a variety of restorative mechanisms, and if such mechanisms fail to "bring back" their husbands, they divorce them.

The wife's infidelity, on the contrary, brings disgrace to the husband who is then a *Keratás*—the worst possible insult for a Greek man—a shameful epithet with connotations of weakness and inadequacy.[3]

[2] While the respondents were asked to *imagine* that they had discovered the infidelity of their spouses, it is highly probable that a large number of the Greek wives—if not the majority—and at least some of the Greek husbands, already had been faced with real infidelity on the part of their partners. Most probably, the confrontation with the real situation has a profound effect on the attitudes held toward marital infidelity as well as on the beliefs regarding appropriate and effective behavior. However, the data in our study do not permit us to distinguish between respondents who have faced actual infidelity and those who have not.

[3] Campbell writes: "In adultery . . . 'She puts horns on him' . . . The implication that the cuckold wears a horn may be an ironical allusion to the sexual potency which his wife's action suggests he does not possess." (1) Or horns may simply indicate the extreme social ridicule that the wife's adultery brings to the husband (12).

The traditional Greek norms entitled such a dishonored man to an "honor" crime; that is, to killing his wife (but not necessarily the other man).[4] In this way he could prove his challenged masculinity by "washing away" with blood the insult on his honor.[5] While for the wife it is socially acceptable to tolerate her unfaithful husband, it is not socially acceptable for a man to tolerate his unfaithful wife and if he does so, he is ridiculed as behaving in an unmanly manner. With such normative pressures placed upon the Greek husband, it becomes extremely interesting to examine the extent to which urban males adhere to these traditional norms and the circumstances under which they would be willing to go against these norms by forgiving their wives' infidelity and maintaining the marriage.

The present study attempts to answer two central questions: (1) What factors determine whether or not a spouse will adhere to the culturally prescribed reaction to spousal infidelity? and (2) What are the chosen alternatives?

METHODOLOGY

The present paper is a part of a larger study on "Family, Social Class, and Attitudes toward Mental Illness" conducted in 1964 in Athens, Greece. A random sample of 250 families was interviewed; in 133 cases the wife was interviewed and in 117 cases the husband.

The questions concerning attitudes toward marital infidelity were asked of both husbands and wives. They were the following:

1. Let us assume now that a wife discovers by chance (without any of her relatives or friends knowing about it), that her husband has a mistress. Meanwhile, she has noticed no change in his behavior; he does not neglect any of his duties and is as tender toward her as he always was. What should this woman do, according to you?

1-a. What would *you* do in her place?

2. Let us now assume that the man discovers that his wife is unfaithful. However, she does not neglect any of her duties and is as tender toward him as she always was. None of his relatives or close friends

[4] According to the traditional Greek culture, a husband not only could, but *had* to kill his wife and her paramour (1). In contemporary Greece, however, it seems that only the killing of the wife is fully acceptable and forgivable by society (12).

[5] Evidence from an analysis of "honor" crimes indicates that rural husbands and urban working and lower-class husbands, who are the most traditional Greek husbands, even now sometimes kill their wives because of an actual or suspected infidelity and are often acquitted—if their suspicion was based on facts.

knows anything about his wife's unfaithfulness. What, in your opinion, should this man do?

2-a. What would *you* do in his place?

It was important to isolate marital infidelity per se apart from its possible side effects which may blur the basic attitudes toward the phenomenon of marital infidelity. For this reason the discovered fact of marital infidelity was separated from the experience of shame which would result if friends and relatives knew of the infidelity (especially in the case of betrayed husbands) and from the disturbing effect of noticeable behavioral changes in the unfaithful spouse in the areas of affection or financial support.

The questions were asked first indirectly and then directly because the pretesting showed that in this way men and women felt comfortable about presenting their personal attitudes.[6] Only the women's answers to the direct question 1-a and the men's answers to the direct question 2-a will be examined in this paper in order to investigate the correlates of the spouses' anticipated behavior in the case of marital infidelity.

The respondents' education, stage of family cycle, marital satisfaction, degree of communication, and marital conflict were examined in relation to attitudes toward marital infidelity committed either by the husband or the wife.

Marital satisfaction was measured on the basis of the expressed degree of satisfaction derived from: (1) the spouse's understanding of the problems and difficulties of the interviewed spouse; (2) the tenderness the spouse showed to the interviewee; (3) the standard of living; and (4) an evaluation of the marriage made by comparing the marital relationship with that of friends and relatives.[7]

[6] The present study indicates that some of the methodological fears expressed by those conducting surveys on attitudes toward marital infidelity do not seem to be borne out. Anticipating difficulties in obtaining answers, those conducting the French survey did not ask at all the direct question, "What would you do?" (See French Institute of Public Opinion, *Patterns of Sex and Love: A Study of the French Woman and Her Morals* [New York: Crown Publishers, Inc., 1961], p. 179.) The Greek data indicate that half of the women and 16% of the men report that their own anticipated behavior in case of their spouses' infidelity would be different from their standards for ideal behavior under the circumstances. The indirect question, then, seems to elicit (at least in the case of women) only their ideal standards.

[7] The actual questions asked (of women interviewees) with regard to marital satisfaction were:

1. Are you pleased with your standard of living; that is, the amount of money you can spend for food, clothes, rent, and entertainment?
   Very pleased _____ Pleased _____ I cannot complain _____
   It could be better _____ I am disappointed _____

The degree of communication was measured on the basis of: (1) the number of "taboo" subjects between husband and wife; (2) the frequency of communication of worries, problems, and troubles; (3) the frequency of exchange of everyday routine happenings; (4) the frequency of joint discussions of financial difficulties; and (5) the frequency of joint discussions of emotional (sentimental) problems and preoccupations.[8]

1-a. For what kinds of things would you like to have more spending money?

2. Are you generally pleased with the way your husband understands your personal difficulties and problems?
   Very pleased _____ Pleased _____ I cannot complain _____
   It could be better _____ I am disappointed _____
3. Everybody needs tenderness. Are you pleased with the degree of tenderness your husband shows you?
   Very pleased _____ Pleased _____ I cannot complain _____
   It could be better _____ I am disappointed _____
4. In comparison with other couples you know, how well could you say you get along with your husband?
   Much worse _____ A little worse than other couples _____
   About the same _____ Better _____ Much better _____

When the interviewee was a man the same questions were asked, except that the word "husband" was substituted by the word "wife." The response "very pleased" or "much better" was coded as 5; "pleased" or "better" as 4; "I cannot complain" or "about the same" as 3; "It could be better" or "a little worse than other couples" as 2; and "I am disappointed" or "much worse" as 1. A cumulative "satisfaction" score was then calculated on the basis of the partial satisfaction scores.

[8] The questions asked of the husbands and the wives interviewed (with appropriate word substitutions for the sex of the interviewee) with regard to "level of communication" were:

1. Some couples discuss everything that happens to them. Other couples prefer to keep silence over some matters. There are also some subjects that are never discussed, because their discussion would create some unease. Are there any subjects that you would rather not discuss with your husband?
   Yes _____ No _____

1-a. If Yes: How many? Many _____ A few _____ None _____

1-b. What are these subjects?

1-c. Why don't you like to discuss these subjects?

2. When your husband has problems, worries, or troubles, do you try to talk to him in order to find out what is the matter and help him if you can? How often?
   Usually _____ Sometimes _____ Seldom _____ Never _____
3. When your husband returns home, does he ask you what kind of a day you had? How often?
   Usually _____ Sometimes _____ Seldom _____ Never _____
4. When you have difficulties in making ends meet with the amount of money your husband gives you for the household, do you discuss your difficulties with him? How often?
   Usually _____ Sometimes _____ Seldom _____ Never _____

The degree of marital conflict was measured in terms of the number of areas of disagreement and the frequency of quarreling. The number of areas of disagreement were measured by the responses to two different questions, one concerning disagreements in any of the eight major family decisions[9] and the other asking, "For what reason do you have quarrels in your family?" The frequency of quarreling was measured on the basis of answers to the following question:[10] "How often would you say that you have quarrels in your family?"

Very often ____ Sometimes ____ Seldom ____ Never ____

FINDINGS

Attitudes Toward Husband's Infidelity

Level of education. The data show that the higher the wife's educational level the less willing she is to tolerate passively her husband's infidelity (22.5% of the more educated and 28% of the less educated) and the more inclined she is to divorce him if her efforts to "bring him back to her" were to fail or if there were no children (27.5% versus 14.6% of the less educated) ($X^2 = 69.429$, $p < .01$).[11] Also, the more

5. Do you talk over these sentimental troubles with somebody else? With whom?

If there was no taboo subject for the spouses they were coded as 3; if some taboo subjects, 2; if many taboo subjects, 1. In questions 2, 3, 4, and 5, if the answer was "usually" it was scored as 4; if "sometimes," as 3; if "rarely," as 2; and if "never," as 1. A cumulative score of "communication" was then calculated.

[9] The eight family decisions refer to: (1) child-rearing, (2) the use of available money, (3) relations with in-laws, (4) use of leisure time, (5) family size, (6) choice of friends, (7) purchase of clothes for the entire family, and (8) purchase of furniture and other household items.

[10] The two questions referring to family quarrels were asked after two more indirect questions which helped put the interviewees at ease in answering the more personal questions. The indirect questions were:

Most families have small quarrels from time to time. What, according to you, are the reasons for which most families quarrel? Any other reasons?
How often, would you say, do most families have quarrels:
Very often ____ Sometimes ____ Seldom ____ Never ____
(The answer "very often" was given a score of 4; "sometimes," a score of 3; "rarely," a score of 2; "never," a score of 1. This score was the actual score of "marital conflict.")

[11] The greater tendency of better educated women to consider divorce as an alternative reflects also their modern attitudes toward marriage and its necessary permanency. Among most uneducated Greek women, who hold the most traditional views and values, divorce could never be considered as a possible alternative because (1) their own values would cause them intense shame if they divorced, or (2) because of pressures exerted by friends and relatives to stay with their husbands, or (3) because of their financial dependence upon their husbands.

educated the Athenian wife, the more inclined she is to discover the reasons for her husband's infidelity, and if she finds herself at fault, to correct her mistakes as well as trying to become a sweeter, more tender and loving wife than before in order to win back her husband ($X^2 = 4.220$, $p < .05$). The above findings become more meaningful in the light of evidence that the higher the education of a Greek woman the more modern is her definition of the husband's role as that of a loving companion and friend (9). A more modern wife's relationship with her husband is disturbed because she expects him to be much more than just a breadwinner. Not only does she expect much more from him but she is also willing to go out of her way in order not merely to maintain the marriage but to improve herself and the marriage as well. However, if she were to fail in her efforts she would not be satisfied with life in a compromised marriage but would consider ending it.[12]

In contrast, the traditional woman who defines her husband's role as mainly that of the breadwinner and authority figure to whom she must submit is not greatly affected by her husband's infidelity as long as he fulfills his financial responsibilities toward his family and does not become violent (beating her or the children). Her relationship with her husband does not necessarily change because of his infidelity, although she may become a little worried lest he start wasting money on the other woman and cause the family to suffer financially. As long as this does not occur she does not feel compelled to do anything either to bring him back or to end the marriage.

[12] It should be noted that in Greece divorce can be obtained on the following grounds: (1) adultery or bigamy; (2) plotting against the life of the plaintiff; (3) malicious desertion for two years; (4) serious impairment of the matrimonial bond, such that life with the other party becomes intolerable; (5) mental illness to a degree prohibiting the effective interaction between spouses and when this mental illness has lasted for four years; (6) leprosy; (7) impotency. The fourth ground for divorce, which is the most vaguely formulated, is the most often used; three-fifths of all decrees were granted on the ground of "serious impairment of the matrimonial bond" (or "incompatible personalities," as it is commonly known in Greece). "Malicious desertion" accounted for one-fourth of all decrees in the same years and adultery accounted for less than one-twenty-ninth of all divorces (and husband's adultery as a ground for divorce has declined sharply in recent years). The spouse found guilty in a divorce suit is obliged to pay alimony; when the divorce is granted on the basis of "mutual culpability" there are no alimony obligations. The divorce procedures are greatly simplified when the divorce is granted on a "mutual culpability" basis. Women, however, tend to avoid this easy form of divorce when they are not financially independent. In about one-third of dissolved marriages the wife is pronounced "at fault"; in about 38% of the cases the husband is at fault; and in about 37% of cases both are pronounced guilty. It is interesting to note that adultery is an unimportant ground for divorce, but actual infidelity, while it may not appear in the official court decisions, may have been the main cause of or the crucial reason for the divorce.

Stage of marital cycle. As can be expected, women at different stages of the marital cycle may become more dependent upon their husbands and therefore more reluctant to divorce them for any reason. A significantly higher percentage of childless women (after five or more years of marriage) than women in any other stage of the marital cycle would unconditionally divorce their husbands in case of infidelity if they had no children (Fisher test, $p < .05$). Thus, the importance of children in deterring women from divorce is firmly established. It is, however, interesting to note that even among childless women, who could more easily consider divorce as an alternative, a large number (42%) would do nothing but wait patiently until, hopefully, their husbands tired of their extramarital affair and returned to them. Probably a variety of intervening factors such as age, level of expectations from marriage, attitude toward divorce, and financial dependence because of lack of skills and education deter women from choosing the alternative of divorce.

In the case of women with children younger than six years of age or children thirteen to eighteen years old the predominant intended reaction to the husband's infidelity would be to try to win him back: to become more tender and loving, to find out their possible mistakes and shortcomings and to correct them (self-improvement and attempts to win back the husband were significantly more frequent than divorce, $X^2 = 48.38$, $p < .01$). About one-fifth, however, of the women with children younger than age six intended ultimately to divorce their husbands if they failed to make them lose interest in the "other" woman. In this case, the wife's relatively high marital satisfaction and higher level of expectations from married life may be responsible for this type of reaction. The second large reaction for women with children thirteen to eighteen years old (31%) was the passive tolerance of infidelity without any overt indication that they are aware of their husband's stepping out.

Women with children six to twelve years old rely relatively more on passive tolerance (28%) than on self-improvement (16%) in handling their husband's infidelity than do the mothers of younger and older children. But they also rely extensively on discussing it with their husbands in a "sweet, civilized" manner (24%) or by protesting (12%).[13]

[13] When the number of children was examined, it was found that women with 3 or more children reacted to their husband's infidelity with passive tolerance more often than did women with fewer children (46% versus 24%). Since the average number of children in urban areas has been estimated to be 1.52 (in Athens, 1.35) and even in the rural areas it has been estimated to be 2.22, women with 3 or more children have large families, according to the Greek norms concerning family size. (See Irene Petrisi-Figa Talamanca, "Demographic Analysis of Census Data," unpublished manuscript.) These women seem to hold

Generally, it seems that the older the woman the more she tends to tolerate passively her husband's infidelity and the less she tends to believe in techniques of self-improvement or discussion that would make the husband return to them ($X^2 = 14.42$, $p < .01$). Possibly, this pessimistic outlook reflects actual experience with facing the husband's infidelity; different techniques may have been used in the past to no avail and finally only patience paid off. Or it may be fear of being left alone in an advanced age when remarriage would be problematic from many points of view. Or is it just habit in a marriage that has lasted fifteen to twenty years or more?

Marital satisfaction. The data on marital satisfaction do not indicate any clear pattern in the wives' intended behavior; the degree of marital satisfaction does not seem to be a differentiating factor in the case of women. The only difference is the fact that twice as many women who are satisfied with their marriage (6%) than dissatisfied (3.7%) intend to divorce their husbands unconditionally ($X^2 = 7.405$, $p < .05$); however, more dissatisfied than satisfied wives intend to divorce if there are no children or if they fail to win back their husbands.

These findings are probably quite inconclusive because other factors such as stage of family cycle, level of expectations from the husband, and other dynamic factors that indicate the type of husband-wife relationship—such as degree of conflict and degree of communication—play a more decisive role in determining the wives' reaction to infidelity.

Degree of conflict. The trends indicated by the data on the frequency of quarreling and the data on the number of areas of disagreements do not agree perfectly, probably because they measure different dimensions of conflict. One couple may disagree in only one area but they may quarrel frequently, while another couple may have many disagreements which lead to a very few quarrels, either because these disagreements do not recur or because mechanisms other than quarrels are used to handle them. In the final analysis, it is frequency of quarreling rather than the number of areas of disagreement that determines more accurately the degree of conflict in the marriage. Therefore, we shall use this as our criterion for judging the degree of marital conflict.

The data show that only wives in harmonious marriages would consider unconditionally divorcing their husbands (8%); it seems that these wives hold high expectations for their spouses and cannot tolerate marital infidelity as easily as women in conflictual marriages. However,

---

the most traditional family values not only with respect to family size but probably also, with respect to divorce, to the level of expectations for husband as well as for a wife's appropriate behavior in case of the husband's infidelity.

the mechanism usually used by women in harmonious marriages (as measured by the frequency of quarreling) is talking it out with their husbands, either by protesting (21.4%) or sweetly and skillfully (29%). This reliance on discussion with the husband may be due to the fact that it is generally possible to discuss even "touchy" issues with him without the discussion ending in a meaningless quarrel. It is important to note than even when discussing with husband is the intended alternative, women in conflictual marriages express this choice much more often in terms of "protest" or "asking explanations" rather than in terms of "talking sweetly and in a civilized manner" which is the more frequent choice of women in harmonious marriages ($X^2 = 16.79$, $p < .01$). In conflictual marriages, however, women predominantly tend to tolerate their husbands' infidelity with passivity ($X^2 = 13.87$, $p < .01$). In highly conflictual marriages a relatively frequent reaction on the part of the women is to worry and cry but do nothing else, a reaction that is never envisaged by women in harmonious or somewhat conflictual marriages. Their tolerance is probably high because they expect very little from their husbands and have to live in an already generally unpleasant marriage to which infidelity does not add much more intolerable behavior,[14] while discussion would only end in more quarreling, which is already too abundant in their lives. That discussions usually end in quarrels in these households is also reflected by the fact that whenever talking with the husband was mentioned as an alternative by women in conflictual marriages it was practically always in the form of "protest" or of "asking explanations" rather than the "sweet and diplomatic talk" much more often mentioned in harmonious marriages.

Degree of communication. Women who have established a very good communication level with their husbands would never consider divorce as a possible alternative. Instead, they would rely heavily on their communication skills to persuade them to change (29%) or to ask explanations (7%). Also, a considerable number of them would try to find out their own mistakes and correct them (21%).

Women who have established a good communication level with their husbands rely to a moderate degree on their communication skills (26%), or tolerate their husbands' infidelity passively (19%), or

[14] It is interesting to note at this point that, in studying the process of defining deviance in the Greek family, it was found that when the marital relationship had always been conflictual and unsatisfactory the "normal" spouse for a long time was not perturbed by the bizarre symptoms of the disturbed spouse (even when these symptoms directly attacked the marital relationship). On the contrary, when the husband-wife relationship had always been good (conflict-free and satisfactory), the "normal" spouse felt hurt, upset, and angry by the symptoms threatening this relationship and quickly defined these symptoms as deviant (11).

divorce them (5% of them unconditionally plus 7% if there are no children).

Finally, women who communicate poorly with their husbands tend predominantly to tolerate passively their husbands' infidelity (40%) or to try to bring him back in any way, including becoming nicer and sweeter (22%). They tend to mistrust the idea of communicating their thoughts and feelings to their husbands (16%). The low level of communication also tends to reflect the low educational level of the spouses and their traditional values, which would dictate a passive tolerance on the part of the wife.

To summarize, the very small minority of wives (seven women out of 133) who would unconditionally divorce their husbands were childless wives or had children over nineteen years old, or they had a very good marriage and very high expectations from it. Their education was low, but since there is not a 1 to 1 relationship between level of education and the holding of traditional or liberal values, it may well be that they also hold modern attitudes toward divorce despite their educational classification.

The majority of women, in case of their husband's infidelity, intended either to pretend that they knew nothing, to say nothing and wait patiently for their husband's infidelity to end, or to go through a process of critical self-examination, correct their "faults" or inadequacies and generally improve themselves by becoming more tender, loving, attractive, and even sexy. The first category of women have three different kinds of rationale for their behavior: (1) If they were to talk to their husbands about his having an affair, the husband, then unmasked, would no longer have to keep up pretenses, and the marital relationship would then deteriorate because the husband might no longer be willing to fulfill even his role as breadwinner and might be more prone to entertaining the idea of divorce. (2) To them, time is the best cure; the husband will get tired of the "other woman" and come back—and then the marriage will resume more smoothly than if unpleasant words have been exchanged. (3) By saying nothing and avoiding creating scenes or plaguing him with nagging and tears, the wife shows her superiority. The husband will eventually realize how superior she is to other women, and by comparing her to the "other woman" he will understand his mistake and come back to her.

This kind of passive psychology is mainly endorsed by older women (or women in their late thirties with young children) with a low educational achievement who hold a low level of expectations from their marriages and communicate very little with their husbands. These women seem to be afraid to react in any other way lest the husband get angry and stop fulfilling his basic duties, thereby breaking up the marriage. It is a typical lower middle, working, and lower class feminine reaction; men in these strata tend to be very authoritarian and to dominate their wives (10). This fact explains the women's fear of saying or doing anything that might make their husbands angry. Also, such women tend to be more dependent upon their husbands because their family of orientation (parents and brothers) have very limited financial resources and, therefore, cannot and will not assume responsibility for her or her children in case of divorce.

The women who try to win back their husbands operate under the theory that a husband does not become unfaithful unless his wife has failed him in some way, either by having become less attractive, or by having "cooled off," or by having neglected her husband and his needs and desires. Therefore, the wife can normally win him back by improving herself in the points of inadequacy or by becoming a "better, more loving and interesting" wife. This is a more typically "middle-class feminine psychology" that precludes the need for variety and change as a motivation for infidelity even in "happy" marriages. Women who react in this way are predominantly young, well educated, and communicate well with their husbands.

Attitudes Toward Wife's Infidelity

Level of education. Divorce seems to be the general normative alternative in the case of a wife's infidelity, particularly among traditional Greek husbands with a high school education or less (43.6% versus 33% of the liberal, well educated husbands).[15] The more liberal Greek husbands (with at least some college education) would only intend to divorce their wives in greater proportion if there were no children, or if they could find no mistake in their own behavior that could have contributed to their wives' deviance or if their wives would not stop their relationship or repeat their "wrongdoing" after having been forgiven the first time. Thus, liberal husbands found a variety of excuses for not divorcing their wives even after they had transgressed a very rigid rule for married women.

However, the findings indicating that even among traditional husbands the divorce norm is not faithfully subscribed to bears an important qualification to the usual stereotype about traditional men in underdeveloped countries. Half of them were willing to go against the imperative cultural norm that dictates divorce. They intended to use, instead, a variety of mechanisms before (if ever) reaching the extreme solution of divorce. It is also interesting to note that among

[15] The relationship between level of education and traditional or liberal attitudes and values is presented in Constantina Safilios-Rothschild, "Marital Role Definitions of Urban Greek Spouses" (9).

the tolerant traditional husbands most (27%) were willing to forgive their unfaithful wives the first time. In light of these findings, one is led to question whether or not traditional men were, to the extent that they are reputed to be, uniformally and consistently, strict with and punitive toward their wives.

Stage of marital cycle. It seems that the stage of the marital cycle is the factor that most differentiates which husbands, and under what conditions, are willing to go against the cultural norm of divorce prescribed for unfaithful wives. It is in the childless marriages (newlyweds excluded) that the husbands adhere most strictly to the cultural norm and are determined to divorce their wives (60%, while an additional 10% would either forgive them or divorce them, depending on their mood). In contrast, when children under twelve were present, husbands had the least intention of divorcing their wives (36%) and were the most inclined to forgive them conditionally; that is, the first time, or if they were at fault ($X^2 = 8.007$, $p < .01$). Interestingly enough, some of these husbands (16.7%) clearly state that they would divorce if there were no children. It is, then, quite well established that the presence of children younger than twelve years of age seriously deters Greek husbands from divorcing their wives. Is it simply because wives are especially needed at this stage for the child-rearing tasks? Or is it the widespread belief that it is "detrimental" for young children to experience the divorce of their parents?

Once the children are thirteen to eighteen years old husbands once again adhere more closely to the cultural norm, since 50% would divorce the unfaithful wife and only a few would forgive her the first time or try to bring her back.[16]

Among husbands with children over nineteen years old (who live with their parents or away from them) a considerable percentage (35%) were willing to forgive their wives. It must be remembered at this point that the average marriage age for all Greek males is 28.6. For urban males, this age is much higher, thirty to thirty-five (median age group) (13). Therefore, among urban married males, the younger ones are in their fifties, and they may be more concerned with family continuity and with security at this point in their lives than with "pure" feelings or absolute cultural dictates. Also at this age, they may have more understanding and may feel more self-assured and not as threatened as are younger men by their wives' infidelity.

What is probably the most interesting finding resulting from the

[16] When the number of children was examined, no definite pattern was found. It seems, then, that husbands are not influenced one way or the other by the number of children in their reactions to their wives' infidelity, but rather by how old the children are.

data on the stage of the marital cycle is that, despite strict cultural norms, the wives' marital infidelity is, in actuality, tolerated by their husbands during the years when such infidelity would be most likely to occur. Since the average marriage age for Greek women is 24.2 (in urban areas it is estimated to be one or two years higher) (13), and women on the average have their first child two years after marriage (14), they are twenty-seven to thirty-nine years old when their infidelity is most tolerated.

Marital satisfaction. The general trend evident from the data is that the more satisfied the husband is with his marriage, the more intolerant he is of his wife's infidelity and the more inclined he is to divorce her ($X^2 = 15.85$, $p < .01$). It must be noted at this point that there is evidence indicating that Greek men consistently tend to rate their marriage as satisfactory much more often than do Greek women.[17] It seems, then, that those husbands who are willing to rate their marriage as unsatisfactory are truly and seriously dissatisfied with it; those husbands who have low expectations from their marital partners tend to be tolerant also of their infidelity (at least the first time) since, in a way, they are prepared for the worst.

Degree of conflict. The data indicate that the more conflictual the marriage, the more willing is the husband to forgive his wife, probably because marital adjustment has been achieved at a very low level of mutual expectations. On the contrary, in "harmonious" marriages in which no quarrel or area of disagreement is reported, husbands are very intolerant of their wives' infidelity ($X^2 = 8.65$, $p < .01$ when degree of conflict is measured by the number of disagreements, but it is not significant when measured by the frequency of disagreements).[18] Furthermore, it seems that when the husband-wife relationship is not weakened by conflicts and disagreements, the wife's infidelity is the determining factor in the husband's decision to divorce her. Because their relationship had been harmonious and predictable it cannot withstand the strain that results from the revealed infidelity which directly attacks the husband-wife bond. In the husband-wife

[17] Two previous studies, one based on clinical interviews and the other on questionnaires as well as on repeated focused interviews, have shown that men, especially working-class and lower-class men, do not expect that all their needs will be met within marriage, and have outlets such as the coffeehouse, male friends, and their work, from which to draw at least some degree of satisfaction. On the other hand, women conceive of marriage as the solution to all their problems and are therefore easily disappointed (5, 11).

[18] One possible alternative interpretation of this finding could be that traditional husbands tend to report little or no marital conflict because they are not willing to admit that their authority is disputed in any way by their wives. Such traditional husbands also adhere to a greater extent to the traditional norm of "honor" crime or the presently more acceptable alternative of divorcing the unfaithful wife.

relationships, however, in which conflicts and disagreements had already undermined the bond, the presence or absence of children played an equally important role in the husband's decision to divorce or not to divorce his wife.

Degree of communication. The lower the communication level between spouses the greater is the husbands' tendency to divorce their wives than to forgive them or to try to bring them back (54% versus 36% of the husbands who have a good or very good communication level with their wives). The contrary is true for husbands who communicate well with their wives. The level of communication between spouses reflects, to a large extent, the traditional or liberal attitudes of the husbands in particular. Thus, the level of communication largely reflects the educational level of the husband.

To summarize, it seems that three sets of conditions tend to render Greek husbands tolerant toward their wives' infidelity. First, education liberalizes Greek men and frees them from the traditional concepts of "honor." Related to education is good communication with one's wife, which also seems to increase the husband's tolerance of infidelity, probably because the existence of good communication between the spouses reflects the husband's high level of education and his more liberal attitudes. The second condition is a low level of expectation from marriage resulting from a conflict-ridden marriage or a generally unsatisfactory marriage. Such disillusionment with marriage tends to increase the husband's tolerance for deviance, including infidelity. Third, the presence of children under twelve years bends the Greek husband's intolerance of marital infidelity, to a large extent out of necessity and for the sake of the young children.

DISCUSSION

The present Greek data suggest the following conclusions which could be expressed in the form of hypotheses to be tested further cross-culturally:

1. The better the husband-wife relationship the least tolerated is marital infidelity, especially a wife's infidelity. The limiting factor is the presence of young children.
2. The greater the utilitarian dependence of one spouse upon the other, the greater the tendency of the dependent spouse to tolerate his (her) partner's infidelity.
3. The higher the spouses' educational achievement the greater their deviation from traditionally prescribed behavior in case of infidelity on the part of the marital partner. The direction of this deviation is

toward greater tolerance on the part of well-educated husbands and toward less tolerance on the part of well-educated wives.

Since, however, in industrialized societies education does not have the liberalizing influence upon men and women that it has in underdeveloped countries, an equivalent factor with the same socio-psychological consequences will have to be found in the case of an industrialized society such as the United States. Probably, some aspect of the husband-wife relationship, such as the power structure, or the division of labor reflecting liberal attitudes in the sphere of male-female relationships, could substitute for the factor of education in the above-stated hypothesis when it is tested in an industrialized society.

Comparative studies of attitudes and reactions toward infidelity should be carried out further in a culture in which divorce is a socially acceptable alternative and the social penalties relatively few (such as the United States), in a culture in which little importance is accorded sexual infidelity (such as Sweden), and in a culture in which a variety of kin is available as a resource for financial, emotional, and social support (such as cultures in the Near East and Far East) in order to clarify and specify the formulated hypotheses so that we would know finally which conclusions are culture-specific and which ones hold universally.

References

1. CAMPBELL, JOHN F. *Honour, Family and Patronage.* Oxford: Clarendon Press, 1964.
2. CHRISTENSEN, HAROLD T. "A Cross-Cultural Comparison of Attitudes Toward Marital Infidelity," *International Journal of Comparative Sociology,* 3 (No. 1), 124–37, 1962.
3. CUBER, JOHN S., and HARROFF, PEGGY B. *The Significant Americans.* New York: Appleton-Century-Crofts Inc., 1965.
4. FRENCH INSTITUTE OF PUBLIC OPINION. *Patterns of Sex and Love: A Study of the French Woman and Her Morals.* New York: Crown Publishers, 1961.
5. GUTENSCHWAGER, MARY, and SAFILIOS-ROTHSCHILD, CONSTANTINA. "Attitudes of Greek Refugee Women Toward Marriage." Paper read at the Mediterranean Conference, Athens, Greece, December 12–17, 1966.
6. KINSEY, A. C., POMEROY, W. B., and MARTIN, C. E. *Sexual Behavior in the Human Male.* Philadelphia: W. B. Saunders, 1948, pp. 583–94.
7. KINSEY, A. C., POMEROY, W. B., MARTIN, C. E., and GEBHARD, PAUL A.

Sexual Behavior in the Human Female. Philadelphia: W. B. Saunders, 1953, pp. 409–45.

8. NEUBECK, GERHARD, and SCHLETZER, VERA M. "A Study of Extramarital Relationships," *Marriage and Family Living,* 24 (August), 279–81, 1962.
9. SAFILIOS-ROTHSCHILD, CONSTANTINA. "Marital Role Definitions of Urban Greek Spouses." Paper read at the National Council for Family Relations Meetings in Toronto, Canada, October 21, 1965.
10. SAFILIOS-ROTHSCHILD, CONSTANTINA. "A Comparison of Power Structure and Marital Satisfaction in Urban Greek and French Families, *The Journal of Marriage and the Family,* 29 (No. 2), 347–49, 1967.
11. SAFILIOS-ROTHSCHILD, CONSTANTINA. "Deviance and Mental Illness in the Greek Family," *Family Process,* Vol. 7, no. 1 (March, 1968).
12. SAFILIOS-ROTHSCHILD, CONSTANTINA. " 'Honor' Crimes in Contemporary Greece," *The British Journal of Sociology,* Vol. 20, No. 2 (June, 1969).
13. SAFILIOS-ROTHSCHILD, CONSTANTINA. "Legal and Statistical Analysis of the Greek Family." Unpublished paper.
14. VALAORAS, V. G., *et al.* "Control of Family Size in Greece," *Population Studies,* 18 (No. 3), 273, 1965.

Hyman Rodman

FIDELITY AND FORMS OF MARRIAGE: THE CONSENSUAL UNION IN THE CARIBBEAN*

It is not always clear what "marriage" is,[1] and as a result it is not always clear what "premarital" and "extramarital" are. Establishing a marriage is a process in which husband and wife and certain of their kin may become progressively more committed to each other through a series of rituals, prestations, and transfers of rights and duties. For example, in former times among the Kgatla, there was an initial ceremony of "entering the hut," after which the boy would visit the girl every night but return to his home in the morning; ceremonies were later held in connection with the girl's move to the boy's parents. Interestingly, Schapera states that after the first ceremony "the couple were now considered married," and after the second ceremony "they were now fully married."[2] If marriage is a process then the question of whether a couple is married makes less sense than the question of what stage in the process are the couple, and perhaps their kinsmen, at—what exchanges have the contracting parties already made, and what rights and obligations have they undertaken?

In many societies marriage is less of a process and more in the nature of a single event. For example, there may be a long series of transactions between the boy and the girl (and their parents and

* I want to thank David M. Schneider and Audrey Smedley for their helpful comments on an earlier draft, even though some of their suggestions will have to be implemented in a future paper.

1 This matter is usually of relatively little interest to members of a community. It is of interest, however, to anthropologists concerned with a universal definition of marriage. See Gough (7), Leach (15), and Gough (8).

2 Schapera (30, p. 73). The actual marriage process was considerably more complicated than what is suggested here, and it involved other ceremonials and considerations.

kin) in contemporary national societies, but there will also be a single act of legal marriage. A legal marriage, as opposed to customary marriage, may therefore make it possible to speak with greater certainty about marital, premarital, and extramarital relationships. On the other hand, we can still ask whether sexual relationships after a declared intention to marry (perhaps through a formal engagement) are still merely premarital? And to what extent would sexual relationships with another partner after a declared intention to marry be considered infidelity and therefore, in a sense, "extramarital"? Moreover, customary marriage also often involves a single ceremonial which represents a clear-cut boundary between the premarital and the marital state. It should therefore be understood that the legal status of a relationship is not the underlying criterion for marriage, and that this criterion has significance only insofar as members of a community see it as the customary and appropriate way of entering a relationship.

It is my intention, in the present paper, to make use of the literature on marriage as a process, and on alternate forms of marriage, in order to help clarify the disputed status of consensual unions in the Caribbean area. I will, in particular, focus upon the question of fidelity as one criterion for marriage, and use this principle of fidelity (along with other data) to help ascertain whether the consensual union is a normative form of marriage or a deviant relationship within the lower-class Caribbean community.

VARYING FORMS OF MARRIAGE

A man and a woman may be involved in a sexual relationship, they may have children, they may be engaged in various types of tasks and labor, and they may participate in various rituals and ceremonies. What sexual, procreative, labor, and ritual rights and obligations do they have toward each other (and each other's kin)? For example, at what point does a man have sexual rights to a woman, and are these rights exclusive? In a lineal society, to whose lineage do the children belong? It is because these rights and duties are handled differently in different societies, and because they may also be handled differently in varying forms of marriage within the same society, that there has been a great deal of difficulty in defining marriage. Also, because marriage is a process, there have been difficulties with the definition of marriage. If we briefly consider some aspects of customary marriage in patrilineal African societies we will be able to see the outlines of the problem more clearly (3, 23, 24).

Analyses of customary marriage in certain patrilineal African societies have singled out the following features: [3] a high involvement of the kinship groups of the man and woman, the institution of bridewealth, and a developmental or processual aspect of the relationship. One of the most important issues centers around the question of securing legitimate descendants, and "in a very large portion of the disputes involving customary marriage law the crucial issue concerns the determination of the question, To which kinship group shall the children belong?" (23, p. xvii) In patrilineal societies various payments of bridewealth are made by the man or his kin to the girl's kin, the girl leaves her kinship group to live patrilocally, the man acquires sexual rights to the girl, and his lineage acquires rights to their children insofar as the bridewealth has been fully paid. In some forms of marriage, however, the man may acquire sexual rights to the woman, but his lineage may not acquire rights to the children. For example, the Verre, Birwana, and Sumbwa recognized alternate marital forms in which lesser amounts of bridewealth were paid but in which the children belonged to the mother's kin group (16, pp. 62, 135).

The discussion by Harris of the Taita is a particularly full account of marriage as a process in which stages in the payment of bridewealth correspond to changes in the relationship between the couple and in the rights that each party has (9). Parts of the bridewealth payment are made during a betrothal period of two years or longer, and during this time the man has sexual rights to his wife. During this period certain livestock transfers, particularly the *kifu* heifer, give a man tentative descent rights over the children—these rights are not fulfilled until the heifer reaches maturity and itself bears a calf. After the payment of a substantial part of the bridewealth the bride's parents give their permission for their daughter to live with the man, and from the establishment of such co-residence the man also has rights to his wife's domestic services. But the relationship between a man and his father-in-law still remains a debtor-creditor relationship, and it is not until the *kifu* heifer's calf is born and the rest of the bridewealth payments are made that a man has validated his claim upon the children. In some extreme cases "a union begun with a formal betrothal is not fully validated until after the deaths of the partners, when their son completes the bridewealth payments." (9, p. 67)

Marriage may therefore be seen as a process, and insofar as it is a process it is sensible to inquire as to the degree to which two individu-

[3] Phillips (23), Fortes (3), Radcliffe-Brown, and Forde (24). This is not an exhaustive list of general features, nor are these features confined exclusively to African patrilineal societies.

als are married at any one stage.[4] This would refer to the nature of the exchange that has taken place, and the rights and duties that have been acquired. At times, however, the exchange takes place at one point in time, and under these circumstances marriage is, formally, a single event. Occasionally, we may be confronted with the question of whether a particular relationship—regardless of whether it is established processually or at one point in time—is a form of marriage. This is the case for the consensual union in the Caribbean. Which criteria might we use in order to determine whether a relationship is a form of marriage? Two important criteria are: (1) the existence of a privileged sexual relationship between the man and the woman, or as it is frequently seen, the man's privileged sexual access to the woman; and (2) community approval of the relationship.

THE FIDELITY PRINCIPLE

It was seen that sexual rights are one of the major elements acquired in the marriage process. These rights are either exclusively confined to the spouses, or are primarily confined to them, but with certain community-sanctioned exceptions.[5] As Fortes has put it, "what distinguishes the conjugal relationship uniquely from all other dyadic relationships, and isolates it as the core of the domestic domain, is the exclusive, or at the minimum privileged sexual rights and claims of the spouses on each other." (3, p. 5)

This exclusive or privileged sexual relationship is generally supported by sanctions, and these are ordinarily more severe for women. Adultery is a transgression of the community expectations of this privileged relationship, and is punished in varying ways, with varying degrees of severity, in different societies. I shall refer to the privileged sexual relationship in marriage, the expectations of fidelity, and the sanctions against adultery as the "principle of fidelity." Since this principle stems from, and supports, marriage, it is possible to use it when one is trying to distinguish between a man-woman relationship that is

[4] It is an awkward but a necessary convenience to impose the alien term "marriage" upon a variety of relationships in different societies. Cf. Gough (7, p. 24), Phillips (23, pp. xi–xiii).

[5] According to Murdock (20, p. 265), "Taboos on adultery are extremely widespread, though sometimes more honored in the breach than in the observance. They appear in 120 of the 148 societies in our sample for which data are available. In four of the remaining twenty-eight, adultery is socially disapproved though not strictly forbidden; it is conditionally permitted in nineteen and freely allowed in five."

marriage and one that is nonmarriage. The components of the principle need to be spelled out more concretely, but it does seem to be a principle that can be used, among other criteria, in determining whether a particular form of union between a man and a woman is a marital union.

The following quotations indicate the way in which elements of the principle of fidelity apply to several different societies:

> Marriage amongst the Mayombe is described as a system by which a man acquires sex access to a woman, and certain clearly defined rights to her services and those of her adolescent children, in return for a substantial payment in money or goods. The Mayombe husband never acquires full authority over his wife or children, as we shall see, but the marriage payment enables him to remove his bride to his own village immediately on marriage; his sex rights over her are exclusive, and payments as damages for adultery are heavy. In the old days, in fact, adultery was a crime punishable by death. (25, pp. 215–16)

> Adultery by a wife, as elsewhere, is not only an infringement of her husband's rights for which in the past both she and her lover might be severely punished, but is also believed to have supernatural consequences. The Cewa believe that if a woman commits adultery the salt which she puts in her husband's food will poison him; so long as this is seriously believed, it is obviously difficult for a wife's infidelity to go long undetected. More widespread is the belief that this is the explanation of difficulties in childbirth, and that they can only be relieved by confession. With the Yao this applies also to adultery by the husband. It is very commonly believed that adultery by the husband on particular occasions, notably while the wife is pregnant, can cause injury to her and her child. (16, p. 98)

Before discussing community approval as a criterion of marriage, I shall turn to a discussion of the data on the consensual union in the Caribbean in order to see whether the principle of fidelity can help us to clear up the controversy about whether the consensual union is or is not a form of marriage.

THE CARIBBEAN CONTROVERSY

The controversy about the consensual union in the Caribbean has been discussed in an earlier paper at some length (28). To add to the sharpness of the dispute, the question is not merely whether or not the consensual union is a form of marriage. In essence, the question is whether in the lower-class community the consensual union is an alternate form of marriage that is normatively approved, or whether it is a deviant, stigmatized relationship. Data have already been presented on the normative aspect of the relationship (28, pp. 675–83), in which it was pointed out that there were two dominant lower-class positions: a majority of the respondents were normatively favorable to the consensual union, while a smaller number were unfavorable. For example, on three different normative questions the percentages favorable were 50%, 66%, and 81%. Moreover, 44% were favorable to consensual unions on all three normative questions, while 22% were opposed on all three questions. In view of the social desirability factor —the lower-class respondents knew that the consensual union was not legal and that it was disapproved of by higher-status individuals and by the churches—it is probably safe to say that these results underestimate the amount of lower-class community acceptance of the consensual union. But even without correction, they show that a large body of respondents see the consensual union as normatively acceptable. It is true that they may prefer conventional marriage, but they also include the consensual union within their normative range (28, pp. 676–81).

What of the attitudes of the respondents toward fidelity in the consensual union? Data were collected on questions on the consensual union (*living*), on the non-cohabiting (*friending*) relationship, as well as on conventional marriage. The full set of data, broken down by social class and sex, are presented in Table 1. If we look at the percentages for the total sample, we can see the overall picture, ignoring for a moment the differences by class and sex.

Questions 1 and 2 are not on attitudes toward infidelity, but deal with the normative status of sexual intercourse before marriage. For both men (62%) and women (51%) there are substantial numbers who state that premarital intercourse is all right. The rest of the questions deal with attitudes toward infidelity. Questions 3 and 4 deal with the non-cohabiting (*friending*) relationship, and here 23% approve of infidelity for men, and 8% approve for women. These figures decline a little in the questions on infidelity within the consensual (*living*) relationship (17% approve for men, 7% for women) and the legal marriage relationship (11% approve for men, 2% approve for women). One striking feature is the double standard that exists, with women expected to adhere to a code of fidelity in all relationships by a greater percentage of respondents. Another striking fact, of special interest in this paper, is that fidelity is expected by a very high percentage of respondents in all three relationships—*friending*, *living*, and married. The major differences are between the first two questions and the last six questions—the differences in expectations of fidelity within the

TABLE 1. ATTITUDES TOWARD INFIDELITY IN VARYING FORMS OF MAN-WOMAN RELATIONSHIPS: PER CENT SAYING *Yes* BY SEX AND CLASS

Attitude	Sex	Class: Upper-lower	Class: Lower-lower	Total Sample
1. Is it all right for a man to have sexual intercourse before he marries?	Female	63	37	
	Male	69	81	
				62
2. Is it all right for a woman to have sexual intercourse before she marries?	Female	50	29	
	Male	56	74	
				51
3. Is it all right for a man to be *friending* with more than one woman?	Female	18	10	
	Male	36	30	
				23
4. Is it all right for a woman to be *friending* with more than one man?	Female	0	2	
	Male	14	13	
				8
5. Is it all right for a man who is living (common-law) with a woman to be *friending* with someone on the outside?	Female	29	7	
	Male	25	20	
				17
6. Is it all right for a woman who is living (common-law) with a man to be *friending* with someone on the outside?	Female	6	3	
	Male	11	8	
				7
7. Is it all right for a man who is married to be *friending* with someone on the outside?	Female	6	5	
	Male	11	18	
				11
8. Is it all right for a woman who is married to be *friending* with someone on the outside?	Female	0	0	
	Male	0	5	
				2
Total number of respondents	Female	17	59	
	Male	36	61	
				181

three marital relationships in Trinidad are minor, although a slightly higher percentage do expect fidelity in marriage than in *living*, and in *living* than in *friending*.

In summary, according to the principle of fidelity alone, we would conclude that all three relationships are marital relationships, and represent alternative forms of marriage to a large majority of the respondents. Two important qualifications, however, must be made. In the first place, the questions assume that it is all right to be in each of the three marital relationships, and merely ask whether it is all right to be unfaithful in that relationship. A respondent who says "No" is, therefore, not directly telling us that he approves of the relationship. It is conceivable that he both disapproves of the relationship and of infidelity within that relationship. However, it must be borne in mind that (1) only one respondent out of 173 rejected the assumption made in the question; (2) this form of questioning perhaps overcomes the social desirability factor and underlines our earlier point about the usual underestimation in interviews of the percentage who normatively accept the consensual relationship; and (3) in any case, the percentage who accept the consensual union on the above-mentioned normative questions is itself quite high. A second, and more serious qualification, is that the infidelity asked about involves entering into a *friending* relationship, which is a relationship involving patterned mutual obligations between a man and a woman. The responses might have been quite different if the questions were asked about infidelity in a less involved relationship, for example, asking about sexual relationships outside the *friending*, *living*, and married relationships.

If we look at the responses for males and females in Table 1, we find that within the lower-lower class there are substantial differences on questions 1 and 2, moderate differences on questions 3, 4, 5, and 7, and slight differences on question 6 and 8. In all the differences there are more men than women who accept sexual relationships outside marriage or infidelity in any relationship. The same trend holds true for the comparison of men and women among the upper-lower class, although the differences are smaller and there is a single reversal on question 5. In short, more men than women accept premarital sexual relationships and infidelity for women as well as for men. These differences are most marked for questions 1 and 2 (though only for the lower-lower class) and 3 and 4. In other words, for questions 5 through 8, dealing with the consensual union and with legal marriage, there is not only a greater expectation of fidelity, but there is also more homogeneity in the attitudes of men and women. This would suggest that these two relationships in particular must be considered marital relationships in terms of the principle of fidelity, as well as in terms of community approval and attitudinal homogeneity.

Looking at social class,[6] we find that the major differences are to be found in the first two questions, along with a difference in question 5 in the response of females. All of the other differences are minor. Curiously, while the lower-lower class males show more acceptance of pre-

[6] See Rodman (28, pp. 679–80) for the operational definition of lower-lower and upper-lower class.

marital sexual relationships (questions 1 and 2), the pattern is reversed for females, and the differences are even more pronounced. The anomalously low figures for lower-lower-class women on the acceptance of premarital sexual relationships is related to their much greater normative acceptance of the consensual union (28, p. 677, Table 1; 29). In short, the class differences on the acceptance of infidelity for *friending, living,* and marriage are relatively minor and suggest that there is substantial community agreement on the principle of fidelity for all three relationships.

COMMUNITY APPROVAL

Kinship or community approval is another obvious indication as to the existence of a marriage or a marriage process. A relationship which is generally condemned or at best tolerated within the community, and which is not maintained in the open, is not a marriage. In the village in which I did field work in Trinidad, *friending* was sometimes a hidden relationship and sometimes an open and approved one —the latter especially in cases where the man and woman were not violating the principle of fidelity and were planning to enter a consensual union. The consensual union and legal marriage were both open and approved marital relationships, and although members of the community knew the marital form each couple was in, few distinctions were made between them (26, 27). Insofar as this interpretation is correct—and the quantitative data on the normative questions and the fidelity questions tend to confirm it—the consensual union must, in general, be seen as an approved marital relationship within the lower-class community.

The conclusion that the consensual union is a form of marital relationship has also been reached by a good many other field workers who have done research in the Caribbean area (2, 10, 11, 13, 18, 19, 32, 33). Goode, however, has critically reviewed the writings of the researchers who have concluded that the consensual union is a community-approved form of marriage (6). If that were true, Goode asserts, then these writings would refute Malinowski's rule of legitimacy —that marriage is a prerequisite for the status of offspring, and that all children must therefore have a sociological father (6, pp. 21–24; 17, pp. 201–8).

Goode makes his point as follows:

> It is precisely with reference to Malinowski's principle that many students of the Caribbean have taken an opposing position—without developing its implications for family theory. The claim has often been

> made for various Caribbean lands that . . . the consensual union is the marriage form of the lower classes in the Caribbean, and is "sociologically as legitimate" as a legal union. It is, in short, a "cultural alternative," as permissible a way of founding a family as any other. If this interpretation is correct, Malinowski's principle would be erroneous, and one of the apparently major functions of the father would have to be redefined as unessential. (6, p. 23)

What Goode ignores should be obvious to even a beginning student of anthropology—that if the relationship is approved by the community, and is an alternate form of marriage, then the rule of legitimacy is in no way challenged.[7] Although Goode is clearly aware of the difference between legal marriage and customary marriage, and uses that distinction elsewhere in his writings, he nevertheless fails to make the distinction in his discussion of the consensual union.

Goode also goes on to try to refute the ethnographic material by stating that the consensual union is stigmatized, and as I have pointed out elsewhere he uses the following five reasons to back up that claim: (1) the consensual union is considered deviant by individuals who are not members of the lower class; (2) it is not as stable as legal marriage; (3) a girl who becomes illegitimately pregnant while living with her parents is punished; (4) most adults eventually marry; and (5) legal marriage is preferred. But not one of these reasons constitutes evidence that the consensual union is considered deviant within the lower class (28, pp. 674–75).

In summary, Goode was wrong in arguing a) that if the consensual union is an alternative form of marriage then it disputes Malinowski's principle of legitimacy, and b) that the consensual union is a deviant and stigmatized relationship. It is an alternate form of marriage found particularly within the lower classes of Caribbean society[8] and fulfilling particular functions for lower-class individuals, in the same way that alternative forms of marriage serve different functions in other societies (1, 4, 5, 12, 14, 21, 22).

[7] There is, of course, an entirely separate question about the general relevance of or importance of the principle of legitimacy. Malinowski developed the idea to account for marriage and paternity in a matrilineal society that did not recognize the physical basis of paternity, and the idea has been little used since that time.

[8] David M. Schneider points out that social surveys cannot by themselves establish cultural facts, although they may be of assistance when combined with anthropological field work using informants. My use, therefore, of both techniques in Trinidad serves to strengthen the argument. Schneider agrees "that the consensual union is a form of marriage, is an alternate form for that society and that culture, is not a form of deviance like homosexuality or theft or buggery" (personal communication). (See also Schneider, 31, Chapter 1.)

CONCLUSION

We have seen that there are varying forms of marriage between societies and often within societies. These varying marriage forms generally fulfill an overlapping set of functions (some are similar, some different), in accordance with the structure of the community under consideration. We have also seen that marriage is, at times, better conceptualized as a process rather than as a single event. As a result, it is not easy to define marriage, and it is not always easy to ascertain whether a particular man and woman are married. Since it is not always clear what marriage is, this also means that it may be difficult to distinguish between what is marital, what is premarital, and what is extramarital.

Among the Tallensi, for example, when a woman leaves her husband and stays one night with another man, do we have an instance of an extramarital relationship? In fact, this is one way for the woman to break up a marital relationship and to enter a new one, and rather than an extramarital relationship we have the establishment of a new marriage (16, p. 142). Among the Ngoni, a couple's marital status may be questioned when the man makes a claim for adultery compensation. Has he paid the full brideprice, and is he entitled to compensation? It is at this point that one gets clarification of whether he is fully married—or rather, one sees that there may be conflicting ideas about whether the marriage is sufficiently validated to determine rights to adultery compensation (16, p. 87). Even in contemporary national societies some apparently completed marriages are annulled, and there is also much legal variation on whether common-law marriages will be recognized.

As a result, anthropologists have come to look at marriage as a relationship in which a variety of rights may be transferred or exchanged, and in which such transference or exchange may take place at one point in time (the marriage ceremony) or be spaced over a period of time (a series of marriage ceremonies). These rights involve, among others, sexual and procreative rights. There is generally sexual exclusiveness or at least sexual privileges that are shared by the man and woman in a marriage, and I have used this to develop the idea of a principle of fidelity—consisting of the sexual privilege in marriage, the expectation of fidelity, and the punishment of adultery. This principle of fidelity—or more specifically the expectation of fidelity—was then proposed as one criterion that might be used in order to determine whether a particular relationship was recognized as marriage or considered to be deviant. It was applied to the debated status of the consensual union in the Caribbean, and on the basis of data presented on Trinidad we found that fidelity is expected within the consensual union. In addition, we pointed to observational data and to quantitative data on normative attitudes toward the consensual union which also provided support for the position that the consensual union was —at least among a very substantial part of the lower class—an acceptable form of marital relationship.

In advancing toward a definition of marriage (and of premarital, extramarital, and deviant relationships), further cross-cultural attention must be paid to at least the following issues: marriage as a process versus marriage as a single event; the principles of fidelity and community approval as criteria of marriage; and the nature, scope, and variations in the exchanges that take place in the different marital and nonmarital relationships.

References

1. Bohannan, Laura. "Dahomean Marriage: A Revaluation," *Africa,* 19 (No. 4), 1949.
2. Braithwaite, Lloyd. "Social Stratification in Trinidad," *Social and Economic Studies,* 2 (Nos. 2 and 3), 1953.
3. Fortes, Meyer (Ed.), *Marriage in Tribal Societies.* Cambridge: Cambridge University Press, 1962.
4. Fortes, Meyer. "Analysis and Description in Social Anthropology." Presidential address, Section H, British Association for the Advancement of Science. *Advancement of Science,* 10 (September, 1953), 190–201.
5. Gibbs, James L., Jr. "Marital Instability Among the Kpelle: Towards a Theory of Epainogamy," *American Anthropologist,* 65 (June), 552–73, 1963.
6. Goode, William J. "Illegitimacy in the Caribbean Social Structure," *American Sociological Review,* 25 (February), 21–30, 1960.
7. Gough, E. Kathleen. "The Nayars and the Definition of Marriage," *Journal of the Royal Anthropological Institute,* 89, 23–34, 1959.
8. Gough, E. Kathleen. "A Book Review of *A Study of Polyandry,*" *Man,* 65 (January–February, No. 23), 30–31, 1965.
9. Harris, Grace. "Taita Bridewealth and Affinal Relationships." In Meyer Fortes, *op. cit.,* pp. 55–87.
10. Henriques, Fernando. *Family and Colour in Jamaica.* London: Eyre & Spottiswoode, 1953.
11. Herskovits, Melville J., and Frances E. *Trinidad Village.* New York: Knopf, 1947.

12. HOWARD, ALAN, and HOWARD, IRWIN. "Premarital Sex and Social Control Among the Rotumans," *American Anthropologist,* 66 (April), 266–83, 1964.

13. KREISELMAN, MARIAM. "The Caribbean Family: A Case Study in Martinique." Unpublished Ph.D. thesis, Columbia University, 1958.

14. LA FONTAINE, JEAN. "Gisu Marriage and Affinal Relations." In Meyer Fortes, *op. cit.*, pp. 113–19.

15. LEACH, E. R. "Polyandry, Inheritance, and the Definition of Marriage," *Man,* 55 (No. 199), 182–86, 1955.

16. MAIR, L. P. "African Marriage and Social Change." In Arthur Phillips (Ed.), *Survey of African Marriage and Family Life.* New York: Oxford University Press, 1953.

17. MALINOWSKI, BRONISLAW. *Coral Gardens and Their Magic.* New York: American Book Co., 1935.

18. MANNERS, ROBERT A. "Tabara: Subcultures of a Tobacco and Mixed Crop Municipality." In Julian Steward *et al., The People of Puerto Rico.* Urbana: University of Illinois Press, 1956.

19. MINTZ, SIDNEY W. "Cañamelar: The Subculture of a Rural Sugar Plantation Proletariat." *Ibid.*

20. MURDOCK, G. P. *Social Structure.* New York: Macmillan, 1949.

21. NUTINI, HUGO G. "Polygyny in a Tlaxcalan Community," *Ethnology,* 4 (April), 123–47, 1965.

22. PAUL, LOIS, and PAUL, BENJAMIN D. "Changing Marriage Patterns in a Highland Guatemalan Community," *Southwestern Journal of Anthropology,* 19 (Summer), 131–48, 1963.

23. PHILLIPS, ARTHUR (Ed.). *Survey of African Marriage and Family Life.* New York: Oxford University Press, 1953.

24. RADCLIFFE-BROWN, A. R., and FORDE, DARYLL (Eds.). *African Systems of Kinship and Marriage.* London: Oxford University Press, 1950.

25. RICHARDS, A. I. "Some Types of Family Structure Amongst the Central Bantu." *Ibid.*, pp. 215–16.

26. RODMAN, HYMAN. "On Understanding Lower-class Behaviour," *Social and Economic Studies,* 8 (December), 441–50, 1959.

27. RODMAN, HYMAN. "Marital Relationships in a Trinidad Village," *Marriage and Family Living,* 23 (May), 166–70, 1961.

28. RODMAN, HYMAN. "Illegitimacy in the Caribbean Social Structure: A Reconsideration," *American Sociological Review,* 31 (October), 673–83, 1966.

29. RODMAN, HYMAN, NICHOLS, FLORENTINA J., and VOYDANOFF, PATRICIA. "Lower-class Attitudes toward 'Deviant' Family Patterns: A Cross-Cultural Study," *Journal of Marriage and the Family,* 31 (May), 315–21, 1969.

30. SCHAPERA, ISAAC. *Married Life in an African Tribe.* Evanston, Ill.: Northwestern University Press, 1966. (First published in 1941.)

31. Schneider, David M. *American Kinship: A Cultural Account.* Englewood Cliffs, N.J.: Prentice-Hall Inc., 1968, Chapter 1.

32. Seda, Elena Padilla. "Nocora: The Subculture of Workers on a Government-owned Sugar Plantation." In Julian Steward, *op. cit.*, pp. 293–94.

33. Smith, Raymond T. *The Negro Family in British Guiana.* London: Routledge & Kegan Paul, 1956.

Gerhard Neubeck

OTHER SOCIETIES: AN ANTHROPOLOGICAL REVIEW OF EXTRAMARITAL RELATIONS

The ground rules by which various societies, cultures, and subcultures have regulated marriage and do regulate marriage have a great deal in common, but they also differ substantially among themselves. Regulations had to be devised because the system of marriage, like all other systems, is fallible. Among the proscriptions, one of the most universal seems to be the one on extramarital relationships. Murdock (1949) reports that in 120 of 148 societies studied, a taboo on extramarital relations was apparent. He is careful to add, though, "In four of the remaining twenty-eight, adultery is socially disapproved, though not strictly forbidden. It is conditionally permitted in nineteen and freely allowed in five. It should be pointed out, however," he goes on, "that these figures apply only to sex relations with an unrelated or distantly related person." While he is careful to make this reservation, he is really not careful enough in setting up criteria as to what is an unrelated or distantly related person. We will see later that other writers have defined this in more precise terms. To cite one other example of the taboo, the fact that the seventh commandment, "Thou shalt not commit adultery," had to be codified, indicates that there seems to have been some affinity in the direction of extramarital relations, which then had to be outlawed. The explanation for this affinity seems obvious to this writer. Sexual and erotic attraction to nonspouses has remained a "Given" for many individuals and therefore has threatened monogamous patterns. There are other motives, economic ones certainly; but the most powerful motive seems always to have been a personal, sexual-erotic one.

The question then became one of how societies have handled this powerful urge, the urge to associate with persons not bound to one another in marriage. Murdock has indicated that the taboo is not a global one, as it appears at first, because a great many societies in fact, allow extramarital relations with certain types of relatives.

Polygamy, of course, has been the legalized solution to the "attraction is a given" problem, as extramarital relations have been the illegitimate outlet. At one time, the Ojibwa Indians of North America practiced polygamy. As this is no longer feasible, a system of extramarital relations has taken over. "Extramarital sex activity was tolerated so long as the partners were unrelated or were in the cross-cousin relationship, and it wasn't a serious enough breach of the mores to cause illness. Faithfulness in marriage was the ideal, especially for women, and certain women were regarded as especially virtuous and good because they had never committed adultery." (2)

It would stand to reason that polygamous cultures had little, if any, extramarital activity, because opportunities for consummation of attraction were systematically provided. Polygamy, however, sooner or later seemed to be impractical and was abandoned and extramarital relations alone have remained the answer. Driver points out that the vast majority of North American peoples practiced polygamy, but that exclusive monogamy was the rule among the Iroquois and a few of their neighbors. The most interesting pattern, of course, of the North American people is that of the Eskimo. Driver refers to the wife-lending phenomenon and describes it in detail:

> Among the Eskimos polygamy was complicated by that form of Northern hospitality called "wife-lending." Any man would lend his wife for a night to a total stranger, and to a friend or relative for longer periods depending on circumstances. In theory, at least, wife-lending eventually terminated. In some cases the wife was a second wife from a polygamous marriage. At the same time, cases of two brothers sharing one wife are widely reported. While details are often wanting the general pattern is that of a younger brother moving in with his married older brother and playing a secondary role. The common procedure in wife-lending was for the visitor to go to bed with the wife of the host in the one-room hut where the host also slept. The only privacy was darkness. Such being the case, we may presume that two brothers shared their wife at home with each other present. The length of time that such multiple unions lasted is seldom reported. However, it is generally agreed that they would not continue for a life time. The arrangement is best regarded as a stop gap in cases where one of the two brothers had no wife.[1]

The anthropological literature includes a good many references to

[1] Harold E. Driver, *Indians of North America* (Chicago: University of Chicago Press, 1961), p. 277. Used by permission of the publisher.

extramarital relations. Since anthropologists have studied family patterns and rituals, taboos would also be observed. In fact, they were hard to overlook, and the important taboos concerning extramarital relations, of course, stood out. But no research in depth has been done to illuminate inter-cultural differences, not to mention explanations for these differences.

Jack Goody in his article, "A Comparative Approach to Incest and Adultery" (7), has contributed a typology which has made somewhat clearer what we are talking about in regard to extramarital relations in other cultures; that is, to delineate more sharply between incestuous extramarital relations and those with non-relatives. Goody, therefore, suggests the following typology for most societies characterized by unilineal descent:

1. Prohibitions on sexual intercourse with a member of the same descent group (intra-group sexual prohibition);
2. With a wife of a member (group-wife prohibition);
3. With another married woman (extra-group prohibition).

In the same paper Goody quotes Rattray, who made this classification:

Adultery with:

1. A brother's wife
2. A son's wife
3. A wife's mother
4. An uncle's wife
5. A wife of anyone of the same *fekuo* (company)
6. A wife of anyone of the same trade or guild
7. A wife of one's own slave
8. Father's wife (other than adulterer's own mother)
9. Wife's sister, married or single

Rattray makes a contribution by explaining that adultery may include various forms of intimacy besides coitus.

Rattray, in his work on the Ashanti, also describes the interesting concept of "Atwe-bene-Fie which means literally having sexual intercourse with 'a vagina that is near to the dwelling house,' and the offense as the title implies, consisted in committing adultery with the wives of certain persons with whom the existing ménage necessarily compelled close social intercourse in constant physical proximity."

Another work Goody quotes is the study by Fortes (6). Fortes describes the Tallensi culture, which he categorized in three different patterns: (1) sexual intercourse with a member of the same patriclan (up to the inner lineage only); (2) sexual intercourse with the wife of a member of the same patriclan; and (3) sexual intercourse with a wife of a non-clansman.

It is interesting, therefore, to see that Goody found that the breaches of the taboo varied not only between societies but also within societies. Goody, in his conclusions, takes psychologists to task, psychologists that is, who have ventured into the cross-cultural field and do not realize that reactions to a breach vary within and between societies. Moreover, he feels that these psychologists have imposed categories derived from their own social institutions on the other societies they have studied. He also accuses anthropologists and sociologists about the ethnocentric nature of their categories, "particularly since they have tended to treat incest," as he says, "as an isolate instead of examining the systems of prohibitions as a whole in relation to the social structure. Thus there is quite a disproportionate amount of literature devoted to incest as compared to adultery. Yet from the standpoint of social problems, the latter would seem to deserve the greater attention, but the lure of the exotic has overcome the attraction of the mundane." This writer agrees with Goody that adultery itself is a problem to be studied and is, therefore, happy about the derivation of a typology, yet even these typologies are not without their limitations. Though in the long run, Goody's point that women who belong to the group and women who are married to its male members must be differentiated from each other, is a workable hypothesis. This writer is more interested in incidents than in typology.

Ford and Beach, in their classic, *Patterns of Sexual Behavior* (5), have a chapter on "Sexual Partnerships," in which they describe sexual liaisons in human society. A sexual liaison is described as referring to partnerships which are relatively impermanent and do not ordinarily involve economic or other non-sexual forms of cooperation. While he describes the usual incestuous relationships, Beach mentions that there are at least two patterns which are excluded from the taboo. First, the instance where, "Mothers and fathers are permitted to masturbate or in some other sexual manner to stimulate their very young children," and secondly, the exception to the taboo in which "a society expects a few individuals of special social rank to cohabit with their immediate descendants. (For instance, the Azande of Africa insist that the highest chiefs enter into sexual partnerships with their own daughters.)" The general tenor of Beach's chapter, however, underlines the strong taboos on incest prohibition. Beach goes on to describe a number of societies which approve of certain liaisons. In his sample, 39% of 139 groups approve of some type of extra-mateship liaison. He mentions the Toda of India, in which a woman may have one or more recognized lovers as well as several husbands. There is no censure of adultery. In fact, the Toda language does not include any word for adultery. Then he describes the Siriono. Among the Siriono a man may have liaisons with his mate's sisters and his brothers' wives and their sisters. Similarly, a woman has sexual access to her husband's brothers and to the husbands of her sisters.

Ford and Beach go on to say that in some societies extra-mateship liaisons take the form of wife-lending or wife exchange (I have described the Eskimo pattern earlier in this paper). "Generally the situation," Ford and Beach say, "is one in which a man is granted sexual access to the mate of another only on special occasions. If the pattern is reciprocal, an exchange of wife occurs. Both wife-lending and wife exchange may be involved in patterns of hospitality." The Chukchee of Siberia are described as follows: "The men often travel to distant communities and each married man generally makes special arrangements with some man in each of the communities he has occasion to visit. These arrangements are such that wherever he goes he may engage in sexual liaison with his host's mate in return for permitting these men the same privileges when they visit his community."

Ford and Beach state, "Sixty-one per cent of their 139 societies forbid a mated woman to engage in extra-mateship liaisons. In some societies the mated man is similarly restricted, although the great majority of these people are much more concerned with the behavior of the mated woman than that of a mated man." The conclusion that Ford and Beach draw is that although 85 societies were classified as restrictive, in at least seventeen of them extra-mateship liaisons appear to be extremely common and are not seriously punished. For many of these peoples, disapproval of liaisons outside of mateship become serious only when an affair is conducted in a flagrant manner. The Bena of Africa furnish a typical example. In this culture mateship is supposed to carry with it exclusive rights to sexual intercourse. But in actual practice mated individuals very frequently enter into liaisons with other members of the community. For both sexes, undetected extramarital seduction is the spice of life. If one mate does apprehend the other in an affair, there is likely to be a furious outburst of temper in which the offending partner bears the brunt of a fierce verbal attack. But the tantrum is soon over and both partners renew the game with the recently caught one determined to be less careless on the next occasion.

Of the many writers who have studied the family in cross-cultural patterns, most have studied some African societies. William Reyburn in his article, "Kaka Kinship, Sex and Adultery," (10) points out, first of all, that "the term 'family' doesn't mean to an African what Europeans and Americans take it to mean to them. The lack of an equivalent term in the language of the South Cameroun for the European elementary family reflects the fact that the Africans do not conceive of the elementary family as being a valid concept." More specifically in regard to adultery, Reyburn quotes a young Kaka as describing his family with lots of fathers and lots of mothers. Some of these mothers, who are obviously not his natural mother, this young man seems to desire sexually, but his fathers have always told him that, "If we had sex relations with a 'mother,' both the mother and the man would die an awful death and no medicine not even the Christian's God could prevent it." Further on he said, "Once one of my 'fathers' dreamed of sleeping with one of his 'mothers.' In the morning he awoke with a fever and after he confessed what his spirit had done in the night he became terribly ill and in a few days was dead." So it seems that even dreaming of intercourse with a person of this kind has dire consequences. Similar feelings for his sisters are described. There is a certain degree of embarrassment and shame about a sister; for instance, the young fellow says that, "If we were to go to bathe after eight or ten years of age and there is a sister bathing, he will pass on and come back after she is gone." As far as uncles are concerned, the young man has free sexual access to his uncle's wife even while the uncle is alive. In fact, they will have intercourse on the uncle's bed, and if the uncle comes home while they are thus engaged, the young fellow would merely call out, "It's taa," and the uncle acts as though he doesn't know what is going on inside.

"There are restrictions on promiscuous relations with my older brother's wives, though he may have relations with my wife's younger sisters, but after these are married this is less frequent." They have definite taboos on in-laws. In fact, the young fellow may never enter the sleeping quarters of the parents-in-law.

The author raises a number of other questions. For instance, "How do premarital sex relations affect extramarital ones?" He answers it by saying that premarital suitors of a girl often continue to seek relations after marriage. The other question raised in broad terms is, "What does a Kaka understand by the term 'adultery'?" The author answers it by saying that sex contacts are defined according to the persons involved. Relations between an individual and his uncle's wife are simply sex relations. This is considered about on the level of paying a social call. Premarital relations are an act in which young people are expected to indulge. It is the way in which girls prepare themselves for the ends to which a woman has been born—to produce children. Extramarital relations is a complex of its own with no exact equivalent in Euro-American societies. It is like a game in which the young fellow wins a comrade, much to his delight, and much to the disgust of the person from which the woman is taken. None of these acts are understood in the same way that Western missionaries take the term adultery. But the Kaka concept of incest is much more serious than the Christian idea of adulterous unions.

The next question the author asks is, "Can the idea of *wandja* (which is the game in which the comrade is won) serve as an equivalent for adultery?" Reyburn says that, while it is true that *wandja* is an offense to the husband of the adulterous female, it is not so because the wife has broken the sacred vows of marriage, nor would a man suspect the paternity of his wife's offspring. The offense is in the thought of having been forced into this kind of relationship which gives the adulterous male a superior position of social prestige. Also important is the fact that if a woman is adulterous it implies that her husband is less potent than some other male. This is a bitter bit of ridicule which no Kaka man can take easily. Consequently, his reputation as a sire of offspring is belittled in the eyes of the other village women and his chances of gaining other *wandjas* for himself are crippled. It often results in the man taking his wife and family and moving from the village. A further factor is the food relationship between a man and his *wandja.* If a husband's meat from the hunt will go to feed his adulterous partner, he will himself suffer and such meat will injure his chances in the hunt, as well as his medicine for the traps. Then comes the question of "Who is actually wronged in a *wandja* relationship?" The author says again that the answer is an economic one. The rights of ownership for the purpose of production paid via the dowry is the thing which is wronged. Then, "How important is the woman's attitude in the adulterous unions?" The author believes that younger and middle-aged women encourage adulterous unions by ridiculing men as impotent if they do not make sexual advances. It is common for a group of women to mock a man and ridicule the size of his genitalia. The natural defense of the male is to subdue one of the women and convince her or them that he is equally as potent as the other men of the village. Last, but not least, the author raises the question, "How do Kaka Christians rate adultery in their moral concept of right and wrong?" He believes that, first of all, the greatest wrong is incest, then stinginess within the family, and then theft. *Wandja*, or adultery, is a wrong against the dowry, but since it is an act into which two agreeing parties enter, it is not looked upon as harmful to any party on the order in which incest, stinginess and theft are.

The term "family" as described earlier in Reyburn's article is the *ddité*, which is a common fireplace.

Schapera, in his classic work, deals with a contemporary society called the Kgatla.[2] He states that adultery is fairly common among both men and women:

> In theory, husband and wife should remain faithful to each other. It is a breach of marital rights if either has sexual relations with any other person. This does not apply, of course, to men who are polygamists, or who cohabit with the widow of a close relative to raise up seed to the deceased. But any man sleeping with a woman other than his wife or wives, except for the reason just given, is still held to be violating his matrimonial obligations, and so is a woman sleeping with anybody but her husband. Like so many other peoples, however, the Kgatla do not take a husband's infidelity as serious as a wife's. They hold that a man is naturally inclined to be promiscuous. "A man like a bull cannot be confined to a kraal," says their proverb.

Schapera goes on to say:

> The reasons men commonly give for their infidelity include some interesting examples of rationalization. Occasionally a man will admit frankly that he is tired of his wife, or is attracted by someone else, or is unable to be satisfied by one woman alone. He will say that at certain times, as we have already noted, he is expected to refrain from sleeping with his wife, and, since he cannot curb his sexual desires, he must seek relief somewhere else. More often than not, however, he will seek to justify himself by pleading that the decay of polygamy, and the prolonged absence of many men in the towns, have led to a preponderance of dissatisfied women at home, and that he is doing them and the tribe a service by consorting with them! There is a widespread impression that fewer children are being born nowadays than before, so that men distributing their favours among several women are actually regarded with approval by some. "They are the bulls of the tribe," said an enthusiastic informant. Even respectable members of the Church, who unknown to their missionary have one or more concubines as well as a wife, have advanced this argument to me as an excuse for their "immoral" conduct. "There are these women," they say, "young and ripe for bearing children, but the laws of the white people will not allow us to have more than one wife. Why should their fertility go to waste, when they can be used to increase the numbers of the tribe?"

Then Schapera quotes a certain Natale:

> As for adultery, I have many concubines. There is R——, and there is M——, and several others as well. I live with the first two as if I

[2] Isaac Schapera, *Married Life in an African Tribe* (New York: Sheridan House, 1941), pp. 204–5. Used by permission of the publishers. Copyright 1941 by Sheridan House, Inc. Renewal copyright R 457951.

were married to them, but the others I sleep with for only one night, and then abandon. And when I go to these other women, my junior wife gets jealous and complains, but the older one does not. And when the junior wife gets angry with me, I buy beer and bring it to her, and we drink together, and when she has drunk it she becomes reconciled to me again. And in any case I once found her also sleeping with a lover, I caught him in her blankets, but I forgave him; this was at the time when the Prince of Wales visited us. (1925)

Schapera also says that, "Sometimes a man's mistress is a woman whose husband is still living," (11, p. 205) but that this affair is generally kept as secret as possible and the meetings are confined mainly to occasions when the husband is away.

The author also believes that one important motive for concubinage is the barrenness of a wife. In the old days this was usually circumvented by the *sororate*, whereby she would get her parents to provide her husband with her younger sister or some other close relative, to bear children in her place.

"Wives vary greatly in their attitudes towards an unfaithful husband," Schapera says. "Often enough a woman is fairly complaisant, or at least resigned, so long as her husband continues to look after her decently, sleeps with her regularly and does not obviously favor his concubine." Schapera, in fact, says that one of his informants said that at his wedding feast he was greatly attracted to two of the girls present, and asked his wife if he might take them as mistresses. Her reply was, in his eyes, eminently reasonable. "Well," she said, "you are still a young man, so I suppose that you need more than one woman, but don't make your affairs too public, and remember that we also must have a baby of our own!"

Schapera believes that this attitude is by no means unusual, though he also says that the wife is not always so accommodating.

As far as the infidelity of the wife is concerned, many a husband, although fully aware of it, prefers to ignore it, especially if he too is unfaithful or if the marriage is barren. In relatively recent times adultery by women seems to have increased considerably as a result of labor migration. Often enough, a husband stays away so long from the Reserve that his wife can no longer control her sexual desires, and begins to look around for a lover.

In conclusion, Schapera believes that there is a good deal of maladjustment within the society, based, to some degree, on labor migration. He apologizes for having stressed the unhappy marriages too much, but he believes that true companionship, upon which a successful union should rest, is not present in the Kgatla society. There are almost always complaints of sexual ill-treatment and infidelity, and he believes that the characteristic female attitude is one of resignation.

Newly married couples are often very much in love with each other, and the wives will speak most affectionately of their husbands, but in a few years little of this remains except in isolated instances. Many women become reconciled to their husband's infidelities and manage to lead a tolerable existence with a not unduly inconsiderate husband; others find some sort of relief by being unfaithful themselves; some are acutely miserable.

It is clear, however, that infidelity, unfaithfulness, or whatever the behavior can be labeled, pervades the Kgatla society.

Ruth Benedict, in another classic anthropological work, *Patterns of Culture*, compared three different societies. While she was not focusing on adultery as such, like other anthropologists she made interesting observations in regard, first of all, to the Pueblos of New Mexico. Here she states that, "They do not meet adultery with violence." On the plains a usual response to the wife's adultery was to cut off the fleshy part of her nose. This was done even in the Southwest by non-Pueblo tribes like the Apache. But in the Zuñi (which is the particular Pueblo tribe that Ruth Benedict describes) the unfaithfulness of the wife is no excuse for violence. The husband does not regard it as a violation of his rights. If she is unfaithful, it is normally a first step in changing husbands, and their institutions make this sufficiently easy so that it is a tolerable procedure. They do not contemplate violence.

Wives are often equally moderate when their husbands are known to be unfaithful. As long as the situation is not unpleasant enough for relations to be broken off, it is ignored. The season before one of Dr. Bunzel's visits in Zuñi, one of the young husbands of the household in which she lived had been carrying on an extramarital affair that had been bruited about all over the pueblo. The family ignored the matter completely. At last the white trader, a guardian of morals, expostulated with the wife. The couple had been married a dozen years and had three children; the wife belonged to an important family. The trader set forth with great earnestness the need for making a show of authority and for putting an end to her husband's outrageous conduct. "So," his wife said, "I didn't wash his clothes. Then he knew that I knew that everybody knew, and he stopped going with that girl." It was effective, but not a word was passed. There were no outbursts, no recriminations, not even an open recognition of the crisis.

Wives, however, are allowed another course of action that is not sanctioned in the case of deserted husbands. A wife may fall upon her rival and beat her publicly. They call each other names and give each other a black eye. It never settles anything, and even in the rare cases when such a battle occurs, it dies down as quickly as it has flared. It is the only recognized fist-fight in Zuñi. If, on the other hand, a woman remains peacefully with her husband while he conducts amour after amour, her family is angry and brings pressure to bear upon her to separate from him. "Everybody says she must love him," they say, and all her relatives are ashamed. "She is disobeying the rules that are laid down for her."

In the Dobu society (the Dobu Islands in the d'Entrecasteaux group off the southern shore of Eastern New Guinea), faithfulness is not expected between husband and wife, and no Dobuan will admit that a man and woman are ever together even for the shortest interval except for sexual purposes. The outsider spouse of the year is quick to suspect unfaithfulness. Usually he has grounds. In the suspicion-ridden atmosphere of Dobu the safest liaison is with a village "brother" or "sister." During the year when one is in one's own village, circumstances are propitious and supernatural dangers are at a minimum. Public opinion strongly disapproves of marriage between such classificatory "brothers" and "sisters." It would disrupt the village to have obligatory marital exchanges between two parts of the settlement. But within this group adultery is a favorite pastime. It is celebrated constantly in mythology, and its occurrence in every village is known to everyone from early childhood. It is a matter of profoundest concern to the outraged spouse. He (it is as likely to be she) bribes the children (his own or any in the village) for information. If it is the husband, he breaks his wife's cooking pots. If it is the wife, she maltreats her husband's dog. He quarrels with her violently, and no quarrel can go unheard in the close-set, leaf-thatched houses of Dobu. He throws himself out of the village in a fury. As a last resort of important rage he attempts suicide by one of several traditional methods, no one of which is surely fatal. He is usually saved, and by this means he enlists his wife's *susu;* in fear of what his relatives might do if the outraged spouse succeeded in his attempts at suicide, they are moved to more conciliatory behavior. They may even refuse to take any further steps in the matter, and the partners to the marriage may remain sullenly and angrily together. The next year the wife can retaliate in the same manner in her own village.

Benedict's societies have been aptly classified in the following way: The Zuñi as Apollonian, moderate, practical, middle-of-the-road, polite and nice as well as generous; the Dobu as Faustian with a great deal of prudery, suspicion and a deep fear that life is magical; the Northwest Coast Indians called the Kwakiutl are described as Dionysian, competitive, status conscious, shaming, self-glorifying, and somewhat paranoid, with particular emphasis on property. In every possible way, marriage was thought of as a business transaction and followed the same peculiar rules. Benedict says very little in regard to adultery in this culture and it seems clear that within this status-ridden society, acts of adultery were very dangerous and attraction to others must have been neutralized.

William N. Stephens in his book, *The Family in Cross-Cultural Perspective* (13), devotes one chapter to "Sex Restrictions." Like this author, he seems to assume that there have always been violations of the monogamous taboo. He covers a number of Indian tribes including the Kwakiutl, about which Ruth Benedict lacked data.

HOPI, ARIZONA

Next to the dance days with singing, feasting, and clown work, love-making with private wives was the greatest pleasure of my life. And for us who toil in the desert, these light affairs make life more interesting. Even married men prefer a private wife now and then. At any rate there are times when a wife is not interested, and then a man must find someone else or live a worried and uncomfortable life. People cannot think that a man is doing wrong if he finds a single woman or a widow so long as he uses her right and rewards her. . . .

If I caught her (my wife) in adultery, I would not fight her lover, but I would be terribly hurt and would speak to his relatives about it. . . . I probably would not have left her for that, but I would have given her a good scolding, and I might even beat her. A husband can't often catch his wife in another man's arms and stay happy.[3]

NAVAHO, ARIZONA-NEW MEXICO

I know all there is to know about such things. I know more about it than all of you people. I know just how it starts and how it happens, because I've been all through it. Lots of times the same thing has happened to me, but I tried never to think about it. I always put it out of my mind, because, when I think of it, it's nothing to me, there's nothing to it. We're all doing just the same to one another. All of you people who are here now are all wishing for another man's wife, even though you have a wife of your own. I know every one of you has been around with another man's wife. Nothing can be done about it. It's always that way, with no end to it. And so I think there's no use talking about it. So we'll drop it and put it away.

One day, when I was driving the horses to the water, I saw a woman riding along on horseback. She was the one we called Woman Who

[3] Leo W. Simmons, ed., *Sun Chief* (New Haven: Yale University Press, 1942), p. 276. Copyright 1942 by Leo W. Simmons. Used by permission of Yale University Press.

Flips Her Cards. She used to snap her cards down when she played, so that's what they named her. She was going after water. As soon as I met her I reached out for the bridle and held it. She said, 'What do you mean by that?' I said, 'I want you to ride away with me.' 'I'm after some water,' she said, 'because there's no water at my home.' I said, 'It won't take us long. We'll be over there in the wash. Nobody'll see us there.' So we went down in the wash, and I got off my horse, and she got down off hers. As soon as she got off she sat down, and as soon as she sat down I went up to her. We both liked it very much. This woman had a husband, and she said, 'You're better than my husband.' I said, 'You mustn't tell on me, because if you do your husband might get after me and kill me.' She said, 'I won't tell on you, because I know, sure enough, my husband would get after you.' I reached down in my pocket and got out two dollars and gave them to her. She liked it and was thankful.[4]

KWAKIUTL, VANCOUVER ISLAND

One thing you don't know is how we get a girl. What I do is tell some friend—maybe a man or maybe a woman. He goes and tells her I want to see her. He sees her husband or father is out of sight when he does this. Then he says that I want to meet her in a certain place in the woods. If it is a woman who is telling her, maybe she tells the girl to come to her house, and I go and sneak into that house to see her. Sometimes when the husband is away from the village, we would make arrangements that I'll go and stay with her at night, and during the night I sneak in very carefully so no one sees me, and I get up before daylight to get out of the house, looking around on both ways from the house to see there is no one seeing me come out of the house. Sometimes someone sees me, and they go and tell somebody, because they think it is a good joke, and then it comes around to the woman's husband. Then there is liable to be trouble between the woman and her husband, and maybe she gets a licking from him.

I give those girls and women presents—sometimes blankets and sometimes money, maybe ten or maybe as much as fifty dollars at the beginning to start with them, and after that if she wants anything she asks for it. How much she wants at the beginning, that is all arranged by my friend. A lot of them wouldn't come with me for less than fifty dollars.

I haven't any idea how many girls and women I spent money on like this. About two hundred, I guess. I think now there wouldn't have

[4] From *Son of Old Man Hat* by Walter Dyk (New York: Harcourt, Brace and World, Inc., 1938), pp. 247, 267. Copyright 1966 by Walter Dyk. Reprinted by permission of the University of Nebraska Press.

been so many after I was married, if I could have married the woman I wanted. Some of the girls I went with when I was young were married. A few weren't, and these were harder to get at, because they were so well watched, unless their parents wasn't alive. Some would be easy and wouldn't ask for anything. Others would be hard, and it seems those are the ones I want most usually. But the only reason I paid fifty dollars for one and not for the other was her business; it doesn't matter to me.

Sometimes there would be two at a time, and sometimes three. I stop when she or I gets tired of each other, and sometimes there is trouble between us. I sometimes gets jealous of her going with someone else, or she gets jealous if she knows I am seeing another girl at the same time. Sometimes, too, she has trouble with her husband, and she won't see me any more. And sometimes if the husband is too good to me, I don't like to hurt his feelings if he finds out I am laying his wife. There were some girls from my own tribe I goes with, but not so many as from other tribes. There was none from my own clan. These is all relatives and friends, and I never had anything to do with them like this. I didn't want to, because they all call me brother or nephew or uncle or cousin. It's all right to marry close, but none of us would go with one of our cousins or aunt or niece unless they are from other tribes. And if I have a very good friend, I wouldn't go and interfere with his wife or the wife of his near relatives either.

My best friend goes between me and the girls and comes back with the answer. They used to be strict in the olden days, though, and the parents wouldn't let the girl out of their sight. The only girls that isn't married and I can get is the ones that doesn't have any parents, and their brothers and uncles is away working. And another thing, the girls that I go to, I don't go to when her folks is awake. I go and hide myself in the corners of the community house till I know that everybody is asleep, and walk from my hiding place then, very careful that I don't step on a stick that will break. When I get near to where she is lying, I could hardly breathe in case that would wake the people near her. When I get to her, I just touch her by the foot and shake her a little. She tries to stay awake, for she knows everytime that I was coming, and I go and lay down with her, and I have to be very careful all the time I am lying with her. Oh, it is a hard time to go with a girl when she is watched! We couldn't talk; we would just whisper as low as we can.

I got caught once, at Fort Rupert. . . .

Girls couldn't go around with men until they were married, and it was a great disgrace, especially to a chief's daughter, if anyone touches them. It doesn't make any difference in the money, but the husband might not like the girl and might not stay with her. The man usually doesn't want her, and when he is asked why he tells them she is not a virgin, and they go and spread it all over the place. They says they know when a girl has been touched, because the private of the girl is already too wide. My wife was all right.[5]

NAVAHO, ARIZONA-NEW MEXICO

That was the last time we did anything, and that was the last time I saw her. Five days later they moved away towards the north, and I never saw her again. I sure did miss her. Every day and night I thought of her and wished she were with me always. But we were far away, and there was no way for me to go and see her.

Two years later I heard she was married. After they held the wedding the boy who married her found out she wasn't a virgin, so he went back to his home and told his father and mother. His father went to where the girl lived and took back all the horses she'd got in marriage. They began asking her who the one was she'd been with, but she wouldn't tell. They tried and tried, asking her for a long time, but she never told anything at all. (3, pp. 149–50)

Stephens also talks about the restrictions on adultery, and states that in his sample of thirty-nine societies, twelve permitted adultery. These were the Baiga, Copper Eskimo, Fiji, Kwoma, Lepcha, Lesu, Marquesans, Murngin, Pakapuka, Siriono, Siwai, and Toda. And he goes on to say:

Fourteen societies have an apparently ineffective rule against adultery. Six societies have harsh penalties for adultery, which apparently effectively restrict it. In six societies, men are allowed to commit adultery but women are not (Ancient Greeks, Ancient Romans, Gusii, Kipsigis, Papago, Tikopia). For one case, a wife's adultery is severely punished, and there is no information about restrictions on men (Brahmins, Hindu India). And two societies have a rule against adultery, with no comment from the ethnographer as to whether or not the rule is effective (Alor and Tiv). In other words, adultery is freely permitted in about 30 per cent of the cases in my sample; adultery seems to be *effectively* restricted in 20 per cent of the sample for men and in about 30 per cent of the sample for women.

Where adultery is permitted, it is usually limited to some special situation, occasion, or kin relationship. The Kwoma, Marquesans, Murngin, Pakapuka, and Siwai have periods of ceremonial sexual license. The

[5] Clellan S. Ford, *Smoke From Their Fires* (New Haven: Yale University Press, 1941), pp. 123–25, 155. Used by permission of Yale University Press.

Copper Eskimo practice wife-lending. The Fijians, Lepcha, Marquesans and Siriono allow adulterous permissive sex relationships (with a cross-cousin, or with a potential spouse via the sororate-levirate).

In a few cases, Baiga, Lesu, Marquesans and Toda, there seems to be little if any bar to any sort of nonincestuous adultery. In Lesu, a woman's lover gives her gifts—*tsera*—which are to be handed over to her husband; adultery is open, fully permitted, and properly paid for (Powdermaker 1933: 244–48; Lesu, New Ireland)

It is interesting that in some of these societies which allow adultery, the jealousy problem still exists; some people are still hurt when their spouses engage in perfectly proper and virtuous adultery. In Lesu, says Powdermaker, "some men are jealous, and some are not. Some men gladly accept the *tsera* from their wives, who have received it from their lovers, and there is no rift in the family. However, others, who are the exceptions rather than the rule, instead of taking the *tsera* fight the wife's lover. There is the same difference in woman's attitude toward her husband's mistresses." (Powdermaker 1933:248). Among the Fijians, Lepcha, and Siriono, permissive sex relationships are carried on with a certain amount of discretion and secrecy, suggesting some danger of jealousy and hurt feelings. And the Murngin, in their ceremonial license, are also discreet; they copulate secretly, in the bush, and tend not to choose the wives of band members or of close associates. (Warner 1937: 64)[6]

Stephens describes behavior patterns of the Kaingang in Brazil, the Tikopia in Western Polynesia, and the Murngin in Australia which make it pretty clear how these cultures deal with the adulterous behavior of their members.

KAINGANG, BRAZIL

Once a couple are married they do not drop the liaisons formed before marriage. Their long training in philandering and the absence of an ideal of faithfulness have not suited them to the stability that marriage implies. Furthermore the absence of binding legal forms or big property stakes, as well as the knowledge that a meal can always be found at one's father's or brother's fire, that one's mother or sister-in-law is ready to cook the food and spread the bed, makes marriage brittle and its rupture is not sharply felt. Yet, in an utterly contradictory manner, the Kaingang believe that a man and woman, once they

[6] William N. Stephens, *The Family in Cross-Cultural Perspective* (New York: Holt, Rinehart and Winston, Inc., 1963), pp. 251–53 (excerpts). Reprinted by permission of Holt, Rinehart and Winston, Inc.

are "sitting together," belong to each other. . . . This theoretical possessiveness comes into constant conflict with the actual sharing in which the young people have taken part all their lives. The young man who for years before his marriage has dallied with the wife of anyone from his father to his second cousin, who has day in and day out enjoyed adultery with an equally delighted adulteress, decides suddenly, once he is married, that his possession should be exclusive. "I left my wife," Yuven told me, "because she took Kanyahe and Kundagn as lovers. She sleeps with everyone. All the women are that way. When their husbands go away they sleep with others. That is why I want to marry a Brazilian woman."[7]

TIKOPIA, WESTERN POLYNESIA

Adultery by a married woman is stated in reply to casual enquiry never to occur, and in actual fact does seem to be very rare; only one case became public during my stay in Tikopia, though I have notes of a few others. . . . A married man, however, has not to suffer this restriction to the same degree. Convention allows him to go among the unmarried girls without suffering any real stigma. He may be chaffed or sneered at by other men for his lecherous conduct, but the only check that is liable to be put on his amorous exploits is that applied by the jealousy of his wife. Fear of a nagging tongue and sharp female nails are probably the most potent deterrent in keeping many husbands faithful. . . .

In such a case, if the husband goes out alone at night the wife does not sleep but watches for him anxiously. When the time draws on and it is near morning, then she knows "he has gone to the women" (the conventional Tikopia expression for lechery). When he returns, he thinks she is asleep, but no, she is waiting for him. She has a stick, with which she bangs him on the back and legs—the head is taboo—and she pinches his flesh until the skin is broken. This he must suffer as quietly as he can, in order not to arouse the whole household.[8]

MURNGIN, AUSTRALIA

A beating is the usual punishment for a wife's adultery. Garawerpa, an old man of the Daiuror clan, put fire on his wives' vaginas, as did

[7] From *Jungle People* by Jules Henry (Richmond: William Byrd Press, 1941), pp. 25–26. Copyright 1941 © 1964 by Jules Henry. Reprinted by permission of Random House, Inc.

[8] Raymond Firth, *We, The Tikopia* (New York: American Book Company, 1936), pp. 132–33. Used by permission of Barnes & Noble, Inc., and George Allen and Unwin, Ltd.

Binindaio when their *galles* copulated with Willidjungo, the medicine man. With the beating goes a severe tongue lashing. An outraged wife who has caught her husband in a sexual relation with another woman resorts to public abuse of her mate for his infidelities. Her obscenity and abuse are usually more proficiently and much more adequately expressed than a husband's.

At noon one day Bruk Bruk, the young and attractive wife of Lika, who had inherited her from an older brother, accused Djolli, a man from a more distant clan, of trying to seduce her in the bush. A tremendous noise was made in the camp. All the relatives of the parties concerned talked at once, and the two men armed themselves with spears, spear-throwers, and clubs and charged at each other, exchanging curses.

Djolli was angry because he claimed to be falsely accused; and so was Lika because he knew something was wrong, for either his wife had defended her virtue against Djolli, or she had succumbed and then accused him. In either case his self-esteem had been injured. Djolli's wife, an older woman, no longer attractive, stood by, and instead of helping her husband, the usual thing for a wife, screamed at him: "You belong to me. I am your sexual partner. You are like a dog. You are incestuous and sleep with your own mothers and sisters. Why don't you keep your penis where it belongs—in me, not other women." [9]

It seems then, that every culture described had to come to grips with the "attraction" problem. These cultures and societies, however, in comparison to our contemporary world, seemed rather simple. The complexity of our modern family system, flexible sex roles, frequent exposure to other people, and a liberal, that is, more tolerant value system, have compounded "attraction" as a given component.

As observed elsewhere in this book, while the taboo is still in existence it hardly seems to be enforced, and restrictions against extramarital relations are today more self-imposed, either because of beliefs that are anchored in the Judeo-Christian tradition or because personal considerations do not allow for transgressions against other persons. And sometimes, of course, these two are identical. When we will be studied by later cultures, we are likely to be seen as an advanced example of the *realistic* societies which recognize that any system is imperfect and that a system composed of male-female partners will be subject to universal patterns of heterosexual attraction. Like other societies, we do not allow extramarital relations, but we do have them. Like *others* before us, *that* is the clue— we are merely the

[9] Lloyd W. Warner, *A Black Civilization* (New York: Harper & Row, 1937), p. 81. Used by permission of the publisher.

most recent society in this chain. As long as there is marriage as a monogamous system, there will be a concomitant system of clandestine relationships, sometimes rivaling and competing with, and sometimes nestling next to, the basic marriage.

References

1. BENEDICT, RUTH. *Patterns of Culture.* New York: Mentor Books, 1934.
2. DRIVER, HAROLD E. *Indians of North America.* Chicago: University of Chicago Press, 1961.
3. DYK, WALTER. *Son of Old Man Hat.* New York: Harcourt, Brace and World, Inc., 1938.
4. FIRTH, RAYMOND. *We, The Tikopia.* New York: American Book Company, 1936.
5. FORD, CLELLAN S. and FRANK A. BEACH. *Patterns of Sexual Behavior.* New York: Harper & Row, Publishers, 1951.
6. FORTES, M. "Kinship, Incest and Exogamy of the Northern Territories of the Gold Coast," In L. H. D. BUXTON, *Custom Is King.* London: Hutchinson, 1936.
7. GOODY, JACK. "A Comparative Approach to Incest and Adultery," *British Journal of Sociology,* 7, 286–305, 1956.
8. HENRY, JULES. *Jungle People.* Richmond: William Byrd Press, 1941, pp. 25–26.
9. POWDERMAKER, HORTENSE. *Life in Lesu.* New York: W. W. Norton & Company, Inc., 1933.
10. REYBURN, WILLIAM. "Kaka Kinship, Sex and Adultery," *Practical Anthropology,* 9, 223–34, 1962.
11. SCHAPERA, ISAAC. *Married Life in an African Tribe.* New York: Sheridan House, 1941.
12. SIMMONS, LEO W., ed. *Sun Chief.* New Haven: Yale University Press, 1942.
13. STEPHENS, WILLIAM N. *The Family in Cross-Cultural Perspective.* New York: Holt, Rinehart & Winston, Inc., 1963.
14. WARNER, W. LLOYD. *A Black Civilization.* New York: Harper & Row, Publishers, 1937.

Part Three

CAUSE OR EFFECT?

It is one thing to describe the extent of extramarital relations, realize their pervasiveness, and describe their various manifestations; but it is another to question the motivation of individuals engaging in these relations and the nature of the social-psychological environment in which these relations take place. We must investigate the latter as well if we are to get a clear picture of the total phenomenon. In this part of the book we are concentrating on today's patterns and people in the United States and on how they behave.

The sociologists and psychologists who contributed to this part of the book come from diverse clinical and research backgrounds.

Research is primarily an attempt to find out what reality is, and the propositions researchers set up are designed to verify hunches and theoretical formulations about these realities. The only one in this group who goes beyond this essential research approach is Albert Ellis. Known for two decades as a crusader for what he calls a rational-emotive stance toward life, his contribution here leads to a comparison of reasons why spouses become involved in extramarital episodes, and advocacy is established by implication. The reader may accept or reject the soundness of Ellis' reasoning. Yet Ellis has not shied away from taking a stand; he is the only one in this book to do so.

Beltz contributes a wealth of case material from what the clinicians call "patients." In the field of therapy today one therapist's "patients" are another therapist's "individuals who are coping with life." As long as emotional disturbance remains a debatable phenomenon, all we can say here is that Beltz's "patients" were persons who felt strongly enough to seek help from a professional psychologist. Their need was obviously severe enough so that they believed they could not handle these problems or feelings by themselves. Whether their extramarital relations were the result of their psychological "brittleness," or their psychological fragility the result of their extramarital relations, is not demonstrated.

Cuber's summary of his previously published work introduces a reality that comes as a bit of a shock to many—the fact that successful extramarital relations can go hand in hand with successful marital relationships. This necessitates giving the term "successful" a good deal of play.

Schletzer and I were able to find some evidence for the hypothesis that moral and psychological factors of personal nature combine with interactional ones to result in extramarital behavior. Primarily, we established that impulsive individuals with little guilt feeling are less worried about observing rules and, consequently, are poor prospects for monogamous relationships.

Whitehurst raises fundamental questions about marriage and sexuality in our culture. He raises more questions than he answers, but, agreeing with most of the other writers, he confirms the idea that personal motivations in a frightfully complex world clash with the concept of eternal fidelity. His introduction of the phenomenon of "alienation" opens the door to further research by sociologists and psychologists.

Robert N. Whitehurst

EXTRAMARITAL SEX: ALIENATION OR EXTENSION OF NORMAL BEHAVIOR*

INTRODUCTION: FREUD, SOCIOLOGY, AND SEX

The most singular event in the history of the behavioral sciences, in terms of our understanding of sexual behavior, has probably been the intrusion of Freudian psychology into this area. There is little doubt that the survival of deeply ingrained Freudian habits of thought and perception have continued to color our viewpoints of sexuality, regardless of the kind of sexuality under discussion. The present paper is an effort toward the clarification of variables which are more sociological in their content as a means of relating psychological variables with sociological ones to increase predictive power in regard to extramarital sexual activities. Possibly one of the reasons the Freudian paradigm has persisted is because of its difficulty in relating the underlying assumptions and notions of the model to an empirical reality, rendering some Freudian notions somewhat unassailable. At any rate, the topic of sex and especially extramarital sex has been well worn as a popular item and rather neglected as a research variable (12).

The purpose of this article then, will be, first, to develop a theoretical rationale which is more consistent with sociological interpretations, and secondly, to test some of these variables in a small-scale research in order to discuss their worthiness in terms of future investigations. In its simplest form, the notion discussed in this paper can be described

* This paper is a revised and extended version of two papers previously presented by the author: "Adultery as an Extension of Normal Behavior: The Case of the American Upper-Middle Class Male," presented at the National Council of Family Relations, October 26, 1966, Minneapolis, Minnesota, and "Extra-Marital Sex, Alienation, and Marriage," a paper presented at the American Psychological Association, September 5, 1967, Washington, D.C.

as follows: for a range of males in American society, it is useful to conceive the outcome of extramarital sexual activities as a response to alienation and opportunity in some combination and that it can best be seen as an extension of normal behavior rather than as a pathological response. A case will be made for the understanding of our societal base as containing a relatively great amount of alienation-potential. If the combination of high alienation plus opportunity is present, a high rate of extramarital sexual activity can be predicted. A sociological rationale will be provided in an attempt to relate certain variables which are cultural and structural to more psychological types of variables traditionally used to explain sexuality.

A sociological interpretation of deviancy varies from the psychological interpretative mode in one important respect—that is, the insistence upon understanding something about the society or tagging agencies which interact with the deviant (and have helped create him), as well as attempting to understand the behavior itself as deviant. It is the social basis of both behavior and the interpretation of behavior which interests the sociologist. Thus, the potential for developing tags and making them stick is sometimes a more relevant source of information pertinent to behavior (sociologically) than the deviant behavior itself. The process of the separation of man from his fellows and the development of categories is ubiquitous.

Society in part is formed and maintained on a moral basis reflecting behavior which must be sanctioned and held as appropriate for most members. One of the means by which society sanctions behavior and operates is by the use of certain boundary-maintaining mechanisms. It is no chance happening that the word "adultery" in our society has a negative connotation but in some other societies does not. The monogamous base of American society is in part maintained by defining as deviant certain acts and people who do not fit the ideal prescribed. Since adultery cannot be openly tolerated in this system, it is necessary to have tags and procedures to identify the deviants and, in a Durkheimian way, develop social solidarity and a sense of rightness of identity for those who remain true to the ideal. It is suggested here that the boundary-maintenance reasons constitute one of the major bases for acceptance of psychological and psychiatric definitions of the adulterer in America. We have equated adultery often with "sick, immature, narcissistic, neurotic" and other names denoting evil. The social function of these names is to assure ourselves that those of us who do not indulge in such behavior are therefore normal, good, etc. We have in fact performed a useful function by indulging in this kind of psychiatric curse-word usage at the bad guys; we have maintained appropriate social definitions and set apart those who are different (11).

Sociologically oriented writers are interested in developing a comprehension of the systems in which the lives of people become enmeshed, asking in effect, "What are the interactive forces creating the probability of this kind rather than another kind of behavior?" The sociologist is also interested in getting behind the social facades of the glib proclamations we make in public and finding out what, indeed, is tolerable, what we rationalize, and what is in actuality going on, and how it differs from what we say ought to be.

FAMILY TEXTBOOKS AND ADULTERY

Among the more sociological textbooks in the field of family books is one by Robert R. Bell (1, pp. 317–23). Bell lists among the "reasons" for sexual infidelity of the male the following: variation in sexual experience, retaliation, rebellion, new emotional satisfaction, development of sex from friendship, spousal encouragement, and the aging factor. Bell's analysis points up the fact that there are real discrepancies between stated attitudes in the society and actual behavior, and that the social attitudes of many prompt not deterrence from nonmarital coitus but participation without great amounts of remorse or guilt. Bell interprets the lack of agreement between the moral norms and sexual behavior as one of the characteristics of a schizoid culture.

A survey of the explanations and interpretations of many other family sociologists and psychologists tends to show much less coverage than the six pages used by Bell to cover the topic, and the explanations become more truncated, as if to dispense with a topic about which we either know the answer or avoid because it is unpleasant or repulsive. A brief coverage of some other writer's interpretations may shed some light on the problem, but little on the solution.

Christensen, in his analysis of the problem of infidelity, claims that although alcohol releases the inhibitions (and the conscience) of the male and often creates the problem of infidelity, a more basic cause is lack of maturity of the male. He is still attempting to live at the narcissistic level (6, pp. 433–34). This kind of explanation is much like many explanations in modern social sciences purporting to explain a variety of problems; that is, it involves the "evil causes evil" fallacy, and since alcohol and immaturity are evils in our society, it is reasonable to expect evil consequences to result from them (17, pp. 697–737, and 7, pp. 77–80). Christensen likewise suggests that unpleasant reactions or uncooperativeness of the mate may drive the spouse into an affair. Thus, infidelity is also a symptom of unmet personality needs. If this be so (and it may be), then we can likewise say that almost all human actions result from some unmet personality need and likewise be correct. The point is, we have in reality explained very little in relation to the phenomenon in question and have little served the ideal of developing measurements.

Bowman, in a fifth edition of a popular marriage text, suggests that a successful marriage takes perseverance and courage, and that man must rise above the times (4, pp. 139, 184). His apparent explanation hinges on the unreadiness of the partner for marriage, again a sign of immaturity. He suggests that the spouse who considers extramarital intercourse thinks in terms of partial commitment and expects to be partly single and partly married. One of the unanswerable questions is the problem of degree, for surely no one in this relatively individualistic society gets married entirely for the spouse's gratification (15). It is the suggestion of this writer that we have laid heavy stress on the qualities of togetherness, sharing, and selfless altruism as virtues to be striven for in marriage while almost totally overlooking the highly secularistic and individualistic nature of the actual world of reality in which we live. In other words, the gap between the cultural achievement level expected and what is realistically probable seems to be a hiatus of some magnitude.

A somewhat more complete coverage (though only listed by the author as "suggestive diagnoses of the situation") is offered by Cavan (5, pp. 399–401). She claims that biologists show how the male sex drive is stronger than the female's (primarily from Kinsey's data) and how the cerebral cortex of the male makes for more rapid arousal. Males, according to this theory, are more or less sexually aroused most of the time when in the presence of sexual stimuli, making them more prone to adulterous behavior. The sociologist tends to look more at the norms (the double-standard that allows more freedom for the male) or differences in sexual mores of the social classes or ethnic groups which make for differential rates of adultery. The psychological explanation views adultery as immature behavior, infantile regressiveness, hostility toward the spouse, deep self-uncertainty, or as a symptom of marital maladjustment at other levels. In her final summary of the topic, though, it is interesting to note that Cavan claims the entire marital relationship should be subjected to expert study, not only the personality of the digressing partner. This statement involves the assumption that this is seriously deviant behavior that should not be expected from normal people in our society, an assumption open to debate on several counts (5, p. 401).

Simpson, in a sociological-psychoanalytic interpretation of family life, cites coital dissatisfaction and levels of anxiety not assuaged by marital coitus as factors basic to infidelity (21, pp. 181–82). He differentiates between types of infidelity, showing that isolated infidelity may be a sign of Satyriasis. His basic psychoanalytic explanation is that marriage permits the woman the acceptance of the originally forbidden love object (the father) through the substitution of the husband for the father. When he deviates sexually, this is a heavy blow to her ego structure, for her sense of self has been built around resolving the Electra problem of wanting to possess the father sexually, and her mode of adjusting to this problem is central to her. Since the husband may then waver in his loyalty, this is more than just plain infidelity; it is a threat to a central part of the self. Simpson claims that this varies with the experiences of the social classes, and alas, no one has figured out how to measure objectively the impact of the Freudian assumptions as these are presumed to affect the growing personality. The unconscious processes must be inferred, and cannot be measured by any kind of scales (at least demonstrated to be valid at acceptable levels) now available.

In an article which originally appeared in the *New York Times Magazine*, Bossard lists eight reasons why marriages go wrong (3). This is a truly enlightening article to read if one is in a position to be inspired by traditional American simplistic philosophy. Item number five is especially revealing of the "cause" of problems, pointing up again our ideal of democratic togetherness: "A married person who seeks individual development of his or her personality is courting trouble." This is a near-classic restatement of the standard sentiments of Americans about marriage. The problem for the sociologist is to understand how accurately the sentiment reflects what really happens. The remainder of this paper will purport to develop a rationale for the understanding of male marital infidelity (EMS) as relatively normal (non-pathological) behavior in the social context in which a great many men live in today's world.

THE PROBLEM

The present paper is conceived as a beginning point for the development of a more sociological approach. Good research in the area of adultery is important for the understanding of family dynamics but has been noteworthy by its absence. Even more disturbing is the fact that until very recently (19) little adequate professional attention was given to the topic except in clinical descriptions involving disturbed spousal relations. It is suggested here that an increasingly large proportion of adultery of certain types cannot be considered a function of seriously neurotic personality disturbances. By this is meant that many persons can and do commit adultery without strong guilt feelings, without underlying intrapsychic complications, or other commonly described neurotic symptoms. Rather, adultery, of the type described in this paper involving extramarital involvements of upper-middle class business and professional people, can be considered an extension of fairly normal (meaning non-pathological) behavior.

The basic assumption underlying the proposed research suggested by this paper is that there are definable and measurable sexual "problems" in the socio-cultural and interactional worlds of the subjects that lead increasingly to the possibility of nonneurotic adultery. These problems and factors leading to this behavior constitute the remainder of the paper.

Neubeck has noted that a low strength of conscience accompanies sexual involvement (19, p. 281). Although "low strength of conscience" is a difficult research variable, it may be interpreted several ways, one of which involves alienation or psychopathy. It is not inordinately difficult to make the point that, in some respects, a psychopathic civilization is rapidly developing in America. Our socialization patterns have been examined by a variety of theorists and have been found lacking in some important respects in terms of preparing people for viable interpersonal or marital relationships. Comments on the semi-adequacy of masculine identification in American culture are rife. Since little boys are frequently told to avoid feminine things, not to cry when hurt, not to express affect, and are given rather early autonomy in some respects, it is possible to view this socialization cycle with suspicion in terms of its potential for marital adequacy. The norms of the peer group do not ordinarily support a humanistic view of the male-female relationship. Rather, exploitation and the double standard tend to prevail as norms to which the average male commits himself. The rather obvious differentiation of normative content in the socialization of males and females in our culture creates disparity in role expectations and the probability of a fairly long period of difficult adjustment interpersonally in marriage as a result of socialization practices. Socialization can be seen rationally to be much more effective for the male as this impinges upon his occupational preparation. As a means of preparing people adequately for human interaction and nonpsychopathic marital relationships, the current American mode can seriously be called into question. The point, most simply put, is: people who mature in American society and become successful adults with good marriages probably do so in spite of the system, not because of it. That many currently feel a sense of alienation from conventional institutions and norms might not be surprising in our kind of world. Alienation, when coupled with a relatively high level of opportunity to interact with others, can be expected to create the stuff of extramarital sexual practice.

Males socialized to a concept of success in the business world can easily transfer some learned norms of fringe legitimacy into their personal worlds of values as these become reflected in alienation from the ideals of society. Complicating this potential and adding to it for the male is the (sociologically relevant) recognition that a double standard of youth and beauty prevails in our culture. Females, much earlier than males in western cultures, tend to outgrow their perceived youthfulness and desirability as sex objects. This increases the possibility of some males' involvement with some females as a normal cultural response to differentiation in valuations of people. As males grow older their cultural valuation does not depreciate nearly as rapidly as does that of their female counterparts. As a male ages he becomes more affluent, more poised, more powerful, and possibly more manly in the eyes of women; his attractiveness does not decrease until much later than his wife's.

Given certain average conditions in the married life of the males involved, it is possible to predict an adulterous outcome for a great number of males between the ages of forty and forty-five that may be created out of natural conditions arising over years of marriage coupled with the differential value notion described above. Recent research shows that marriages, contrary to the togetherness notions extant in our culture, do not, through time, become characterized by increasing depth and intensiveness of marital communication. Instead, there is some evidence that time takes its toll in regard to the importance of the relationship (13, p. 306; 2, pp. 263–67; 16).

Not only has communication in depth decreased through time, but both husband and wife often tend to develop separate identities involving quite distinct kinds of ventures in life. The husband may become more interested in his work for a variety of reasons, chief among which may be personal anxieties relating to success, need for money and status (these also placate the spouse), and lastly, he may become more involved with work as a way to avoid significant interaction with the wife, whom he perceives as somehow having changed through the years from the blushing bride he once knew who could keep him entertained in many ways. In short, the retreat to work may have many advantages of one sort or another for the male who has few other respectable means of withdrawing from significant family interaction. The wife may retreat into neighborhood club routines, civic work, etc. ad infinitum for a like variety of reasons. Some of these may have to do with the decreasing sense of real contact with the spouse (as well as loss of maternal functions as children grow up). In any case, husbands and wives often (without either in reality being the "bad guy") find themselves going in separate directions more frequently as the time of the marriage lengthens. Whatever the basic causes of the lessened interdependency, few would doubt that it is real in a number of marriages existing for ten to twenty years. It is at this point in the life of the male that his personal value system begins to become more fluid: he has lost much, if not most, of his youthful idealism and has faced up to the cold, hard world of reality in business, if not in his personal life. The point here is that the operation on the periphery of legitimacy is so much a part of the American pattern, that it is not at all unreasonable to expect some of this "fringe legitimacy" to carry over into his personal philosophy. Alienation in some form is a usual rather than an unusual problem. Thus, we have set the stage culturally and socially for the male in middle-class society to begin a varyingly adequate career of philandering. It is very difficult at this point to believe that the person subjected to the set of social and cultural pressures described is either "sick" or maladjusted in any significant way, or is even immature. He has certainly shown all of the other manly virtues and has acted on the standard values of his society, but when he makes the next logical step in the sequence of his life, we brand him as a sexual delinquent, an immature person unready for or unfit for marriage. The contention of this writer is that his subsequent behavior as an adulterer (in many cases) has very little to do with his marriage, excepting as noted above.

In summary, the phenomenon of extramarital male infidelity can as easily be conceptualized as a cultural-social problem with a high probability of involvement for many males as it can be seen as either a problem in the marital relationship or in the personality of the deviant (although all levels may be involved in any particular case). In its essence, the behavior should be quite frequently expected, and if expected and explained as a social-structural and cultural problem, it may then be construed much more nearly as normal rather than as abnormal behavior in the kind of society we now experience.

CONCEPTUALIZING THE PROBLEM

Other variables considered by Neubeck but of lesser interest for this paper would involve routinization of marriage experience, boredom, the developing of an unserious self concept (this may also be a defense and may be involved in alienation; that is, a "fun" concept of life as unserious business helps protect one against the ugliness of life and one's inability to cope). Thus, the playful person, for whatever reason, is more likely to present himself as a prospect for EMS. Neubeck is also concerned with the ground rules of marriage. As an aside, it is possible that the youthful penchant currently in vogue for honesty in interpersonal relations may lead to more, rather than less, adultery. One bit of evidence for this direction in our society might be suggested from the tone of the 1966 Groves Conference in Kansas City, much more than ever concerned with the meaning of newly-emerging "wife-swapping" habits of certain middle-class American couples. The point is that possibly a new morality may be emerging which does not always preclude EMS but prescribes the rules for it.

Whether Americans who indulge in EMS are more or less stupid, moral, or neurotic is not really the question posed by this paper. Rather it is this: "How can EMS be explained from the vantage point of the social psychologist or from a social systems viewpoint?" The tentative answer suggested here (and of necessity needing data to verify or reject the notion) is that, increasingly, EMS in certain socio-economic settings can be viewed as an expected outcome of alienation involving life-cycle variations, socialization, and changes in values, which when coupled with a fairly common decrease of meaning as related to family life (and concomitantly an increase in importance of the career of the male), the outcome (given the opportunity) is quite likely to be an extramarital affair. (See figure 1.)

FIGURE 1. VARIABLES RELATING TO EMS POTENTIAL

Independent (Alienation) Factors	Intervening (Opportunity) Factors	Dependent
Loss of youthful idealism, conditioning to business world and its fringe ethics. "Reality" as a personal construct of the male changes. (Anomie, self-estrangement, powerlessness, isolation.) This amounts to a *change in the value configuration* of some males in American society.	Increased work participation. Less meaning in marital ties and communication. Separateness of marital roles and functions. Differential perception of relative worth of males and females (with increasing age).	EMS

THE STUDY

A middle-class sample of males in service organizations was used in the collection of the data. A structured questionnaire was used involving measures of alienation, extramarital sexual experiences (frequency and depth of relationships), opportunity, and marital type as measured by Cuber's typology (self-rated [8]).

The specific purpose was to test through non-parametrics the relationships among the variables under consideration. No conclusions beyond the nonrepresentative sample are claimed other than the assumption that if significant differences were to be found then the variables would have some utility for further research. The design, basically, should become implicated in the future of research involving the impact of cultural forces as these change males from relatively stable and unalienated persons into ones more alienated, with reference group support for extramarital deviancy when opportunity occurs.

SAMPLE AND METHODOLOGY

The sample consisted of 112 upper–middle class Midwestern business and professional men who were members of service organizations in a metropolitan area of about 175,000. Total samples were used when service clubs volunteered the use of their membership at a specific meeting for purposes of responding to the questionnaire. After the subjects filled out the questionnaire anonymously, a discussion period was held to outline the purposes of the study and to discuss any questions. At this time, the purposes and viewpoints of the researcher were clarified in terms of the goals of the study. After the formal meeting, some respondents were interviewed for longer periods of time on a volunteer basis. As part of the questionnaire, short descriptive statements were included describing Cuber's marriage types as found in *The Significant Americans* (8, pp. 43–65). Subjects were asked to indicate the marriage type they felt most accurately reflected the kind they had most of the time. The alienation scale was an adaptation of one previously used by Neal and Rettig and included subscales of powerlessness, meaninglessness, normlessness, and social isolation (18). Although the sample was nonrepresentative and was small, it was deemed legitimate to attempt, through non-parametrics, to relate levels of alienation to marital adjustment and extramarital sexuality. The basic hypothesis tested in this small group involved dichotomization of alienation into high and low alienation groups and then comparing them on several variables, including self-rated marital adjustment and extent and variety of extramarital sex experiences. It is hypothesized that those males who are older, have been married for longer periods of time, and who have poorer marital adjustment as indicated by their choice of one of Cuber's negative types, will be differentiated on the variable of alienation (and therefore EMS). Subjects from the upper–middle class were selected on the assumption that family change often is initiated at this level, and that what is happening here might be an indicator of future changes in other strata in the social system (14, p. 144).

FINDINGS AND DISCUSSION

For this sample, 80% of all of the extensive extramarital involvement (anything beyond admitted "playing around either at parties, with office help, or others, but no serious sexual involvement") was indulged in by the high alienation group. Those in the high alienation group also had more isolated and passing affairs, as well as more short affairs, than those in the low alienation group. There was a significant difference between these two groups in regard to self-rated type of marriage. The low-alienation group indicated more frequently that their marriages were "vital" or "total" ones than did the high alienation group.

When subjects were asked to respond in terms of what they felt were the reasons they themselves deviated sexually, 79% of those who scored low in alienation said that the strength of their sex drive was primarily responsible for extramarital involvement. When asked why others deviated sexually, only 29% of this low alienation group felt that sex drive was responsible for the deviation of others. In other words, a common view appears to be that one's own sex drive could be considered responsible for one's own deviation, while there must be other reasons for other males' deviation from conventional sex norms. One interpretation of this may be that one's own sex drive intensity may be used as a rationalization to cover up for one's own EMS involvement, while other reasons are seen as the usual ones for other males to deviate from conventional norms about fidelity. For example, roughly one-third felt that either opportunity to indulge in sex undetected, or dissatisfaction with sex from one's wife were factors which would account for the prevalence of EMS.

Of those scoring low in alienation, 83% claimed that they remained true to their wives for religious and moral reasons or for reasons of family responsibility. On the other hand, 68% of the high alienation group claimed that their current level of adjustment in marriage could be seen as an important factor responsible for their sexual deviation. It is probable that the high alienation scorers may have a less stable commitment to their marriages. This would seem to follow, since a poor marriage probably is related to alienation (although cause and effect may be confounded).

When the low and high alienation scorers are compared on the dichotomized variable of *no* extramarital sexual experiences (EMS) and sexual experience of any variety, there was a significant difference between the low and high groups as measured by the McNemar test (9, p. 139). One of the interesting findings of the activities that the sample group had indulged in related to one of the responses described as "some playing around, either at parties, with office help, or others, but no serious sexual involvement." In answer to this alternative, 70% of the low alienation respondents claimed to have indulged in these kinds of experiences, while only 30% of the high alienation scorers had done so. One possible interpretation is that those who are less alienated may frequently find themselves in a position that enables them to become marginally deviant with some borderline playful sexual involvement, while those who are relatively more alienated may go beyond this point more frequently and find other kinds of sexual relationships in terms of seeking meaning, or, for some other reason not evident in the low alienation population, seek other sexual responses.

Approximately 41% of the study sample claimed that the places and the people they were with which presented opportunity to indulge in extramarital sex was a crucial factor in determining fidelity to one's wife. The expression of this response was inconsistent with the proportion of vital and total marriages indicated by the sample. It may merely indicate, however, that males become conditioned to the problem of opportunity, and that our social structure in general does not provide great amounts of opportunity for extramarital expression as is sometimes supposed. It also means that opportunity is conditioned by the social structure. Opportunity appears to be dependent upon the social situation in which the male operates. For example, the male's ability to convince his wife regarding working hours, and the nature of the significant others one is involved with are either supportive of extramarital activities or in some significant ways tend to limit opportunity severely. If reference group support is lacking (and, most significantly, from male peers) a male will be less likely to find opportunity unless he is a singular deviant who operates in terms of hiding his behavior from practically all others. It is suggested here that the latter case (hiding one's behavior from practically everyone) involves much more severe pathology and is more truly deviant behavior than the type discussed before in which there is reference group support for deviancy. Possibly, those scoring low in alienation avoid opportunities for EMS by enveloping themselves in a social structure which supports conformity (in some significant sense, this creates an impossibility for deviation extramaritally because of the web of social control with which this kind of person surrounds himself).

Even though sociological writers talk about mass society and the aloneness of the individual in the social structure, it is quite easy to underestimate the efficiency of the web of social control as a device in preventing EMS, even in the kind of society in which we find ourselves operating today. Men who are reasonably well-known in a community, and who might otherwise seek EMS kinds of experiences, find themselves chastened by the thought that neighbors or acquaintances may see them in embarrassing places with someone they know is not their wife. Opportunity, as a multifaceted intervening variable to be developed in the understanding of EMS, is important in terms of its relationship to the differential social structure in which males find themselves operating.

Apparently, people who experience higher alienation tend to seek extramarital sex as a relationship. Of those in the present sample who could be characterized as having claimed to have indulged in sex as a manner of seeking a relationship, 85% were in the high alienation category. Although the sample was small, this may mean that sex may at times be involved as a seeking, self-validating venture to solve alienation problems.

When the alienation scores were separated on the basis of each subscale, those subjects with some extramarital sexual experience scored relatively higher in all categories, but scored highest on the powerlessness dimension of alienation. This raises an interesting question about the relationship of powerlessness to seeking extramarital sexual situations. Possibly EMS in some ways is a response to powerlessness; since a male placed in an EMS situation can be said to be exerting power over another, this may be an important link to the understanding of EMS. It has long been suggested that the need to certify masculinity and to assert virility are motives for EMS. In some ways not well-understood, powerlessness may well be reflected in the seeking of EMS experience since females may be seen as one of the minority groups in our society over which power in some ways may be exerted fairly readily. If these variables can be correlated in the future, the dimension of powerlessness may prove fruitful in further understanding of the motivation for extramarital sexual activities.

When the mean scores were derived for each of the alienation subscales, and the low and high groups compared, the greatest single difference found between the low and high alienation groups was in social isolation. Again, this raises the question of felt isolation from others as a motive to establish meaningful contact with other human beings, sexuality being that kind of unique experience which may be seen as an intimate possibility to decrease social isolation, and often to establish meaningful contact with others.

In terms of decreasing frequency of occurrence, the following extramarital sexual behavior was described as being within the experience of the respondents: none whatever of any variety (67%); some "playing around," either at parties, with office help, or others, but no serious sexual involvement (9%); isolated and passing sex experience involving a personal relationship with someone attractive (6.5%); heavy petting, necking, or other sexual activities, but no sexual intercourse outside of marriage, and isolated and passing experiences involving personal relationship (4.5% each); and a smaller proportion had experienced longer affairs, something like husband-wife relationships (2.7%).

SUMMARY AND CONCLUSIONS

Although the low and high alienation groups could not be differentiated on the type of experiences extramaritally, when dichotomized as those who had experienced some kind of EMS versus those who had none, the high alienation group was statistically differentiated. The general hypothesis also received some support for the notion that increasing age and length of marriage is associated with higher alienation (which, in turn, presumes a higher risk of extramarital involvement). The notion that the marriage type, primarily the negative marriage type, is associated with extramarital activities, and the notion that opportunity is a crucial variable in understanding extramarital involvement, also received some support. Further research is necessary to develop a better understanding of the structure of opportunity for extramarital involvement as this relates to significant others and reference groups of the subjects. Although the present sample appears to be inordinately well adjusted as measured by Cuber's self-rated types, and appears to have experienced less than average extramarital sexual involvement, this may be related either to the methodology or to the halo effect present in the middle classes. It may also be a function of a conservative community as reflected in socially desirable responses. Nonetheless, the findings tend to raise questions which could be profitably pursued in further research. Questions relating to the problem of opportunity, the role of reference group support, and the ways in which powerlessness and social isolation affect EMS are among those which need clarification by further research.

From personal interviews with a limited number of the subjects, the following conclusions seem tentatively warranted. The subjects may, in some instances, stretch the truth about the positive attributes of their own marriages, but this appears to be more a function of their need to have good marriages as a self-concept validating device, and is not merely a ruse to fool the interviewer or is only a halo device to give socially desirable responses. These subjects were thoroughly convincing in their middle-class orientations and their desires to live a reasonably convenional life. Most of the subjects seemed to be moralists, even when describing their own extramarital activities.

By "moralists" is meant something that can be picked up from the following expression, which was one man's expression of a dilemma he felt he faced: "Those (females) I can get to go to bed with me I don't really like or feel positively toward, and those I could like, I can't get to go to bed with me." This seems to indicate the inability to dissociate sex completely from affectional ties in our culture. The suggestion here is that there appears to be strongly rooted in American socialization patterns a relationship between sex and love which is possibly less frequently violated by recourse to prostitution and impersonal sexual acts than is often thought to be the case. Our cultural association of sex with affection may be one of the chief reasons for the minimizing of EMS dalliance. Other subjects expressed the opinion that shallow relationships, when associated with sex, are seen as somehow not morally right and are often considered psychopathic or prostitutional (author's interpretation). It seems that sex is often tried out extramaritally for purposes of validating something about one's virility and masculinity, or that the need for variety pushes men into EMS situations, especially when supported by outside reference groups. It appears that sexual experience soon pales unless the male can cover his dalliance with the norm of emotional protectiveness and affect as these may become involved in EMS. Since this is difficult to do in our culture, it is likely that the moralistic aspects of perception of EMS situations create a failure to legitimize these activities. Thus it is this writer's conclusion that males, at least of the variety indicated by this sample, are often moralists of a sort, even though they indulge peripherally in EMS activities.

Apparently, Americans are deeply concerned with the problem of love, which they tend not to be able to separate neatly from sex. The continued existence of the Bohemian response in the United States, and especially the current wave of hippyism, may be implicated in current and future trends involving our extramarital activities. The cult of the collective love response of the hippy may in some ways be seen as creating a relatively normalizing influence on certain varieties of sexual experience outside marriage. American ministers appear to be seeking a better in-depth understanding of deviant subgroups such as the hippy types, and no longer thoroughly castigate sexual deviancy as an outgroup phenomenon. The fact that the American concept of morality is being broadened through a variety of social forces is a matter of no small significance.[1] It might be well to note that contem-

[1] Possibly the January 24, 1964, issue of *Time* (in which the weekly essay was titled, "Sex in the U.S.: Mores and Morality,") may be seen as a harbinger of a new era marking a frank openness of discussion which has been pursued with a vengeance by the American popular press. Recent issues of practically all the leading pop magazines have carried headline articles on nudity, youth cultures

porary sermonizing tends to *follow* contemporary mores and does not seriously become involved in the *making* of contemporary mores. This may be an indicator of a basic acceptance as a part of our cultural pattern of some sexual deviations from the absolute norm of monogamous fidelity. The totality of social forces which increases the probability of deviancy from this absolute norm is without doubt proliferating and is being more deeply impressed upon the average American consciousness. Given current trends, this complex of factors, then, must be seen as having an inevitable outcome of loosening sexual mores in many respects. Basically, the tendency to be able to develop varied opportunity structures as acted upon by alienated modern man implies a certain safety in the prediction of more sexual deviancy which will, in turn, be less frequently seen as deviancy at all.

In conclusion, it is suggested that there is some basis for pursuing further research, using the following variables to develop a research model: Alienation, and perhaps especially the dimensions of powerlessness and social isolation, may prove fruitful to use as independent variables. Further, alienation may be related to age, business success, and type of marriage relationship. As an intervening variable, opportunity seems to be warranted in so far as opportunity can be understood to be a function of the social structure, meaning either reference group support for, or to oppose indulgence in extramarital activity. The dependent variable would be extramarital sexual activities. It may be that a typology of extramarital activities would be useful, following the model of previous researchers in an attempt to relate extramarital sexual involvement to the same kinds of personal or social factors as has been done previously (10).

References

1. BELL, ROBERT R. *Marriage and Family Interaction.* Homewood, Ill.: The Dorsey Press, 1963.
2. BLOOD, ROBERT O., and WOLFE, DONALD M. *Husbands and Wives.* Glencoe, Ill.: The Free Press, 1960.
3. BOSSARD, JAMES H. S. "Eight Reasons Why Marriages Go Wrong." In

and their impact on suburbia, the "anything goes" society (*Newsweek,* November, 1967), and the impact of the new morality. There is an apparent increase in serious discussions in the more specialized and professional journals as well which may be interpreted as being implicated in social change in some ways. A tentative conclusion (at least plausible) is that sex talk is at times at least followed by a freeing of the potential for action.

Ruth Shonle Cavan (Ed.), *Marriage and Family in the Modern World.* New York: T. Y. Crowell Co., 1960, pp. 368–74.

4. Bowman, Henry A. *Marriage for Moderns,* 5th ed. New York: McGraw-Hill, 1960.
5. Cavan, Ruth Shonle. *The American Family,* 3rd ed. New York: T. Y. Crowell, 1963.
6. Christensen, Harold T. *Marriage Analysis,* 2nd ed. New York: The Ronald Press, 1958.
7. Cohen, Albert K. "Multiple Factor Approaches." In Marvin E. Wolfgang, Leonard Savitz, and Norman Johnston, *The Sociology of Crime and Delinquency.* New York: John Wiley, 1962.
8. Cuber, John S., and Harroff, Peggy B. *The Significant Americans.* New York: Appleton-Century-Crofts, Inc., 1965.
9. Downie, N. M., and Heath, R. W. *Basic Statistical Methods.* New York: Harper & Row, 1959.
10. Ehrman, Winston W. *Premarital Dating Behavior.* New York: Henry Holt, 1959.
11. Erikson, Kai. "The Sociology of Deviance." In Edward C. McDonogh and Jon E. Simpson (Eds.), *Social Problems: Persistent Challenges.* New York: Holt, Rinehart, and Winston, 1965, pp. 457–64.
12. Gagnon, John H. "Talk about Sex, Sexual Behavior, and Sex Research." From a paper delivered at the Groves Conference, 1966, in Kansas City, Missouri.
13. Hunt, Morton. *Her Infinite Variety.* New York: Harper & Row, 1965.
14. Kirkpatrick, Clifford. *The Family,* 2nd ed. New York: The Ronald Press, 1963.
15. Kols, William L. "Sociologically Established Norms and Democratic Values," *Social Forces,* 26, 452–56, 1948.
16. Luckey, Eleanore Braun. "Number of Years Married as Related to Personality Perception and Marital Satisfaction," *Journal of Marriage and the Family,* 28 (No. 1), 44–48, 1966.
17. Merton, Robert K., and Nisbet, Robert A. *Contemporary Social Problems.* New York: Harcourt, Brace and World, 1961 (especially Chapter 15).
18. Neal, Arthur G., and Rettig, Solomon. "On the Multidimensionality of Alienation," *American Sociological Review,* 32 (No. 1), 54–64, 1967.
19. Neubeck, Gerhard, and Schletzer, Vera M. "A Study of Extramarital Relationships," *Marriage and Family Living,* 24 (No. 3), 279–81, 1963.
20. Neubeck, Gerhard. "The Dimensions of the Extra in Extra-marital Relations." (See pp. 12–24).
21. Simpson, George. *People in Families.* New York: T. Y. Crowell Co., 1960.

Gerhard Neubeck and
Vera M. Schletzer

A STUDY OF EXTRAMARITAL RELATIONSHIPS

INTRODUCTION

Many persons enter marriage with an idealized notion of the rewards they will receive from the relationship. While these anticipations differ from country to country, in the United States marriage is expected to provide emotional rewards along with satisfaction of sexual and perhaps spiritual needs. We have not understood these emotional factors too well, although the studies of Burgess and Cottrell (2), Locke (8), Strauss (11), Terman (12), and Winch (13) have produced some insight.

Monogamy implies that one man and one woman sufficiently meet mutual needs so that there is no necessity for either to be simultaneously married to another individual. Can we not assume, however, that there are always needs in one spouse which cannot completely be met by the other? Men and women have probably sought and received satisfactions outside the marriage for a variety of needs, as we have realized from literature through the ages, and modern divorce rates must attest to the fact that needs often are not met in marriage.

While a number of investigators have concerned themselves with extramarital sexual relations—in fact, the term extramarital relations is often understood to mean extramarital sexual relations—only a handful of writers have speculated as to the overall problems.

Kinsey (6, 7) reported that about half of all married males have sexual intercourse with women other than their spouses during some time

"A Study of Extramarital Relationships," by Gerhard Neuback and Vera M. Schletzer. Reprinted by permission from *Journal of Marriage and the Family,* 24:3 (August, 1962), pp. 279–81. (Delivered at the XIV International Congress of Applied Psychology, Copenhagen, Denmark, August, 1961.)

while they are married, and 26% of married women have intercourse with men other than their spouses by age 40. Burgess and Locke (3), quoting a subject as saying, "I am attracted to other women," may point to a basic truth as to the animal nature of the male, yet most writers seem to perceive neurotic personality needs as Guyon (5) did when he suspected characteristics such as "aggression," "phallic-type," "infantile development" behind extramarital relations. Astley (1) infers that people have breaking points in the mutual satisfaction of neurotic needs and then turn to someone who seems less harsh and more tender or more accepting and admiring. He does, however, accept that mature people show *playful* interests in others, though he warns of the dangers of duplicity. Duvall (4) among others, writes that variety and experience may be appealing. These writers all seem to be agreed on what Astley has made explicit and what the Judeo-Christian tradition really contends: Mainly, that the exclusive one-to-one relationship is an ideal rooted in the deepest longings of each human being.

The study reported here is the result of the senior author's interest in the psychological interaction of marriage partners and in factors which influence their involvement with non-spouses. The authors choose to consider the extent of need satisfaction in marriage, the kind and extent of involvement with non-spouse persons, and the degree of conscience present to act as an inhibitor. These three variables are defined by the methods of observation used.

MEASURES AND PROCEDURES

The subjects in this study were 40 couples, one or both of whom, as students, had taken the course, "Preparation for Marriage," at the University of Minnesota about 1948. They were chosen because of their willingness to cooperate in this and in a previous research project. They were about 30 years of age at the time of the study. Seventy-four of the 80 had attended the University of Minnesota. Most of the husbands were in occupations such as salesmen, contractors, engineers, architects, and lawyers. The wives were primarily housewives. They lived in Minneapolis or its suburbs in homes which they owned. Most couples had three children. All were first marriages. This was not a random sample of all married couples.

To measure involvement, a structured interview was used. Questions were designed to elicit information concerning what we called (1) actual involvement, which included sexual and emotional involvement and (2) fantasy involvement, which included potential and projective involvement. If there was actual involvement, the person was questioned as to when and where it took place, its duration, the age and other characteristics of the party involved, whether the involvement was sexual in nature, and the extent to which there was revealing of self. This information concerning revealing of self was used in the characterization of emotional involvement. Potential involvement was assessed by asking about fantasies concerning third parties. Projective involvement was inferred by the interviewer asking for reactions to the following situations:

"Suppose you were living next door to people with whom you had become very close friends. As it happened, your wife (husband) has gone on a visit in another part of the country to her (his) folks perhaps, and she (he) has the children with her (him). Also, the husband (wife) next door is away on a business trip and the wife (husband) is by herself (himself). How would you feel about 1. going out to dinner with her (him); 2. spending an evening or evenings in your or their living room with her (him); 3. dancing with her (him) to the radio?"

Responses were recorded by the interviewer and two judges were asked to divide the subjects into groups of involved or not-involved along the four dimensions described above through a three-part rating scale: involved, somewhat involved, not involved. A third judge was used to break ties. The subjects classified for analysis as involved included those judged to be somewhat involved. Finally, potential and projective involvements were combined into the category we called fantasy involvement.

Need fulfillment of marital satisfaction was measured by a modification of a scale devised by Anselm Strauss (10) at the University of Chicago. The scale was designed to measure the numerous ways in which persons were aware of their personality needs. The subjects responded to the following fifteen statements: My spouse loves me, confides in me, shows me affection, respects my ideals, appreciates my goals of achievement, understands my moods, helps me make important decisions, stimulates my ambition, gives me self-confidence, stands back of me in difficulty, appreciates me just as I am, admires my ability, makes me feel I count for something, relieves my loneliness, and is someone to look up to. To each statement, the respondent could check "completely," "fairly much," "somewhat," "little," or "not at all." In order to have numerical scores for statistical analysis, values ranging from four ("completely") to zero ("not at all") were arbitrarily assigned. Since there were fifteen items on the scale, the highest possible score was sixty. Scores obtained ranged from 30 to 60. The mean total score for men was 49.08 with a standard deviation of 6.04. The mean total score for women was 48.43 with a standard deviation of 6.42. The scores were dichotomized at the mean to provide the measure of satisfaction in marriage. Satisfied persons were those with scores above the mean for their sex. Low satisfaction in marriage is attributed to those whose scores were at or below the mean.

The last measure needed was for degree of strength of conscience. For this variable, the Psychopathic Deviate (PD) scale of the Minnesota Multiphasic Personality Inventory was used. The Manual of the MMPI (9) describes this scale as follows: "The PD scale measures the similarity of the subject to a group of persons whose main difficulty lies in their absence of deep emotional response, their inability to profit from experience, and the disregard of social mores . . ." A T-score of 60 was used as cutoff point so that persons falling below a PD score of 60 were regarded as possessing more conscience and those over 60 less so. The authors were not completely satisfied with this means of measuring conscience but felt it served the purpose.

All analyses were made regardless of the sex of a given subject.

FINDINGS

While statistical analysis of the interrelation of all three variables was not possible because of the small number of subjects, it is clear that those who become sexually involved obtain high PD scores but also score among the high on satisfaction. Those who do not get sexually involved score low on PD regardless of their satisfaction scores. As we will see later, this is statistically confirmed by the results obtained from measuring two variables, PD and sexual involvement. Similarly, those who get emotionally involved obtain high PD scores but also score among the high on satisfaction. Those with low PD scores, regardless of the satisfaction scores, get less involved emotionally.

Seven analyses were made with the use of the Chi-square technique. The results are as follows: There is no significant difference between those highly satisfied with their marriage and the low satisfaction group in regard to becoming sexually involved or emotionally involved.

However, as Table 1 shows, a significant difference exists between

TABLE 1. FANTASY INVOLVEMENT

	Fantasy Involvement	Not Involved	
High Satis.	4	34	38
Low Satis.	12	30	42
	16	64	80

X^2 = 4.05920 Significant at .05 level.

the high and low satisfaction groups in regard to fantasy involvement. The less satisfied persons seek more satisfaction in fantasy.

As Table 2 shows, a significant difference exists between groups having high and low PD scores insofar as sexual involvement is concerned. Persons with high PD scores are more apt to become sexually involved than persons with low PD scores. However, there are no significant differences between persons having high PD and low PD scores with regard to emotional and fantasy involvement, respectively.

TABLE 2. SEX INVOLVEMENT

	Sex Involved	Not Involved	
High PD	6	15	21
Low PD	3	52	55
	9	67	*76

$X^2 = 7.77860$ Significant at .01 level.

* For four persons, there were no Mult profiles available or possible to get.

There was no significant difference between the high and low satisfaction groups in relation to their PD scores.

CONCLUSIONS AND COMMENTS

While most previous writers, in their concern with moral issues and focus on sexual infidelity, have seen weak family structure or neurotic inclinations as primary motives of infidelity, these analyses point to three specific conclusions: 1. Low strength of conscience accompanies sexual involvement (which confirms previous findings about the PD scale), yet lower strength of conscience does not seem to accompany emotional or fantasy involvement. 2. Individuals who are rated as the low satisfaction group seek fantasy involvement rather than actual sexual or emotional involvement. 3. Strength of conscience as measured by PD scores is not directly related to the way in which persons responded to the statements on the need-satisfaction blank.

Another way of looking at the interrelationships is to point out that there may be various ways in which marriage partners try to deal with their dissatisfactions. One group, because of reasons of conscience or "superego," seeks satisfaction by fantasy rather than real involvement. Another group not so controlled by their consciences tends toward variety of a sexual nature rather than substituting fantasy or an emotional involvement.

These findings are not really surprising. The environs of marriage are obviously too narrow for impulse-ridden individuals, and clinicians have known about the active fantasy life of many of their clients. (Excursions into fantasy, however, may not be unusual for many spouses.) While marriage partners of the less-satisfied group should be encouraged to seek help with basic problems, fantasy outlets may not necessarily be destructive to the relationship.

While this study has thrown some light on the phenomenon of extramarital relations and suggests multiple causation, further research should be directed toward other dimensions of the problem. First, what is the effect of the kind and degree of involvement on the other spouse? Second, what makes for tolerance of the spouse's involvement with a third party? Third, after an involvement has taken place, how will the behavior and attitude of the other spouse affect future involvements? The phenomenon of extramarital relationships is challenging and is wide open for psychological research.

References

1. Astley, M. Royden C. "Fidelity and Infidelity." In *Man and Wife.* New York: W. W. Norton and Co., Inc., 1957, pp. 80–96.
2. Burgess, W., and Cottrell, L. S. *Predicting Success or Failure in Marriage.* New York: Prentice-Hall, Inc., 1939.
3. Burgess, Ernest W., and Locke, Harvey J. *The Family.* New York: American Book Co., 1945.
4. Duvall, Sylvanus M. *Men, Women, and Morals.* New York: Association Press, 1952.
5. Guyon, René. *The Ethics of Sexual Acts.* New York: Alfred A. Knopf, 1958.
6. Kinsey, A. C., Pomeroy, W. B., and Martin, C. E. *Sexual Behavior in the Human Male.* Philadelphia: W. B. Saunders Co., 1948.
7. Kinsey, A. C., Pomeroy, W. B., Martin, C. E., and Gebhard, Paul A. *Sexual Behavior in the Human Female.* Philadelphia: W. B. Saunders, 1953.
8. Locke, H. J. *Predicting Adustment in Marriage: A Comparison of a Divorced and Happily Married Group.* New York: Henry Holt, 1951.
9. Minnesota Multiphasic Personality Inventory. New York: The Psychological Corporation, 1951.
10. Strauss, A. L. "A Study of Three Psychological Factors Affecting Choice of Mates" (Ph.D. Thesis), Chicago: University of Chicago, 1945.
11. Strauss, Anselm. "Personality Needs and Marital Choice," *Social Forces,* 25 (March, 1947), 332–35.

12. Terman, L. M., *et al. Psychological Factors in Marriage Happiness.* New York: McGraw-Hill, 1938.

13. Winch, R. F. *Mate-Selection: A Study of Complementary Needs.* New York: Harper & Row, 1958, pp. xix–349.

Albert Ellis

HEALTHY AND DISTURBED REASONS FOR HAVING EXTRAMARITAL RELATIONS

Psychologists and sociologists, as Whitehurst points out in his chapter, tend to look upon extramarital relations as an unusual or deviant form of behavior and to seek for disturbed motivations on the part of husbands and wives who engage in adulterous affairs. Although there is considerable clinical evidence that would seem to confirm this view, there are also studies—such as those of Kinsey and his associates (11, 12) and of Cuber and Harroff (1)—which throw considerable doubt on it. In my own observations of quite unusual adulterers—unusual in the sense that both partners to the marriage agreed upon and carried out extramarital affairs and in many instances actually engaged in wife-swapping—I have found that there are usually both good and bad, healthy and unhealthy reasons for this type of highly unconventional behavior (4); and if this is true in these extreme cases, it is almost certainly equally true or truer about the usual kind of secret adulterous affairs that are much more common in this country.

Let me now briefly review what I consider to be some of the main healthy and disturbed reasons for extramarital unions. My material for the following analysis comes from two main sources: (1) clinical interviews with individuals with whom I have had psychotherapy and marriage and family counseling sessions; (2) unofficial talks with scores of non-patients and non-counselees whom I have encountered in many parts of this country and who are presumably a fairly random sample of well-educated middle-class adults, most of whom have been married for five years or more. Although the first group of my inter-

This paper was first presented at the American Psychological Association Convention, September 5, 1967, in Washington, D.C.

viewees included a high percentage of individuals whose marriages were far from ideal and were in many cases quite rocky, the second group consisted largely of individuals who had average or above-average marriages and who were, at the time I spoke to them, in no danger of separation or divorce.

From my talks with these individuals—some of which were relatively brief and some of which took, over a series of time, scores of hours—I am inclined to hypothesize the following healthy reasons for husbands and wives, even when they are happily married and want to continue their marital relationships, strongly wanting and doing their best to discreetly carry on extramarital affairs:

Sexual varietism. Almost the entire history of mankind demonstrates that man is not, biologically, a truly monogamous animal; that he tends to be more monogynous than monogamic, desiring one woman at a time rather than a single woman for a lifetime, and that even when he acts monogynously he craves strongly occasional adulterous affairs in addition to his regular marital sex. The female of the human species seems to be less strongly motivated toward plural sexuality than is the male; but she, too, when she can have varietistic outlets with social impunity, quite frequently takes advantage of them (5).

A healthy married individual in our society is usually able to enjoy steady sex relations with his spouse; but he frequently tends to have *less* marital satisfaction after several years than he had for the first months or years after his wedding. He lusts after innumerable women besides his wife, particularly those who are younger and prettier than she is; he quite often enhances his marital sex enjoyment by thinking about these other women when copulating with his spouse; he enjoys mild or heavy petting with other females at office parties, social gatherings, and other suitable occasions; and he actually engages in adulterous affairs from time to time, especially when he and his wife are temporarily parted or when he can otherwise discreetly have a little fling with impunity, knowing that his spouse is not likely to discover what he is doing and that his extramarital affair will not seriously interfere with his marriage and family life. The man who resides in a large urban area and who never once, during thirty or more years of married life, is sorely tempted to engage in adultery for purposes of sexual variety is to be suspected of being indeed biologically and/or psychologically abnormal; and he who frequently has such desires and who occasionally and unobtrusively carries them into practice is well within the normal healthy range.

Love enhancement. Healthy human beings are generally capable of loving pluralistically, on both a serial and a simultaneous basis. Although conjugal or familial love tends to remain alive, and even to deepen, over a long period of years, romantic love generally wanes in from three to five years—particularly when the lovers live under the same roof and share numerous unromantic exigencies of life. Because romantic love, in spite of its palpable disadvantages, is a uniquely exciting and enlivening feeling and has many splendid repercussions on one's whole life, a great number of sensible and stable married individuals fall in love with someone other than their spouses and find, on some level, a mutual expression of their amative feelings with these others. To be incapable of further romantic attachments is in some respects to be dead; and both in imagination and in practice hordes of healthy husbands and wives, including those who continue to have a real fondness for their mates, become involved in romantic extramarital affairs. Although some of these affairs do not lead to any real sexual actualization, many of them do. The result is a great number of divorces and remarriages; but, in all probability, the result is an even greater number of adulterous love affairs that, for one reason or another, do not lead to legal separation from the original mate but which are carried on simultaneously with the marriage.

Experiential drives. Loving, courting, going to bed with, and maintaining an ongoing relationship with a member of the other sex are all interesting and gratifying experiences, not only because of the elements of sex and love that are involved in these happenings but also because the sex-love partners learn a great many things about themselves and their chosen ones, and because they experience thoughts, feelings, and interchanges that would otherwise probably never come their way. To live, to a large degree, is to relate: and in our society intimate relationships usually reach their acme in sex-love affairs. The healthy, experience-hungry married individual, therefore, will be quite motivated, at least at times during his conjugal life, to add to the experience which he is likely to obtain through marriage itself, and often to return to some of the high levels of relating with members of the other sex which he may have known before he met his spouse. His desires to experiment or to re-experience in these respects may easily prejudice him in favor of adultery—especially with the kinds of members of the other sex who are quite different from his mate, and with whom he is not too likely to become closely related outside of his having an extramarital liaison.

Adventure seeking. Most people today lead routinized, fairly dull, unadventurous lives; and their chances of fighting the Indians, hunting big game in Africa, or even trying a new job after working in the same one for a decade or more are reasonably slim. One of the few remaining areas in which they can frequently find real excitement and novelty of a general as well as a specifically sexual nature is in the area of sex-love affairs. Once this area is temporarily closed by marriage, child-rearing, and the fairly scheduled pursuits that tend to accompany domestic life, the healthy and still adventure-seeking person frequently looks longingly for some other outlets; and he or she is likely to find such outlets in extramarital relationships. This does not mean that all life-loving mates must eventually try to jazz up their humdrum existences with adulterous affairs; but it does mean that a certain percentage of creative, adventure-seeking individuals will and that they will do so for reasonably sensible motives.

Sexual curiosity. Although an increasing number of people today have premarital sex experiences and a good number also have sex affairs between the time their first marriage ends by death or divorce and their next marriage begins, there are still many Americans, especially females, who reach the age of forty or fifty and have had a total of only one or two sex partners in their entire lives. Such individuals, even when they have had fairly satisfactory sex relations with their spouses, are often quite curious about what it would be like to try one or more other partners; and eventually a good number of them do experiment in this regard. Other individuals, including many who are happily married, are driven by their sex curiosity to try extramarital affairs because they would like to bring back new techniques to their own marriage bed, because they want to have at least one orgiastic experience before they die, or because some other aspect of their healthy information-seeking in sexual areas cannot very well be satisfied if they continue to have purely monogamous relations.

Social and cultural inducements. Literally millions of average Americans occasionally or frequently engage in adultery because it is the approved social thing to do at various times and in certain settings which are a regular part of their lives. Thus, normally monogamous males will think nothing of resorting to prostitutes or to easily available non-prostitutes at business parties, at men's club meetings, or at conventions. And very sedate women will take off their girdles and either pet to orgasm or have extramarital intercourse at wild drinking parties, on yacht or boat cruises, at vacation resorts, and at various other kinds of social affairs where adulterous behavior is not only permitted but is even expected. Although Americans rarely engage in the regular or periodic kinds of sex orgies which many primitive peoples permit themselves in the course of their married lives, they do fairly frequently engage in occasional orgiastic-like parties where extramarital affairs are encouraged and sometimes become the rule. This may not be the healthiest kind of adulterous behavior but it is well within the range of social normality and it often does seem to satisfy, in a socially approved way, some of the underlying sensible desires for sexual experience, adventure, and varietism that might otherwise be very difficult to fulfill in our society.

Sexual deprivation. Many husbands and wives are acutely sexually deprived, either on a temporary or permanent basis. They may be separated from each other for reasons beyond their control—as when the husband goes off on a long business trip, is inducted into the armed forces, or is in poor physical health. Or they may live together and be theoretically sexually available to each other, but one of them may have a much lower sex drive than the other, may be sexually incompetent, or may otherwise be an unsatisfying bed partner even though he or she is perfectly adequate in the other aspects of marital life. Under such circumstances, the deprived mate can very healthfully long for and from time to time seek out extramarital affairs; and in many such instances this mate's marriage may actually be benefited by the having of such affairs, since otherwise acute and chronic sexual deprivation in the marriage may encourage hostilities that could easily disrupt the relationship.

The foregoing reasons for engaging in extramarital affairs would all seem to be reasonably healthy, though of course they can be mixed in with various neurotic reasons, too. Nor do these reasons exhaust the list of sane motivations that would induce many or most married individuals to strongly desire, and at times actually to have, adulterous liaisons. On the other side of the fence, however, there are several self-defeating or emotionally disturbed impulses behind adultery. These include the following:

Low frustration tolerance. While almost every healthy married person at times desires extramarital affairs, he does not truly need to have them, and he can usually tolerate (if not thoroughly enjoy) life very well without them, especially if his marriage is relatively good. The neurotic individual, however, frequently convinces himself that he needs what he wants and that his preferences are necessities. Consequently, he makes himself so desperately unhappy when he is sexually monogamous that he literally drives himself into extramarital affairs. Being a demander rather than a preferrer, he then usually finds something intolerable about his adulterous involvements, too; and he often winds up by becoming still more frustrated, unhappier, and even downright miserable and depressed. It is not marriage and its inevitable frustrations that "bug" him; it is his unreasonable expectation that marriage should not be frustrating.

Hostility to one's spouse. Low frustration tolerance or unrealistic demandingness leads innumerable spouses to dislike their partner's behavior and to insist that the partner therefore ought not be the way he or she is. This childish insistence results in hostility; and once a married person becomes hostile, he frequently refuses to face the fact that he is making himself angry. He vindictively wants to punish his mate, he shies away from having sex with her (or encourages her to shy away from having sex with anyone who is as angry at her as he is), and he finds it much easier to have satisfactory social-sexual relations with another woman than with his wife. He usually "solves" his problem only temporarily by this method, since as long as he remains anger-prone, the chances are that he will later become hostile toward his adulterous inamorata, and that the same kind of vicious circle will occur with his relations with her.

Self-deprecation. A great number of spouses are so perfectionistic in their demands on themselves, and so self-castigating when they do not live up to these demands, that they cannot bear to keep facing their mates (who are in the best positions to see their inadequacies). Because they condemn themselves for not being excellent economic providers, housekeepers, parents, sex partners, etc., they look for outside affairs in which fewer demands will be made on them or where they will not expect themselves to act so perfectly; and they feel more "comfortable," at least temporarily, while having such affairs, even though the much more logical solution to their problem would often be to work things out in their marriages while learning not to be so self-flagellating.

Ego-bolstering. Many married men feel that they are not really men and many married women feel that they are not really women unless they are continually proving that they are by winning the approval of members of the other sex. Some of them also feel that unless they can be seen in public with a particularly desirable sex partner, no one will really respect them. Consequently, they continually seek for conquests and have adulterous affairs to bolster their own low self-esteem rather than for sexual or companionship purposes.

Escapism. Most married individuals have serious enough problems to face in life, either at home, in their work, in their social affairs, or in their attitudes toward themselves. Rather than face and probably work through these problems, a number of these spouses find it much easier to run to some diverting affairs, such as those that adultery may offer. Wives who are poor mothers or who are in continual squabbles with their parents or their in-laws can find many distracting times in motel rooms or in some bachelor's apartment. Husbands who won't face their problems with their partners or with their employees can forget themselves, at least for an afternoon or an evening, in some mistress's more than willing arms. Both husbands and wives who have no vital absorbing interests in life, and who refuse to work at finding for themselves some major goal which would give more meaning to their days, can immerse themselves in adulterous involvements of a promiscuous or long-term nature and can almost forget about the aimlessness of their existences. Naturally, extramarital affairs that are started for these reasons themselves tend to be meaningless and are not vitally absorbing. But surely they are more interesting than mah-jongg and television!

Marital escapism. Most marriages in many respects leave much to be desired; and some are obviously completely "blah" and sterile and would better be brought to an end. Rather than face their marital and family problems, however, and rather than courageously arrange for a separation or a divorce, many couples prefer to avoid such difficult issues and to occupy themselves, instead, in extramarital liaisons, which at least sometimes render their marriages slightly more tolerable.

Sexual disturbances. Sexual disturbances are rather widespread in our society—particularly in the form of impotence or frigidity of husbands and wives. Instead of trying to understand the philosophic core of such disturbances, and changing the irrational and self-defeating value systems that usually cause them (2, 3, 6, 7, 8, 9, 10), many husbands and wives follow the line of least resistance, decide to live with their sexual neuroses, and consequently seek out nonmarital partners with whom they can more comfortably retain these aberrations. Thus, frigid wives, instead of working out their sexual incompatibilities with their husbands, sometimes pick a lover or a series of lovers with whom they are somewhat less frigid or who can more easily tolerate their sexual inadequacies. Impotent husbands or those who are fixated on some form of sex deviation, rather than get to the source of their difficulties and overcoming them in their relations with their wives, find prostitutes, mistresses, or homosexual partners with whom they can remain "comfortably" deviant. In many instances, in fact, the spouse of the sexually disturbed individual is severely blamed for his or her anomaly, when little or no attempt has been made to correct this anomaly by working sexually with this spouse.

Excitement needs. Where the healthy married person, as shown previously in this paper, has a distinct desire for adventure, novelty, and some degree of excitement in life and may therefore be motivated to have some extramarital affairs, the disturbed individual frequently has an inordinate need for excitation. He makes himself, for various reasons, so jaded with almost every aspect of his life that he can only temporarily enjoy himself by some form of thrill-seeking such as wild parties, bouts of drunkenness, compulsive moving around from place to place or job to job, or drug-taking. One of the modes of excitement-seeking which this kind of a disturbed person may take is that of incessantly searching for extramarital affairs. This will not cure his basic jadedness, but will give him surcease from pain for at least a period of time—as do, too, the alcohol and drugs that such individuals are prone to use.

If the thesis of this paper is correct, and there are both healthy and unhealthy reasons for an individual's engaging in extramarital sex relations, how can any given person's motives for adultery be objectively assessed? If Mrs. X, a housewife and mother of two children, or Mr. Y, a business man and father of a teenage son, get together with other single or married individuals and carry on adulterously, how are we to say if one is or both are driven by sane or senseless motives? The answer is that we would have to judge each case individually, on the basis of much psychological and sociological information, to determine what the person's true impulses are and how neurotic or psychotic they seem to be. To make such judgments, however, some kind of criteria have to be drawn up; and although this is difficult to do at present, partly because of our still limited knowledge of healthy individuals and social norms, I shall take a flyer and hazard an educated guess as to what these criteria might possibly be. Judging from my own personal, clinical, and research experience, I would say that the following standards of healthy adulterous behavior might be fairly valid:

1. The healthy adulterer is non-demanding and non-compulsive. He prefers but he does not need extramarital affairs. He believes that he can live better with than without them, and therefore he tries to arrange to have them from time to time. But he is also able to have a happy general and marital life if no such affairs are practicable.

2. The undisturbed adulterer usually manages to carry on his extramarital affairs without unduly disturbing his marriage and family relationships nor his general existence. He is sufficiently discreet about his adultery, on the one hand, and appropriately frank and honest about it with his close associates, on the other hand, so that most people he intimately knows are able to tolerate his affairs and not get too upset about them.

3. He fully accepts his own extramarital desires and acts and never condemns himself or punishes himself because of them, even though he may sometimes decide that they are unwise and may make specific attempts to bring them to a halt.

4. He faces his specific problems with his wife and family as well as his general life difficulties and does not use his adulterous relationships as a means of avoiding any of his serious problems.

5. He is usually tolerant of himself when he acts poorly or makes errors; he is minimally hostile when his wife and family members behave in a less than desirable manner; and he fully accepts the fact that the world is rough and life is often grim, but that there is no reason why it *must* be otherwise and that he can live happily even when conditions around him are not great. Consequently, he does not drive himself to adultery because of self-deprecation, self-pity, or hostility to others.

6. He is sexually adequate with his spouse as well as with others

and therefore has extramarital affairs out of sex interest rather than for sex therapy.

Although the adulterer who lives up to these criteria may have still other emotional disturbances and may be having extramarital affairs for various neurotic reasons other than those outlined in this paper, there is also a good chance that this is not true. The good Judeo-Christian moralists may never believe it, but it would appear that healthy adultery, even in our supposedly monogynous society, *is* possible. Just how often our millions of adulterers practice extramarital relations for good and how often for bad reasons is an interesting question. It is hoped that future research in this area may be somewhat helped by some of the considerations pointed out in the present paper.

References

1. CUBER, JOHN S., and HARROFF, PEGGY B. *The Significant Americans.* New York: Appleton-Century-Crofts Inc., 1965.
2. ELLIS, ALBERT. *Reason and Emotion in Psychotherapy.* New York: Lyle Stuart, 1962.
3. ELLIS, ALBERT. *The Art and Science of Love.* New York: Lyle Stuart and Bantam Books, 1969.
4. ELLIS, ALBERT. *Suppressed: Seven Key Essays Publishers Dared Not Print.* Chicago: New Classic House, 1965 (especially Chap. 4).
5. ELLIS, ALBERT. *The Case for Sexual Liberty.* Tucson: Seymour Press, 1965.
6. ELLIS, ALBERT. *Sex Without Guilt.* New York: Lyle Stuart and Grove Press, 1966.
7. ELLIS, ALBERT. *The Search for Sexual Enjoyment.* New York: Macfadden-Bartell, 1966.
8. ELLIS, ALBERT. *If This Be Sexual Heresy.* New York: Lyle Stuart and Tower Publications, 1966.
9. ELLIS, ALBERT, and HARPER, ROBERT A. *Creative Marriage.* New York: Lyle Stuart and Tower Publications, 1966.
10. ELLIS, ALBERT, and HARPER, ROBERT A. *A Guide to Rational Living.* Englewood Cliffs, N.J.: Prentice-Hall, Inc., 1967, and Hollywood: Wilshire Books, 1967.
11. KINSEY, ALFRED C., *et al. Sexual Behavior in the Human Male.* Philadelphia: W. B. Saunders, 1948.
12. KINSEY, ALFRED C., *et al. Sexual Behavior in the Human Female.* Philadelphia: W. B. Saunders, 1953.

Stephen E. Beltz

FIVE-YEAR EFFECTS OF ALTERED MARITAL CONTRACTS (A BEHAVIORAL ANALYSIS OF COUPLES)

The growing prevalence of extramarital sexual behavior in our culture and its high incidence of occurrence among clients in marriage counseling requires that we develop an understanding of its effects, over time, to the marriage relationship. Heretofore, there was much speculation as to the long range effects of openly acknowledged, mutually agreed upon, extramarital sexual behavior. It has been said that such patterns do not always destroy a marriage, and under some circumstances, can even seem to strengthen a shaky marriage. While the data in this chapter do not offer conclusive evidence as to outcomes, they do raise serious doubts concerning such a contention.

Many cultures, even in modern times, have contained subgroups that maintain open and mutually acceptable patterns of extramarital sexual behavior. Those patterns the author is familiar with reflect a sterility and superficiality that mark them as significantly different from the idealized marriage pattern goals of our own culture. The significant question is not whether or not a couple maintains its legal relationship as spouses but *what kind of day-to-day behavior is exhibited toward each other*. It will be the contention of this study that, by the very nature of the alteration in a marriage contract that allows for acceptable extramarital sexual behavior, a deep and complex relationship is impossible. That is, it is virtually impossible, in our culture today and with our current courting system, for extramarital sexual behavior occurring over a long period of time to strengthen a marriage. In fact, a behavioral assessment of such a marriage relationship reveals its essential flaw, which can be stated as: a contingency (or agreed-upon marriage contract) which allows for extramarital sources of social, sexual, or affectional peer reinforcements will yield *different* behavior repertoires from one which does not. The effects of and the nature of these differences will be the subjects of this chapter.

MARITAL BEHAVIOR

Behavior utilized upon a signal from a spouse and under the control of consequences which in part are provided by the spouse can be thought of as *marital behavior.* Many of the behaviors utilized in relation to the spouse are also utilized in relation to other people. Some behavior is restricted for use only in relation to the spouse. This total group of behaviors (which also include behaviors in an individual's repertoire which are possibly of use, although not being utilized currently) comprises the *marital behavior repertoire.*

All *marriage behavior* can be thought of as being learned after marriage. Although each individual has had greater or lesser opportunity to emit and modify behaviors in the process of learning to be an adult, and although these behaviors have come under the control of signals derived from social interaction and are controlled by the consequences of other people's behaviors, the contingencies which produced the learning were different before the marriage.

Contingencies established prior to marriage do not include lifelong monogamy by commitment or by social contract, so that the unique features of marital behavior are primarily developed after marriage.

Some of the important points contained in this type of total contract or contingency are as follows:

1. Sexual and heterosexual peer affectional positive consequences will be controlled solely by the spouse.
2. Behaviors are to be emitted that will make these available. (Even in the "traditional" marriage contract a man had to bring home a paycheck to demand his "rights.")
3. New behaviors must be continually developed to meet changing conditions, and new types of positive consequences will develop to maintain them.
4. New signals will come to have control over increasingly complex and subtle behaviors.
5. The behavior repertoires of each spouse will expand and the behaviors emitted by each spouse will increasingly come to be positive consequences to the other (deepening love).

Because of the extreme difficulty of this complex process and the poorly developed or large number of unadaptive behaviors in one or both spouse's repertoires, the process may fail. A reverse effect takes place whereby the high frequency behaviors emitted by each spouse become increasingly negative consequences. Sometimes one or both spouses, either by open mutual decision or surreptitiously without an open change of the marriage contract, begin extramarital behavior (not necessarily extramarital *sex*).

Any behavior normally considered restricted to the spouse and emitted toward a source of social positive consequences other than the spouse may be considered an extramarital behavior because:

1. It acknowledges sources for social, sexual, and affectional positive consequences from persons other than the spouse.
2. It allows for the by-passing of the shaping process designed to deepen marriage.
3. It tends to foster development of an entirely incompatible repertoire of social behaviors.
4. It minimizes the enrichment of positive consequence properties of the spouse and does not lead to greater differentiation of signal controls.

A marriage can be defined, then, as a *contingency environment* where part of the contract or contingency is legally set at the beginning of the marriage. It is a complex contingency whose rules are only discovered as one goes through the situation. The laws of the legal contractor are known—a spouse must love, honor, and cherish. But a new husband doesn't always know the types of contingencies set up by his spouse. It is a process that takes fifty years to discover all that she expects of him and all that he expects of her (and both of their expectations will also change). Sometimes there is a radical change in the contract on the part of one or both spouses in a covert way (secret or unacknowledged). Sometimes either one or both spouses, by an *open and mutual decision*, will change the marriage contract. When the marriage contract changes, the behavior will also change. Once the rule by which a spouse can obtain positive consequences, or once the source from which a spouse can find positive consequences changes, the behavior patterns and repertoires that the spouse emits will also change.

The change under study in this chapter is the change to extramarital sexual behavior; that is, where the spouse's consent to permit sexual behavior with persons other than themselves. When the spouses acknowledge other sexual sources, both a change and a fixation of sexual behavior patterns takes place. One of the things that can be observed is a by-passing of the development of complex marital behaviors. The marriage behaviors tend to remain much as they were at the point of change; perhaps even a simplification of already established patterns can be seen. The development of an entirely incompatible repertoire of social behavior can also be observed, much more similar to dating behavior than to long-term companionship or other stable marital behaviors. The individual now has to develop or to reestablish a repertoire of search behaviors; he must become more charming; must learn where to find the new extramarital sources. Very often, these behaviors are incompatible with the very difficult job of learning marital behavior.

One other very important development also occurs: this changed pattern tends to minimize the enrichment of the positive consequence properties of the spouse. One of the things that a spouse learns, if restricted to a single sexual or affectional source, is to look more and more deeply into what is available in that individual. A husband or wife comes to value the spouse for many more subtle kinds of positive consequences than initially. However, once a spouse begins to allow himself to keep seeking the same types of positive consequences in other places, the legal source (spouse) does not continue to develop deepening and enriching positive consequence properties.

LONGITUDINAL DATA

During a five-year period near a large Midwestern city it became possible to study five couples who explicitly altered their marriage contracts during counseling. At the onset of the counseling relationship with them, they could be described as fairly typical representatives of the white, Anglo-Saxon, Protestant, suburban, middle class. They were a well educated group, with a stable marriage pattern. They had all been married more than ten years at the time counseling began. The age range of the group was from the early thirties to the mid-forties. They came for counseling for various reasons; most did not come for marriage counseling but came because of a problem child, personal problems, or certain conflicts of attitudes which they could not reconcile within themselves. It became possible to observe this group as they developed social contacts between themselves, among themselves, and with others in their environment, and to observe the effect of their individual alterations of the marriage contingency. That is, as each couple began either tacitly or overtly to allow for extramarital sources of what were usually the positive consequences restricted to the spouse, the effects were observed at frequent intervals over a five-year period.

In order to reduce the complexity of the five years of observation, this report will restrict itself to only two main dependent variables. In each case, the primary independent variable was a decision to allow for extramarital sex *openly* both within the group that formed and also outside the social group. The dependent variables are the number of sexual extramarital contacts that developed and the stability of the marriages. Brief descriptions will be given of each couple and of some of the changes in their behavior repertoires.

The first nine diagrams deal with each group member's sexual behavior prior to counseling and during counseling over a two-year period. The final diagram reflects the results of an additional three-year follow-up.

The thesis of this study was that major shifts in behavior would occur with each minor change in a marriage contingency. The data were collected in a significant way. Direct inquiries were not made as to sexual activity. Each individual, in the course of talking about other experiences, would report sexual activity almost casually. Other couples in the wife-swapping complex would also report their sexual activity, so that reliability checks from the people who were actually experiencing these behaviors were possible. This tended to eliminate the kind of problem which so often occurs in social research: the desire to please the investigator, to magnify events, or to provide fantasy descriptions.

It was found, for example, that there were many reports that did not check out and, of course, are not included in the data reported in the diagrams. For example, one individual reported that "Boy, I was really drinking at that party and I got laid." Everybody else at that party said that this individual passed out after a few drinks and didn't do anything but sit there and snore. If his verbal report had been trusted without cross-checking, an additional line would have been entered in the diagrams. Sexual contacts, for the most part, were recorded only after having been confirmed by other participants. Thus, the number of contacts recorded overall tends to err on the conservative side.

The follow-ups were part of the routine all the clients experienced and no special effort was exerted to obtain sexual information other than a casual inquiry as part of routine questioning. Again, only cross-checking data were reported wherever possible. Since the group remained friendly and was used to talking about each other during counseling, an amazing number of cross-checks were possible. Wherever there was uncertainty about sexual behavior, question marks are used in the diagrams.

In Diagram 1 we are introduced to the first two couples in the developing sequences. Mrs. C referred herself for counseling because of a strong homosexual attraction to Mrs. D, with whom she had en-

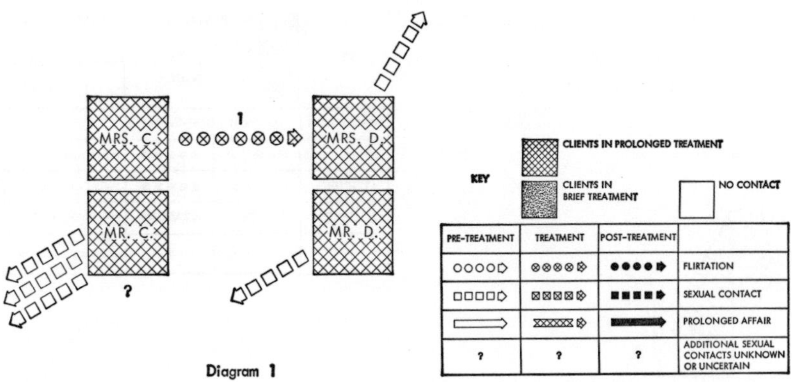

Diagram 1

gaged in a flirtation which was threatening to become physical. She was confused and concerned and she wished to discuss her problem. She had had no previous history of either homosexual or heterosexual relations either prior to her marriage or during the course of her marriage. Somewhat later, Mr. C also requested counseling because of the urgent insistence of his wife that he develop more effective marital behaviors. Mr. C had had three known sexual affairs prior to marriage. There was no premarital intercourse with Mrs. C because of her strict religious background and lack of experience. Although there were no confirmed reports of extramarital sexual behavior on the part of Mr. C, some uncertainty remained and this is reflected in the question marks next to his name in the diagram. Mrs. C referred Mrs. D fairly quickly for help with the management of Mrs. D's children. It developed that while she had a stable marriage, she felt inadequate to stimulate her husband and was dissatisfied with their lack of social life. Mr. D later entered counseling for help concerning vocational problems since he had been unable to progress in his job, was seriously overweight, and lacked interest in life. Neither Mr. D nor Mrs. D expressed any serious dissatisfaction with their marriage. Both Mr. and Mrs. D had had one heterosexual experience each prior to their own premarital intercourse. Neither had experienced any extramarital sex throughout the course of their marriage. Both of these couples had children and were somewhat isolated from participation in the social life of their neighborhood and community. This first phase of the development of what later became a complex social group was marked only by the flirtation between Mrs. C and Mrs. D. This first change came about because their husbands were uncommunicative, lacked social skills, and were poor lovers. So the two women had made an individual decision to seek companionship, affection, and understanding from a source other than their spouses.

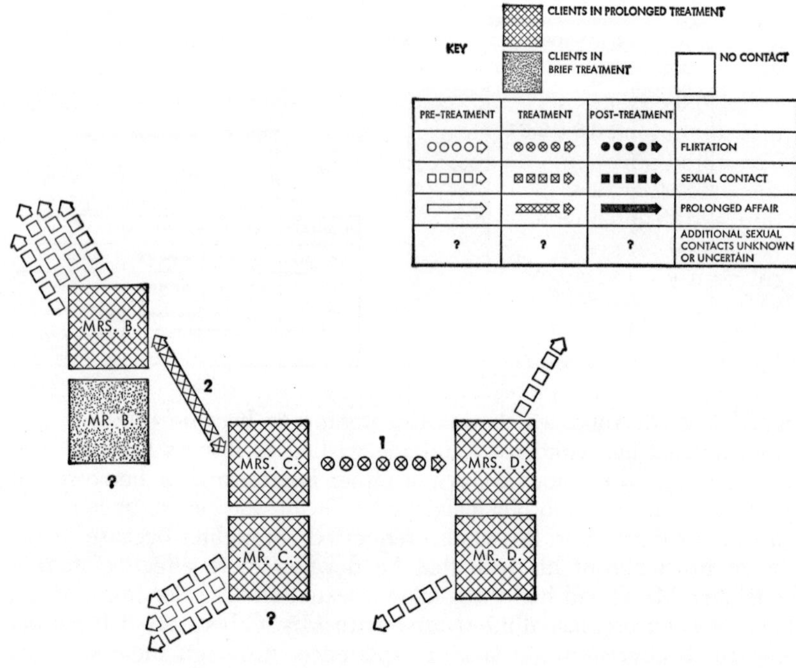

Diagram 2

Mr. and Mrs. D, in this second phase of the development of the social circle, moved to another neighborhood close by, though without any diminution of social contact with Mr. and Mrs. C. Mr. and Mrs. B then moved into the C's neighborhood, which permitted the easy development of a relationship between Mrs. C and Mrs. B as the new neighbor. Mrs. B was referred for counseling in relation to a general dissatisfaction with life, some problems relating to the management of her children, and a general desire to resolve certain specific conflicts within herself. Mrs. B had had some, but not extensive, prior counseling in another state. While she also expressed some dissatisfaction with her marriage, no evidence was given of a desire to terminate the relationship. Mr. B was seen briefly in conjunction with some problems with his children, but refused to participate in any form of counseling. Mrs. B's premarital experience included only a pseudo-rape (which she had provoked), and no premarital intercourse with her husband. There were at least four sexual affairs that took place after her marriage, although only three were reported in sufficient detail to warrant inclusion. Mr. B's background, both prior to and during his marriage, is unknown, although it is extremely likely that extramarital sexual behavior was continually occurring, since his occupation required him to be away from home for long periods of time under circumstances quite conducive to extramarital sexual activity. The relationship between Mrs. C and Mrs. B became highly intense, ultimately culminating in a series of homosexual experiences. The initial unilateral decision to seek affection and understanding from someone other than the spouse by Mrs. C progressed during this phase into a decision that homosexual behavior was permissible to satisfy her sexual desires and would in no way jeopardize the total marriage relationship. On the part of Mrs. B, her initial alteration of the marriage contract permitted heterosexual relations outside her marriage, and under Mrs. C's urging, further altered her unilateral change to include affectional companionship and sexual activity on a homosexual basis. While all three husbands resented the time spent by the three wives away from the family, it was accepted as a minor change in the previous stable and somewhat isolated marriage patterns.

In Diagram 3 we see the results of the movement toward social grouping that occurred in previously isolated marriage patterns. Mrs. C, in attempting to expand her social life in order to develop more adequate social skills, met and added to the circle Mr. and Mrs. A. Mrs. A and Mr. A entered counseling when a long history of a very stable marriage suddenly erupted into a great deal of tension surrounding Mrs. A's gradual attraction for alcohol. Mrs. A blamed her husband for her drinking and forced Mr. A to come for counseling to become a more effective husband and person. Mr. A's background from a Midwestern rural area predisposed him to be very withdrawn and to seek employment in a field that required little interaction with people. The original marriage between Mr. and Mrs. A had occurred because of Mrs. A's desire to find security and to escape from a rather wild and difficult youth. Her background included numerous premarital experiences. After marriage she had occasional extramarital affairs which she effectively managed to conceal from her husband because of his almost total lack of perception or desire to comprehend the situation. Mrs. A entered counseling reluctantly because, as was later discovered, of an intense sexual affair she was having with a Mr. X. Mr. X was seen briefly and it was ascertained that he had had a long history of sexual affairs while maintaining what appeared to be a stable marriage. Throughout the counseling, Mrs. X's behavior remained completely unknown. There was no reason, however, to suspect extramarital sexual behavior on her part because the marriage appeared to be of the traditional sort based on the satisfaction of security desires and relatively minimal interaction. During the course of Mrs. A's and Mr. X's sexual affair, she engaged in numerous flirtations and several secondary sexual affairs, thus altering both her marriage and

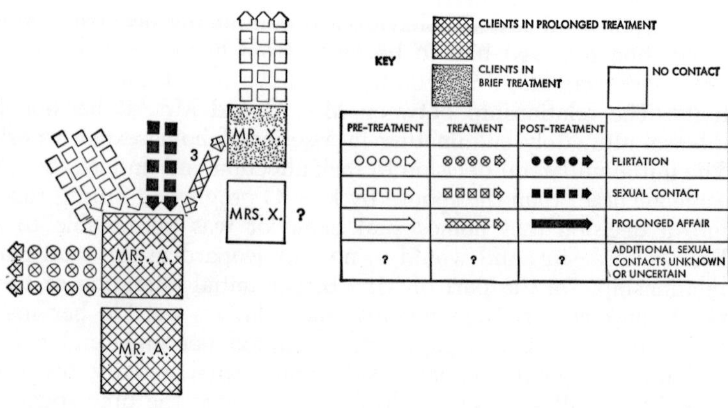

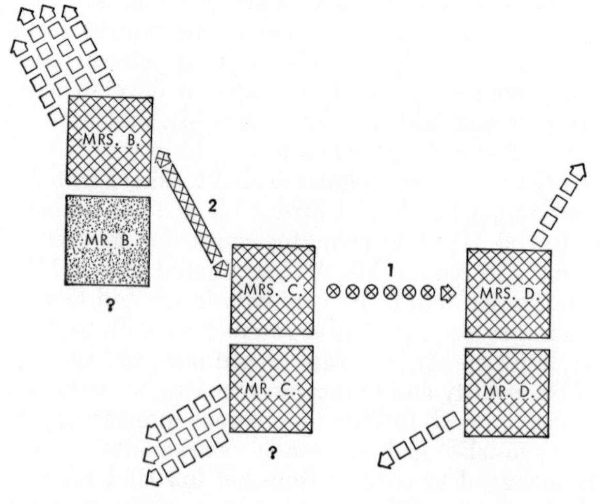

Diagram 3

paramour contracts to include sexual activity with whomever was immediately available or desirable. Mr. X, on the other hand, seemed to be maintaining the paramour contract and his own altered marriage contract. At this point, only Mrs. A had a completely open sexual contract (although on a unilateral basis). No organization was present in the group except for the developing social interaction which began to increase in frequency.

The next phase of the alterations developed primarily because of a unilateral decision by Mrs. D. This occurred following a radical change in Mr. D. Counseling had been most effective in helping him to improve his physical appearance from that of an obese, sluggish, and immature man to a poised, slim, self-confident, and strikingly handsome individual. He had changed jobs, moving from a low-paying poor-future position to a highly competitive, very demanding position which required him to be away frequently on extended business trips. Mrs. D had concurred in this change because of the higher salary involved. She, too, had developed the beginnings of poise and self-confidence. However, she made a critical decision to alter her marriage contract to allow for casual sex with available neighbors during the time her husband was away. Her reasoning was that this type of sexual activity would in no way detract from her marriage relationship since it would only occur when her husband was totally unavailable and would not include any strong emotional ties with paramours. She began these contacts with two men in her neighborhood. During this period, the group's contacts with each other remained casual, with little flirtation occurring at parties. The only sexual interaction among the four primary couples was that between Mrs. C and Mrs. B.

The next phase in the development of the social group again centered around Mr. and Mrs. D. Mr. D became aware of Mrs. D's decision when she informed him of it. Rather than reacting negatively, his response was to encourage it and to suggest an alteration of the marriage contract on a mutual basis. That is, he not only suggested that he too engage in extramarital sex while his wife was unavailable, but that exchanging partners with another couple on the weekends he was home would also not be detrimental to their marriage relationship and would reflect their "modern, enlightened attitudes about marriage." Mrs. D was at first reluctant to agree to try this alteration. The first exchange was arranged with a peripheral couple, Mr. and Mrs. Z. While this couple did participate occasionally in social activities hosted by Mr. and Mrs. D, they never became part of the primary group that formed. The exchange of partners with Mr. and Mrs. D threw a great strain on the Z's marriage and led Mr. and Mrs. Z to seek counseling to discuss this change in their own marriage contract (which had been engineered during a drunken weekend by Mr. and Mrs. D). Mrs. Z had had an affair prior to her marriage but there had not been any other extramarital activity. Mr. Z's behavior patterns were not fully explored and remain unknown. Ultimately, Mr. and Mrs. Z terminated the exchanges after a few sporadic occurrences over a period of time. Thus, the first *mutually* decided alteration of the marriage contract had taken place in one of the primary couples following a series of minor alterations throughout the forming group. At this stage of the game all of the couples were becoming more socially skilled and seeking more stimulation and excitement in social activities. Flirtations, while not openly displayed on a one-to-one

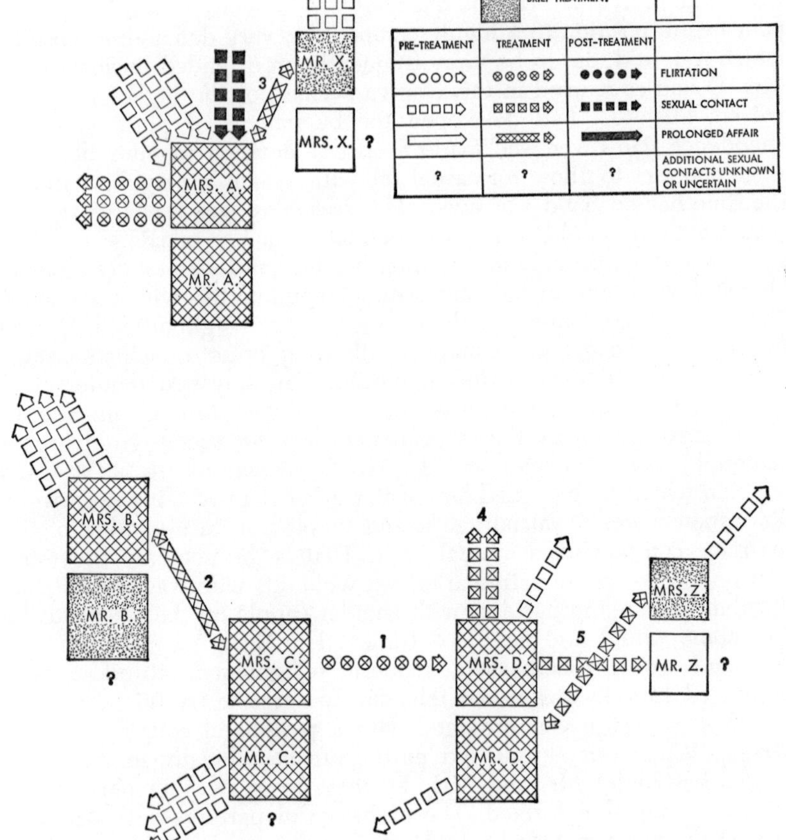

Diagram 4

basis, were indirectly occurring through changes in the group's activities. Discussions of sexual topics increased. Most noticeable were changes in dress, particularly in the emphasizing of sexual characteristics. At a swimming party, many of the female guests removed their bras while they were intoxicated.

In Diagram 5 it can be seen that the activity of Mr. and Mrs. D with regard to extramarital sexual behavior began to increase at a rapid rate. Mr. D was away from home for extended periods of time, and, although he worked long hours, he managed to initiate a series of sexual contacts that continued to occur at a fairly moderate but

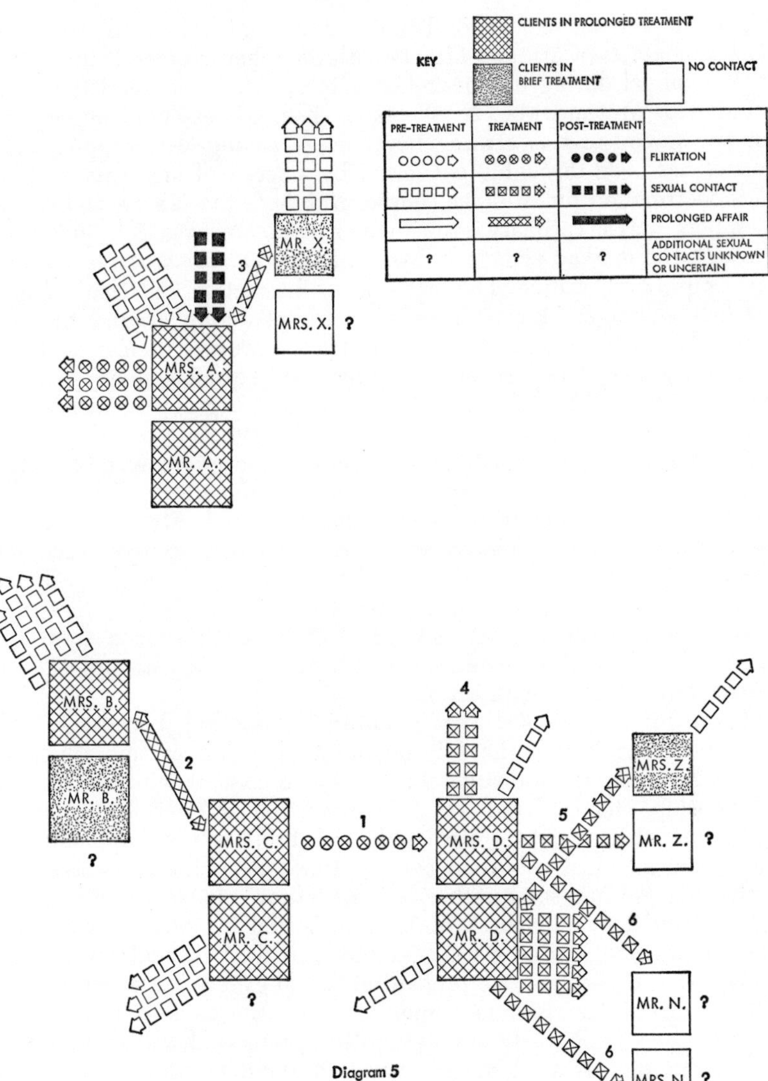

Diagram 5

constant rate (until much later when the ultimate break-up of the marriage appeared imminent, when they increased greatly). At this phase, the extramarital sex was seen by Mr. D as supplementing his marriage.

A Mr. and Mrs. N became involved at this point—a couple highly experienced in the exchange of partners and older than Mr. and Mrs. D. The contacts of Mr. and Mrs. D with the other couples of the group were minimal during this period as much of their weekend time was spent with Mr. and Mrs. N. We have then, the essential ingredients for the spread of this contingency change among the group. A core couple has been throughly converted by a series of incidents, leading to indoctrination by an older couple. Although the N's never became members of the primary group, their influence was felt indirectly through the marked change in Mr. and Mrs. D. The scene is set now for a rapid acceleration. The first year of interaction had resulted in a gradual alteration of established patterns centering around the primary change from restricted to unrestricted sources of marital types of gratification. The first signs of organized sexual activity had appeared and the actual formation of a social group dedicated to sexual stimulation and sexual gratification began.

Simultaneous with the changing mores of the group was the introduction of a previously peripheral couple to the status of full membership. These members were introduced through Mr. and Mrs. A, with whom they had been friendly. The other three couples accepted them readily, and a close attachment formed among the five women. A close relationship, amounting almost to a homosexual flirtation, developed between Mrs. A and Mrs. E. As can be seen from the diagram, Mrs. A also carried on a flirtation with Mr. E, and Mrs. E carried on a flirtation with Mr. C.

A word about the E's. Mrs. E entered counseling because of dissatisfaction with life. She felt unable to develop as an individual within her marriage although she was quite content with her marital relationship. Her husband was in a profession and earning an excellent living; their marriage was stable and, to all external appearances, they were an ideal suburban couple. Her husband was an assertive individual and had some rather bizarre sexual behaviors and interests which tended to alienate Mrs. E from sexual experiences with him (although there was no significant break in their marital sexual relations). Mrs. E had had one premarital sexual experience and no extramarital experience prior to counseling. Mr. E was seen briefly only once or twice and freely admitted many premarital and extramarital sexual activities. It would be impossible in the diagram to indicate the large number of casual sexual contacts he freely admitted to and of which his wife knew nothing at this time. It is interesting to note that at no time during the formation of this group did he do more than flirt with members of the group. This was, in part, a function of his discretion and his extensive activity apart from his social circle, and in part because of his rejection by the females in the group. Although handsome and charming, the women in the group found him cruel and

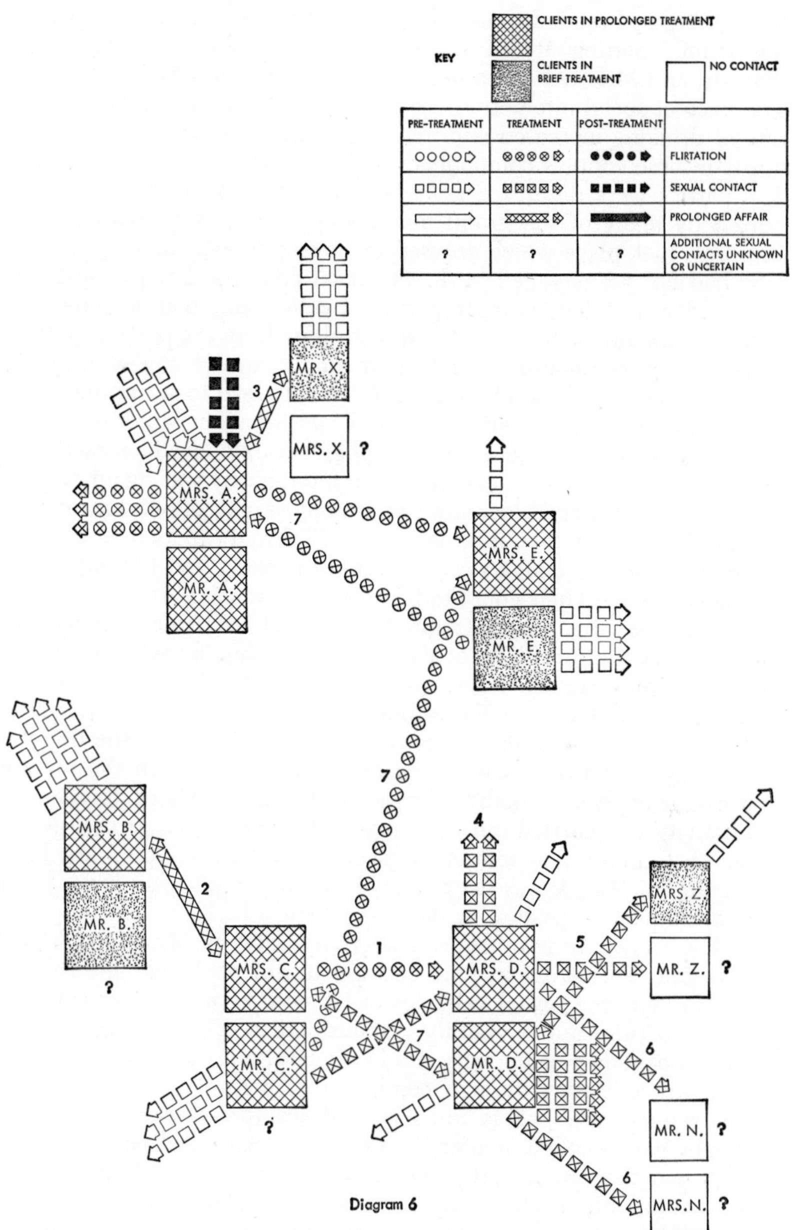
KEY
CLIENTS IN PROLONGED TREATMENT
CLIENTS IN BRIEF TREATMENT
NO CONTACT
PRE-TREATMENT
TREATMENT
POST-TREATMENT
FLIRTATION
SEXUAL CONTACT
PROLONGED AFFAIR
ADDITIONAL SEXUAL CONTACTS UNKNOWN OR UNCERTAIN
MR. X.
MRS. X.
MRS. A.
MR. A.
MRS. E.
MR. E.
MRS. B.
MR. B.
MRS. C.
MR. C.
MRS. D.
MR. D.
MRS. Z.
MR. Z.
MR. N.
MRS. N.

Diagram 6

frightening and tended to avoid anything further with him than necking or mild petting. It can also be seen during this phase of activity that Mr. and Mrs. D had arranged for swapping with Mr. and Mrs. C. The pace of social interaction was stepped up during this period. The rate of drinking increased enormously, to the point where all of these upper-income couples complained of their extremely high liquor bills. The parties were described as "wild" or "fast," and a feeling was reported by many of the group members of being on a roller coaster. Incidents took place which aroused feelings, primarily among the men, who had not yet engaged in direct sexual contacts. For example, Mr. A would report incidents of petting by his wife that angered him greatly, although he took no step to withdraw from the party situations. Occasionally, the couples would pair off for an evening of drinking, which in the case of the D's and the C's would lead to swapping.

Next we see the pace quickening still further, again centering around the D's, who have added a new peripheral couple and increased their individual activity. The pace of all the interactions was again stepped up. Mrs. C and Mrs. B increased their homosexual activity during this period. Although it cannot be said that *full* sexual experiences between them ever reached a high rate, the rate of necking and petting did increase markedly. Their going to bed together was in part prevented by circumstances, Mrs. B's hesitation, the high rate of sexual activity with the D's, and the flirtations at the parties. It should be noted at this point that only serious flirtations involving extensive petting are reported in these diagrams. Every one of these individuals was reported to have engaged in various forms of flirtation with all of the opposite sex members. It would have been impossible to diagram the number and extent of these sexually charged interactions. Where definite sexual activity was carried out extensively at parties, such as oral-genital contacts, fondling and mutual orgasm without coitus, they are listed as flirtations. Mrs. A was deeply involved with Mr. X and limited herself to the party activities, as did Mrs. E and Mr. B.

In Diagram 7 we see that sexual activity between Mr. A and Mrs. B had begun. This arose in part because it was no longer possible for Mr. A to deny the sexual behavior of his wife as well as her complete rejection of him and of family responsibilities. This change marks a radical breakdown of the very rigid unilateral marriage contract under which Mr. A lived. Although coming from a rural background, with strong fundamental beliefs and a great desire to preserve his marriage, he finally had been led to alter his own *unilaterally* held position (since Mrs. A had only superficially agreed to monogamy, and had, in effect, been maintaining a paramour for the entire previous year). Although Mr. A did not openly acknowledge his awareness of this, it was apparent that he had at last recognized the pattern of events. The alter-

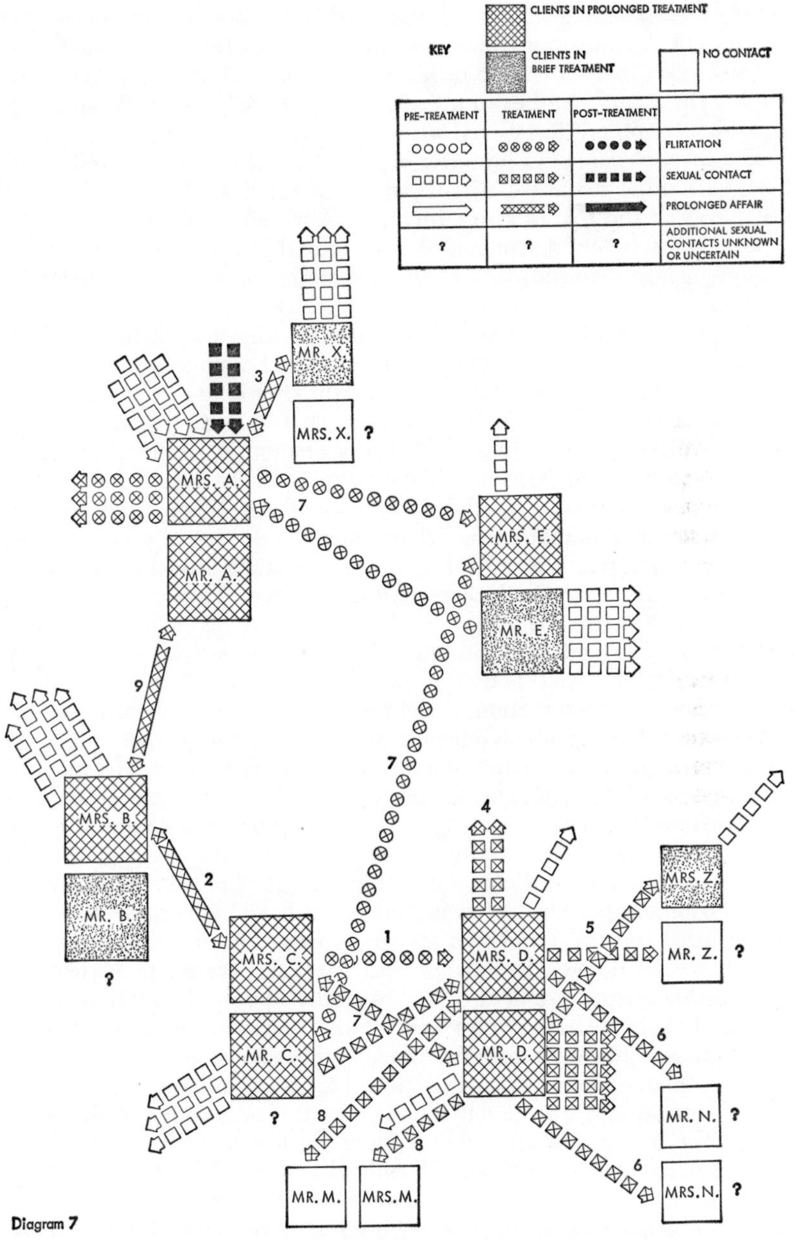
KEY
CLIENTS IN PROLONGED TREATMENT
CLIENTS IN BRIEF TREATMENT
NO CONTACT
PRE-TREATMENT
TREATMENT
POST-TREATMENT
FLIRTATION
SEXUAL CONTACT
PROLONGED AFFAIR
ADDITIONAL SEXUAL CONTACTS UNKNOWN OR UNCERTAIN
?
MR. X.
MRS. X.
MRS. A.
MR. A.
MRS. E.
MR. E.
MRS. B.
MR. B.
MRS. C.
MR. C.
MRS. D.
MR. D.
MRS. Z.
MR. Z.
MR. N.
MRS. N.
MR. M.
MRS. M.
1
2
3
4
5
6
7
8
9

Diagram 7

ation of his marriage contract was made reluctantly and under the pressure of growing resentment and desperation. He had resigned himself to the ultimate break-up of his marriage and engaged in the activities of the group. He began a prolonged affair with Mrs. B, although he also attempted flirtations with other group members. Since he lacked most social skills, he never at this phase got beyond mild flirtations with other members. Mrs. B, on the other hand, had seen herself previously in the role of sympathetic teacher and enjoyed helping Mr. A develop self-confidence and better sexual skills. No other major change occurred during this phase, although the group continued its parties.

The cohesion of the group continued to increase, with members maintaining almost daily contact in the form of bowling, bridge parties, telephone conversations, dinner parties, drinking bouts, coffee clatches, and the like. The women, particularly, shared most intimate confidences and were instantly aware of any change in each other's marriages or patterns of behavior. They were quick to respond with aid, support, and discussion of the various problems. They tried to help each other, to eliminate what they considered Mrs. A's unadaptive drinking, Mrs. B's, C's, and E's failure to communicate with their husbands, and Mrs. D's lack of self-confidence. Thus, when Mr. E revealed an intense love affair with Mrs. W to his wife, the entire group was electrified with the news. After concealing for many, many years his outside sexual activity, under the pressure of the intensification of the sexual interaction of the group, he revealed to his wife his pattern of activity and his current affair. The change that began in their marriage at this point was striking. Mr. E became violent and abusive toward Mrs. E, and at one point tried to run her over with his car. He rejected her utterly and flaunted his mistress at her at every opportunity. He made no attempt toward reconciliation and instead attempted to maintain their relationship only for the sake of his status in the community. Mrs. W was known to have had many previous affairs, while her husband was known to have had none. During this period and subsequently, Mr. W and Mrs. E became good friends, sharing the mutual problem of spouses who openly flaunted their rejection of their marriage vows and of their partners. At this point all five marriages were in serious difficulty. Tensions were arising and showing themselves in open rejection, bickering and quarreling, and in both sexual and affectional fantasies centering around other members of the group and around peripheral figures as well. At this time the two marriages in most serious difficulty were the A's and the E's. The other three couples were still ostensibly working at the resolution of the problems which had been exposed or developed, although more

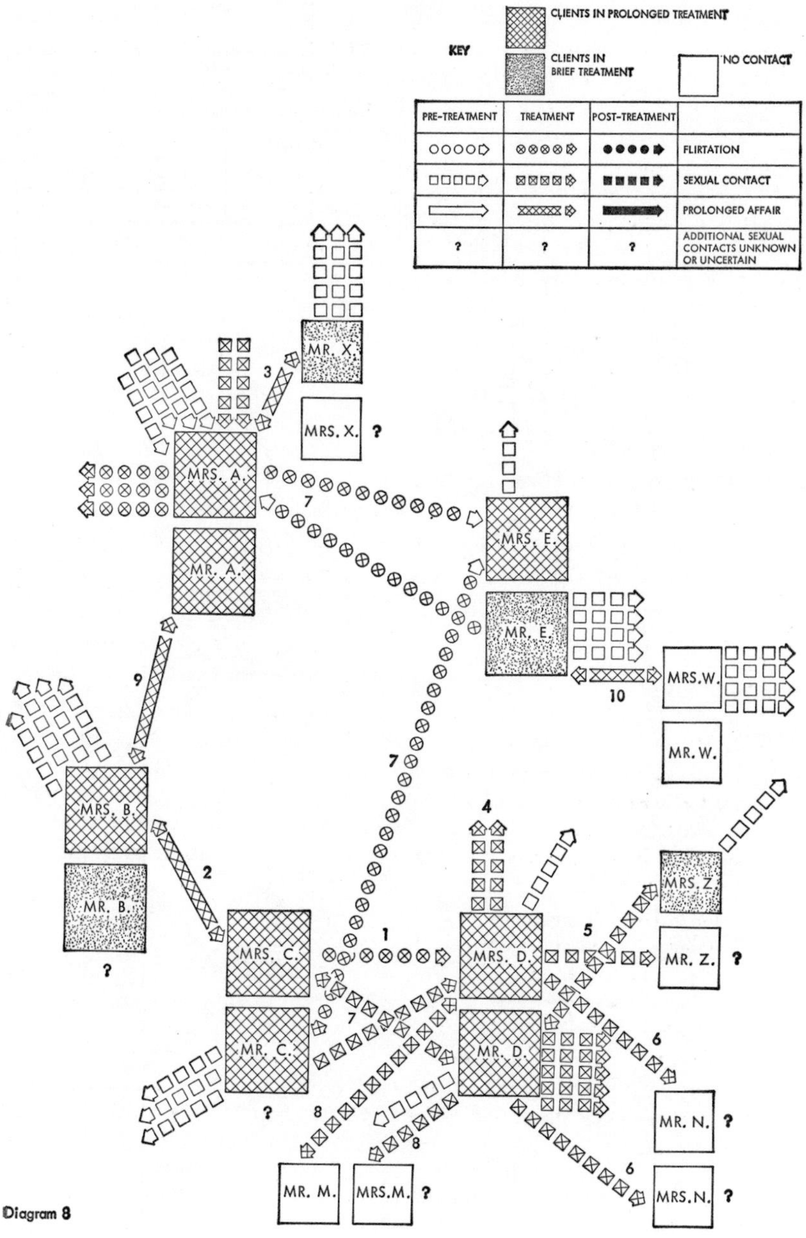
KEY
CLIENTS IN PROLONGED TREATMENT
CLIENTS IN BRIEF TREATMENT
NO CONTACT
PRE-TREATMENT
TREATMENT
POST-TREATMENT
FLIRTATION
SEXUAL CONTACT
PROLONGED AFFAIR
ADDITIONAL SEXUAL CONTACTS UNKNOWN OR UNCERTAIN
MR. X.
MRS. X.
MRS. A.
MR. A.
MRS. E.
MR. E.
MRS.W.
MR. W.
MRS. B.
MR. B.
MRS. C.
MR. C.
MRS. D.
MR. D.
MRS. Z.
MR. Z.
MR. N.
MRS. N.
MR. M.
MRS.M.
1
2
3
4
5
6
7
8
9
10

Diagram 8

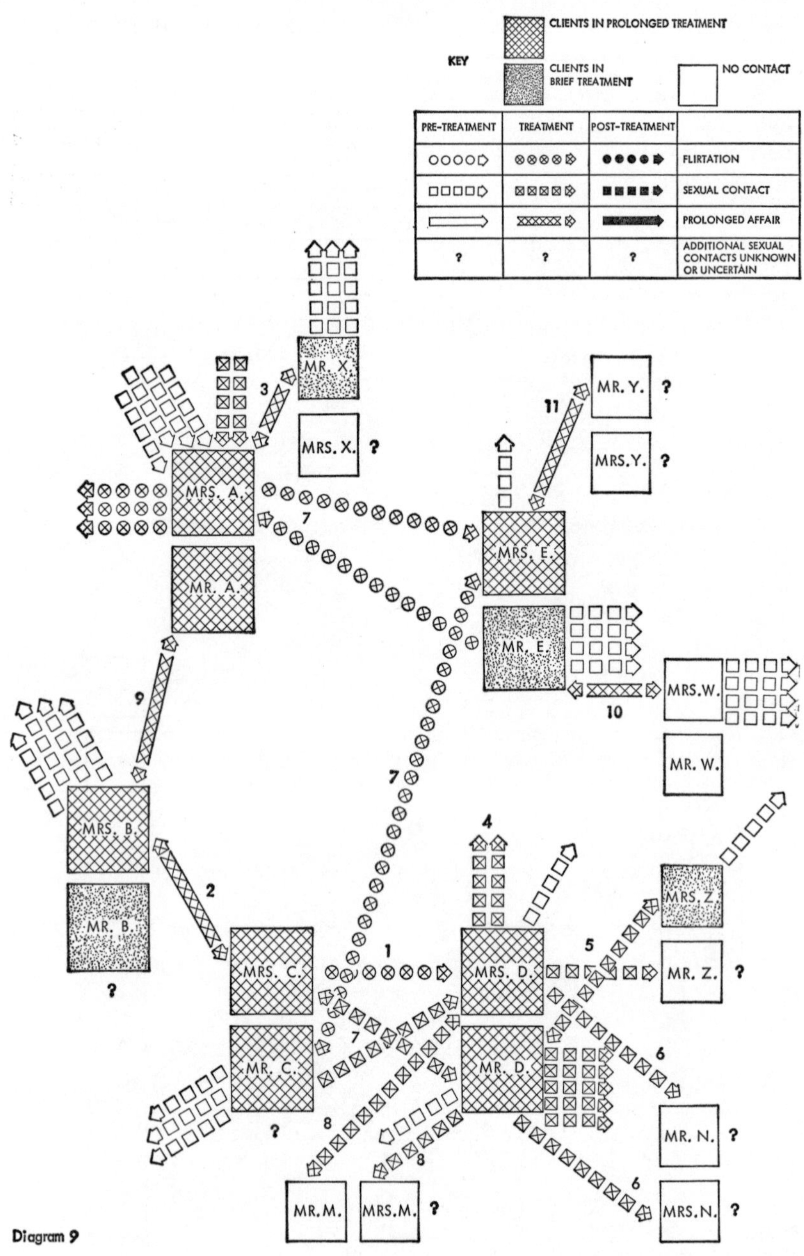

KEY
CLIENTS IN PROLONGED TREATMENT
CLIENTS IN BRIEF TREATMENT
NO CONTACT
PRE-TREATMENT
TREATMENT
POST-TREATMENT
FLIRTATION
SEXUAL CONTACT
PROLONGED AFFAIR
ADDITIONAL SEXUAL CONTACTS UNKNOWN OR UNCERTAIN
MR. X.
MRS. X.
MRS. A.
MR. A.
MR. Y.
MRS. Y.
MRS. E.
MR. E.
MRS. W.
MR. W.
MRS. B.
MR. B.
MRS. C.
MR. C.
MRS. D.
MR. D.
MRS. Z.
MR. Z.
MR. N.
MRS. N.
MR. M.
MRS. M.

Diagram 9

effort was certainly being exerted in charming people other than their spouses.

By this time, general repertoires of nonmarital behavior among all members of the group had shown significant improvement. Mrs. D had become involved in community activities, Mrs. C had become reinvolved quite successfully in her vocation, Mrs. B had become involved in church work, Mrs. A had also obtained employment within her specialty, and Mrs. E was seriously contemplating further education. The men had, for the most part, showed increasing skills at work leading to promotions, job changes, or increased income. The couples' relationships with their children had all significantly improved. In general, it could be said that, apart from their strange sexual behavior and the breakdown in their marriage relationships, they were achieving their goals as individuals.

Diagram 9 reveals the final change which took place in the pattern of the group. At this point, in the light of Mr. E's behavior, Mrs. E had decided upon active alteration of her marriage contract. Mrs. E consummated an affair with Mr. Y which she had been contemplating for a considerable period of time. Mr. and Mrs. Y were never seen, and although it is suspected that Mr. Y had had previous affairs, this could not be confirmed.

It must be pointed out that all of these final phases took place within a short period of time, so that at the termination of counseling the intensity and frenzy which had built up during the year had begun to subside. The next few months led to the gradual termination of counseling by each couple, arriving, in each case, at a mutual termination point with the counselor.

SUMMARY OF THE FIRST TWO YEARS

Mr. and Mrs. A had initially come in order to help Mr. A be a more interesting person and to respond more emotionally to life experiences. This led to Mrs. A's entering counseling reluctant to improve her marriage but determined to eliminate her anxiety and her drinking problem. Mr. A had indeed achieved his individual goal and was a much more outgoing, friendly, and emotional individual who had modified many of his rigidities. Mrs. A had fluctuated drastically throughout the counseling. At the termination of the counseling she had become stabilized to the extent that she was working, although drinking more heavily than desirable, and was not managing her life as well as she or the counselor would have preferred. The significant aspect of their experience to this point was the determination, mutually decided, upon divorce.

Mr. and Mrs. B had had to move from the geographical area and had effectively terminated their relationship with the group and with counseling. However, Mrs. B's initial goal had been realized. She had experienced marked self-improvement and an ability to tolerate what she had come to see as an incompatible marriage. Mr. B had never entered counseling with his wife and had resented her engaging in it throughout its duration. There was no plan for divorce at this time although it had been contemplated by Mrs. B on numerous occasions. The forced change of location prevented any immediate possibility of a move in this direction on Mrs. B's part.

Mrs. C had initially entered counseling because of her homosexual impulses. Mr. C, entering later, had expressed a desire to strengthen his marriage and to improve himself. While Mrs. C had indeed acted out her homosexual impulses, she had also developed heterosexual interests and had grown enormously as a human being. She was again working at her profession, had resolved to eliminate or drastically limit future homosexual interests (since Mrs. B was no longer available) and was working diligently to improve her marriage. Mr. C had experienced moderate improvement in his ability to relate to others and in his role as a husband. It is important to note that, at this point Mr. and Mrs. C jointly decided voluntarily to withdraw from all extramarital sexual activity. They avoided the parties and the open suggestions for sexual activity. They resolved to develop their marriage and to return to the original monogamous marital contract.

Mr. and Mrs. D were moving very markedly in the direction of divorce, although they were attempting alternate solutions such as "We'll relate as though we are having an affair." That policy would allow either Mr. D or Mrs. D to spend weekends away, bring paramours home, maintain a separate apartment, and, in general, to develop a rather unusual marriage pattern. They had finally decided upon this "affair type marriage" and were planning to enact it. It was impossible for Mr. D to continue counseling because of his work schedule and termination seemed indicated for Mrs. D since she had achieved most of her initial goals. When Mr. and Mrs. D had entered counseling, they could have been described as a rather stodgy couple. Mr. D had been obese, sullen, and socially incompetent, while Mrs. D had been mousy, anxiety-ridden, and ineffectual as a parent. They now represented a strikingly handsome and poised couple with few moral scruples, a total lack of interest in marriage or their children, and a general ability to dominate any group of which they were members.

Mr. and Mrs. E were definitely on the road to divorce. What little cooperation Mr. E had contributed to his wife's and family's counseling had disintegrated. His behavior toward a new paramour had removed him from his family. Mrs. E, for the first time in her marriage, was developing confidence, poise, and direction in life. Like Mr. A, Mrs. B, and Mr. and Mrs. C, she had developed an adaptive set of social behaviors which enabled her to function with her children, friends, and community in an increasingly mature fashion. Her affair with Mr. Y was conducted maturely, in the sense that she was aware of consequences and limited future potential and had no plans to continue it beyond the exploratory stage. She was attempting to redefine herself as a woman and as a sexual partner and had chosen a good friend who was available and interested in such a relationship. The group was in the process of dissolving after its two-year build-up and its short period of frenzied sexual interaction. Plans for follow-up were made and contact was retained with the five couples wherever possible.

FOLLOW-UP

Diagram 10 represents the three-year follow-up on the five primary couples. For greater clarity the darker lines marked Number 12 indicate the events that took place after termination of counseling.

For Mr. and Mrs. A, marked changes had taken place in the direction of sexual contacts and in their relationship. As a divorced couple, they remained in close contact, Mr. A continuing to fulfill his obligations as a father. Interestingly enough, he had now become a friend to Mrs. A. His own sexual behavior, however, showed a marked change. He had engaged in a brief sexual affair with Mrs. D and was becoming active in a Parents without Partners group. He was now described by members of this new group (several of whom also came for counseling) as warm, understanding, and highly developed in social skills—a marked difference from his original behavior patterns. Mrs. A, on the other hand, was also engaging in many sexual affairs and was no longer following even her paramour contract. She was drinking intermittently but very heavily and, in general, floundering badly in a fashion similar to her premarital behavior (but not further complicated by the presence of her children). Mr. A was helping to support her both financially and with attempts at guidance and other help. Her relationship with Mr. X was now marked by many of the problems she had encountered with Mr. A and she had developed a subsidiary paramour using the same kind of justification she had used to alter her marriage contract. The looseness of her behavior patterns reflected the looseness of the contingencies under which she was operating.

The feed-back about Mrs. B came in the form of letters which were corroborated by letters to other members of the group. No direct follow-up was possible since she was unavailable for an interview. However, her reports indicated a series of sexual affairs of a heterosexual

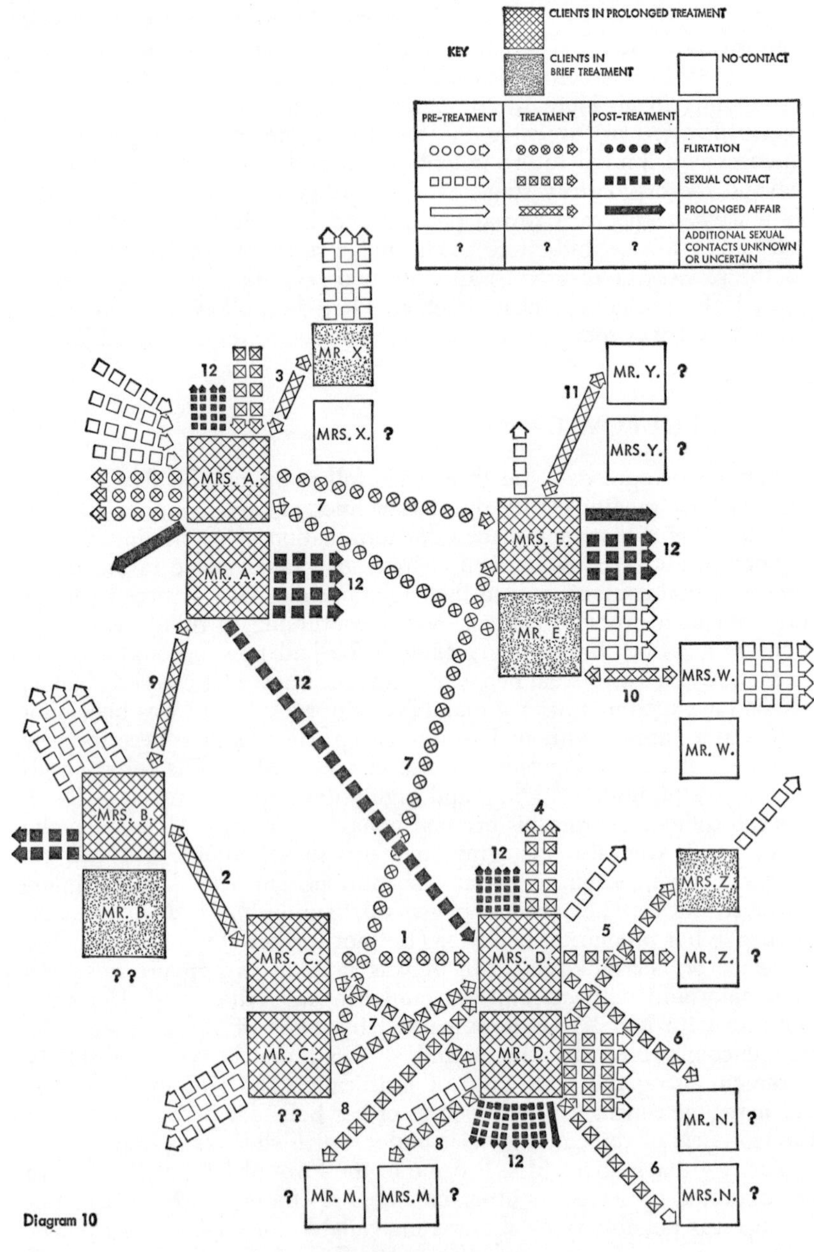
KEY
CLIENTS IN PROLONGED TREATMENT
CLIENTS IN BRIEF TREATMENT
NO CONTACT
PRE-TREATMENT
TREATMENT
POST-TREATMENT
FLIRTATION
SEXUAL CONTACT
PROLONGED AFFAIR
?
?
?
ADDITIONAL SEXUAL CONTACTS UNKNOWN OR UNCERTAIN
MR. X.
MRS. X. ?
12
3
MRS. A.
MR. A.
12
7
MR. Y. ?
MRS. Y. ?
11
MRS. E.
12
MR. E.
MRS. W.
10
MR. W.
9
12
MRS. B.
MR. B.
? ?
2
7
4
12
MRS. C.
1
MRS. D.
5
MRS. Z.
MR. Z. ?
MR. C.
7
MR. D.
6
? ?
8
8
12
MR. N. ?
6
MRS. N. ?
? MR. M.
MRS. M. ?

Diagram 10

nature and a continuation of the status quo of her marriage. Expectations were that the marriage was unstable so that it had to break up ultimately, although a follow-up after a three-year period, reported no change. There are additional factors that would prevent any steps toward divorce at this time and also, because of the family's present location, divorce would be very difficult.

Mr. and Mrs. C had achieved a much higher degree of marital interaction, a return to stable family life, continuation of their individual progress, and a definite absence of extramarital behavior of any sort on the part of Mrs. C. This was completely confirmed by other members of the group. Although no cross-confirmation could be obtained concerning Mr. C's lack of extramarital behavior, it is reasonable to assume that there was an absence of such behavior on his part, too. However, a question mark has been put on the diagram to indicate lack of confirmation.

Mr. and Mrs. D passed through a series of phases during which Mr. D developed an intense relationship with one paramour whom he used as an alternate wife. He became active nationally and internationally in a series of wife-swapping groups. A high-point of this activity was a six-week period during which he had intercourse with 30 different women. Considering the fact that Mr. D worked many long hours at a difficult work schedule this is indeed an indication of the extent to which his social behavior had been shaped to a high degree of effective dating and seductive patterns. Mrs. D also engaged in a variety of sexual contacts, although she formed no intense relationship during this period. Her interaction with group members was confined primarily to Mr. A since most of her social life had now moved in other directions. The ultimate outcome of these patterns and phases of Mr. D's and Mrs. D's behavior was divorce. The divorce action was friendly and quite unemotional, and resulted more from indifference and inconvenience than any other reason. This couple, perhaps, shows the most marked transition in conformity with the altered marriage contingencies. Their reports to the group and to the counselor contain the information that they had discovered other people very much like themselves in their new behavior patterns who "thought as they did."

Mr. and Mrs. E completed their divorce with much bitterness and increasingly bizarre behavior on the part of Mr. E. Mrs. E allowed herself a number of well-managed sexual interactions which involved more than physical sex. Of all of the women in this group, she seemed to have developed the most complex sexual patterns, in that her lovers were involved with her on many levels and sex was a secondary part of the relationship and not a primary one. She had developed an ongoing sexual relationship with an individual with whom she was building a lasting friendship, although there was no intention of marriage by either party. It seemed apparent that this relationship, while not likely to end in marriage, would be the stepping stone to a more effective remarriage for Mrs. E. Mr. E's relationship with his paramour had been stormy and bizarre, and at the time of follow-up had not culminated in marriage but had led to the establishment of a "secret love nest" which was open knowledge to all parties, including its location. Mr. E, however, would use elaborate precautions and pretenses to enter or leave the premises. This information was obtained from detective reports and from Mrs. E, who had hired the detectives. Mr. E's behavior without the support of the marriage contract (to which he had paid some lip service) continued to acquire more and more unusual and asocial characteristics.

Of the peripheral couples, the following information is known. The X's and the Y's remained in unstable marriage patterns, with no divorce but an explosive potential constantly present. According to reports from Mrs. A and Mrs. E, Mr. X and Mr. Y continue their dual life with a constant drifting toward greater and greater dissatisfaction and nearer and nearer to discovery by the two wives, Mrs. X and Mrs. Y. At the time of the three-year follow-up, however, there had been no divorce.

Mr. W and Mrs. W were divorced. Mr. W remained a good friend of Mrs. E although no sexual contact took place between them.

Mr. and Mrs. Z had come close to divorce but continued to make efforts at improving their marriage relationship, and like the C's, had decided on a return to the monogamous marriage contract. At the time of follow-up, their chances of salvaging their marriage seemed reasonably good.

Of the other identifiable peripheral couples, the M's and the N's, no information was obtainable concerning their present status. The many other individuals involved in this interactive network could not be followed up. The final diagram does not adequately reveal the number of other individuals and families touched by these five couples.

At the time of follow-up, partying among these five couples had ceased. Their social interaction had almost entirely disappeared except for well-defined and well-structured interactions which totally lacked the frenzy and sexual excitement so prevalent a few years earlier. The group itself had reflected the instability of its patterns and the contingencies which had brought it together had contained even then the seeds of the group's destruction.

Of the five primary couples, then, three had ended in divorce and one additional divorce was not unlikely. While no final generalization can be made from this limited sample, it appears to be clear that the independent variable was crucial in producing very marked and different patterns of sexual behavior in the social group studied, behavior which ultimately proved incompatible with a classic marriage relationship.

SUMMARY AND DISCUSSION

One purpose of this chapter was to introduce the language of behavioral psychology as applied to marriage behavior, in other words, to see if the more precise language of behavior modification could help to reduce the apparent complexities of human behavior in the marriage setting to enable better understanding of the interactive processes. The position is taken that behavior modification has much to contribute to the thinking of professionals working in the fields of marriage or divorce counseling. A few basic principles were reviewed as a prelude to the examination of some data accumulated over a five-year period concerning the changes in sexual patterns among five suburban couples. Since the modern behaviorist tries not to utilize mentalistic terms and avoids the types of labels which becloud the situation, the variables under study dealt with altered marriage contingencies and their effect on observable, emitted behaviors. As the dependent variable, the number of sexual contacts could be counted and, as the independent variable, the verbalizations of altered marriage contracts could also be observed and recorded. The diagrams revealed some of the changes in role and direction of sexual behavior over the five-year period. It is apparent that new behaviors were learned and old behaviors reduced in frequency and probability of occurrence. It is beyond the scope of this chapter to assess the total repertoires of these individuals, the signals which controlled their occurrences, and the complex positive consequences which maintained them. A thorough behavior analysis or assessment would be too extensive at this time. The data, however, which have been reported shed light on the prevalent notion among many laymen and professionals that extramarital sex could improve the nature of a marriage. The evidence here is overwhelmingly in the opposite direction and could have been predicted on the basis of learning principles. Many conclusions can be tentatively drawn from both the analysis of marriage as a contingency and the effects of alterations in the contingencies revealed in this study. The conclusions must remain tentative until further research. The tendency toward labeling on a global basis using such terms as personality, happy marriage, communication, alienation, and the like, tend only to becloud the issues. Substitution of concepts derived from operant conditioning and the applied field of behavior modification such as behavior repertoires, adaptive and unadaptive behaviors, frequency and probabilities of occurrence, and the scientific rules of functional relationships would greatly improve the usefulness and accuracy of future studies.

Individuals maintain in their repertoires previously learned behaviors and, like Mrs. A, may tend to reestablish them under similar contingencies of reinforcement although they may be, in a larger sense, quite unadaptive. The C's amply demonstrated that a return to original contingencies can bring about a return to original behaviors. But perhaps the most important conclusion revealed by this analysis is that extramarital behavior of any kind is strengthened and increased according to the acknowledged contingencies established by the partners. When mutual alteration of the marriage contingency occurs to the extent that extramarital sex is condoned and permitted, new patterns of behavior will arise. These patterns are most similar to the dating and seductive patterns of courtship, and their use over time seems to result in their intensification on a constantly accelerating basis. By virtue of their contradictory nature with stable marriage patterns, the conflict between the two repertoires will become of such a nature that either reduction of the alteration must take place to maintain the marriage or dissolution of the marriage in the form of divorce must ultimately occur. It does not appear possible, within our cultural setting, to maintain a marriage where extramarital sex is condoned and permitted. While rational arguments can be made for other forms of marriage relationships based on tribal patterns, polygamous marriages, or even new definitions of groupings, these must remain speculative until the actual effects of such contingencies can be studied over time. The "hippy" movement in the United States expresses an attempt to resolve and define old and new relationships among people. It would be interesting to examine the results of those altered contingencies in the same way in which this study was conducted, in order to compare both the resultant patterns of behavior and the stability of the relationships. The rules that define possible marital relationships, the behaviors that must be emitted for maximum success, and the sources and nature of effective reinforcement available need a great deal more empirical investigation. Much of the sophistry that passes as scientific reasoning is useless to the marriage consultant, who must help a couple toward resolution of marital conflict. Practical applications of the principles of behavior modification can lead toward direct and effective techniques not only usable by the professional marriage consultant but teachable to the marriage partners themselves. The process of behavioral architecture and behavioral engineering possible under effective self-management and self-determination by marital partners is the most exciting hope of the future development of marriage counseling. If the marriage counselor can teach the partners a simple language and a set of procedures and techniques for the establishment of effective marital behavior, a major reversal of the divorce rate and family break-up within our society may become possible. Furthermore, if the technology available today, which is based on the language and the principles of operant conditioning, were to be made available prior to marriage through some societal institution such as the schools, churches, or mass media, selection of partners could certainly be improved. Successful marriages are neither made in heaven nor produced by art. They are the result of fortuitous application of behavior principles in clearly examinable and specifiable ways that can be taught. It is always more difficult to teach new behaviors in the presence of competing unadaptive behaviors. It should be the goal of the professional to develop and teach the principles of self-management of effective marriage behaviors before unadaptive ones develop.

John F. Cuber

ADULTERY: REALITY VERSUS STEREOTYPE

Although there has been concern about adulterous relationships throughout history, this concern has been more moralistic than empirical, more hortatory than analytic. And even today, despite a pronounced verbal stance at being objective, there is still, even among the more scientific, a clear tendency to concentrate on negative aspects and to present them more vividly. At the same time, most analysts tend to underestimate the incidence of adulterous behavior and, perhaps worst of all, to overlook the enormous variations in adulterous experience with respect to its function in the lives of the participants, its relationship to marriage, and its impact on the mental health of the participants. Insofar as these dimensions have been given attention, that attention has been focused overwhelmingly on the narrowly sexual aspects of adultery; the effects on the marriage of the adulterous spouse have been presumed always to be destructive, and the effects on the mental health of all participants have been assumed to be deleterious. Probably the most categorical exception to the foregoing generalization has occurred among the literary artists who have at least sometimes portrayed the adulterous situation in holistic terms.

The chief basis for this paper has been a study of 437 distinguished white Americans between the ages of thirty-five and fifty-five who were studied through an intensive and unstructured depth interview technique. These people constituted a completely nonclinical sample, none having had psychotherapy in any form, or, in the opinion of the interviewers, clearly requiring it at the time of interview. It should be understandable that the use of such a "normal" population would show results quite different from the results taken from studies of adulterous behavior among persons in clinical situations or caught in life crises (1).

Throughout this study we did not concern ourselves with a *count* of the incidence of adulterous episodes. We were more concerned with context than with number. This was partly by intent and partly a result of the procedure which we chose to follow. We learned early that a mere count of adulterous behavior yields a useless, if not a seriously spurious, statistic because the concept of *adultery* is a moralistic-legalistic-theological one which lumps together heterogeneous and contradictory dimensions of behavior which, when treated together, can lead only to error. In such a category we would have the person who has had "one too many" at the office party, the one who "lives off the land" at every opportunity, the lecher in the literal sense of the word, as well as the one who feels mismated but trapped and finds warmth and comfort where he can, and the one whose marriage is so seriously destructive that he desperately seeks and clings to another meaningful relationship which sustains him. Such an encompassing category contributes nothing but a moralistic label which obscures more discriminating understanding of behavior.

I

Several important distinctions regarding adulterous behavior came to our attention. The first of these, which should have been anticipated from the more general studies of sexual deviation by Kirkendall (2), Reiss (3), and others, is to the general effect that there is an important qualitative difference between the sexual act which constitutes virtually the sum total of the interaction and coital behavior which takes place in the course of a more or less continuous, affectionately meaningful, totally companionable relationship. Despite a lifetime of attention to marital triangles in counseling situations, I have been surprised at the relatively high incidence of this latter type of relationship, sometimes lasting a decade or two, in the lives of these relatively self-actualized people. Aside from this latter comment, our study merely validates what other students have pointed out, namely, that this dichotomy is apparently a true one and that the behavioral dimensions of these two types are utterly different.

Since *The Significant Americans* was concerned with the whole man-woman world and only incidentally with the question of nonmarital sex, we were soon alerted to the relationship between adulterous behavior and marriage itself. Our data seemed to us to suggest strongly that there are at least three types of relationships between adulterous behavior and the marriage of one or both of the participants. In Type I the adulterous relationship simply compensates or substitutes for a defective marriage. By a defective marriage we mean that, *for the partner involved,* a judgment has been reached that the marriage is seriously frustrating or at least not fulfilling in some important dimension, and that the adulterous relationship compensates for whatever is missing, lacking, annoying, or hurtful in the marriage. We learned again the hard lesson, which behavior analysts always say they have learned and which their judgment often betrays they have not learned very well; namely, that reality is subjective to the actor. This is a very old point in behavior science, but, apparently, it has to be learned over and over again. For example, if a man says that his wife is frigid, it is of little practical use to point out to him that by technical definition she may not be so at all. As Cooley says, "The imaginations which people have of one another are the solid facts of human life." Another formulation of the same idea is that even mistaken judgment is real in its consequences. The standardizing principle for this type of adulterous relationship, then, is that the relationship with the spouse has some serious lack but not serious enough to terminate the marriage and that the other person compensates for the lack in a satisfactory manner. In a society which places so much emphasis upon the mere maintenance of an established marriage and exacts for so many people such serious sanctions for its termination, it is small wonder that so many maintain essentially loveless marriages and find their sexual and affectional fulfillments somewhere else. Qualitative analysis of long-term extramarital relationships shows that they are strikingly similar to good marriages in their psychological dimensions. There are strong emotional and sexual bonds, continuity in the relationship, monogamous sentiments, intense sharing of a variety of ideas and activities, and mutual emotional supports.

Type II is fairly well understood and probably constitutes a set of circumstances which people are most likely to "forgive." This is the behavioral configuration in which a married person of either sex experiences a discontinuous marriage in its face-to-face aspects. Discontinuities in our society typically result from long absence for military duty or extended periods of residence away from home in connection with career or profession. It is startling to realize how many millions of Americans live for prolonged periods in foreign countries in connection with their professional and occupational roles. And, of course, there are the periods of travel for recreational purposes—particularly where both husband and wife are employed and, sometimes by intent, extended vacations are taken separately. Under these conditions, we found that substantial numbers of contemporary Americans of the upper middle class consider themselves freed from the bonds of monogamy for the duration of their absence from home, although the expectation in such a case is that the encounter be a relatively brief one and not a sustained, meaningful relationship which may threaten the marriage.

In Type III we find the true Bohemians. These are people who simply do not accept the monogamous commitment with respect to their personal lives, although they still feel committed to and fulfilled in marriage and parenthood (4). If this sounds like the old double standard, it should quickly be added that we found that *if* there is a double standard in the upper middle class today, it is not so much between men and women as between the more Bohemian men and women and the other men and women.

II

A prevailing preoccupation, again rooted in folklore but also present among professionals with a primarily clinical experience, is with the effects of adulterous behavior on the spousal relationship. Here again, some distinctions must be made at the outset. It matters enormously (a) in the first place, whether the adultery is carried on furtively or is known to the spouse; (b) whether the married partners agree to the propriety or expediency of such behavior; (c) whether one or both participates; and (d) whether the condonement is genuine and based on principle or is simply the result of an ultimatum by one of the two parties. Despite all the possible permutations, a few generalizations from our data appear to be defensible. These are mostly counter-generalizations in the sense that they call into question some almost universally assumed propositions about the effects of adulterous behavior on marriage. The first of these is that the assumption that such behavior is necessarily furtive does not square with the facts. A considerable number of spouses have "levelled" with their mates, who cooperate in maintaining a public pretense of monogamous marriage. We have found a number of truly empathic spouses of this sort, and others, as would be expected, who merely reluctantly go along and say that they are surprised at how good their marital relations continue to be, even though there is involvement with another person. This leads to a second generalization counter to the notion that such triangles are *necessarily* destructive of the marriage. Not so. Both for cases in which the spouse knew about the affair and where the affair was secret, we can document with a long list instances in which the spousal relationship remains at least as good qualitatively as within the average pair without adultery. It is a common mistake, when a couple with a poor sex life is seen clinically, to assume that if one or the other had not been adulterous the sex relationship would have been better. Yet, it is widely known among professionals that abysmally poor sexual adjustment can exist and endure in the completely monogamous marriage. Our study, incidentally, richly documents the latter point.

A different comparison involves the sexual relationships between the married partners before the adultery and afterward. Here again, we found all three theoretical possibilities—sometimes the marital sexual relationship deteriorated, sometimes it improved, and sometimes it remained unchanged. Differences among these three categories seemed not great enough to warrant any comparisons other than making the important point that adultery does not *necessarily* result in deteriorated spousal relations. We found the same for the more total aspects of the spousal relationship—all three possible outcomes occur in fact and none is rare.

A related concern has to do with the effect of adulterous behavior upon the mental health and functioning of either or both of the participants, as well as upon the spouse concerned. Here again, we have inherited a morbid legacy which vigorously asserts that because of the guilt and deception involved for the participants and the feelings of humiliation and rejection experienced by the spouse, the net effect is necessarily negative to mental health. The evidence presented is invariably from clinical cases and here is probably the source of the stereotype. People who have the same experiences as the clinical cases but who don't come to "bad ends" aren't included in the sample under surveillance. Our non-clinical sample would justify almost the opposite conclusion, although not without exception by any means. Overwhelmingly, these people expressed no *guilt* with respect to what they were doing, although sometimes they acknowledged *regret* over practical consequences. The "offended" spouses were often not offended at all; sometimes they were even relieved to be "out from under" a relationship which was personally frustrating and, because of the adultery, they were able to maintain the marriage for other reasons. We were struck by the sizeable group of people who were involved in adulterous relationships of many years standing, who were enriched and fulfilled through the relationship in much the same way that intrinsically married people are, whose health, efficiency, and creativity remain excellent—many of these pairings are in effect *de facto* marriages.

The dynamics of adulterous relationships also break with conventional stereotypes about them which generally run to assertions that such relationships typically follow a cycle which begins in infatuation, has a relatively short decline, ends in disillusionment, a new partner is found, and the cycle is repeated. We found examples fitting this model, to be sure, but typically the cases were otherwise. The most conspicuous contrast is, of course, the brief, emotionally uninvolved "sexcapade," commonly known as the "pickup." There is no cycle; partners are typically relative strangers, even names may not be known; neither expects any continuity or wants it. And even in the prolonged adulterous relationships, there is often no more a "cycle" than there is to marriage—the relationship often is monogamous, continuous "until death . . ." Where there is a cycle in any real sense, it tends to be like the cycle in a goodly number of marriages. In both cases relationships move from vitality and a strong erotic accent to a more matter-of-fact, comfortable kind of interaction. Surprisingly enough, many "affairs" have settled into a kind of apathy which makes one wonder why they go on, since there are no institutional obligations involved. But perhaps sentiment and a quiescent kind of attachment may be stronger bonds than external social sanctions.

It is a moot question to what extent the long standing adulterous relationships are vulnerable because one or the other may find a new partner. We certainly would be disinclined to make any sweeping generalizations other than to point out that such a conclusion from our data would indeed be riskful. When speaking about quality rather than the mere fact of continuity, all relationships, marital or otherwise, are vulnerable. To assert that either is more susceptible than the other is to go beyond the data.

III

Perhaps the most important theoretical overall generalization which our study supports is the great heterogeneity masked in the monolithic word "adultery." A companion generalization points up the strong parallels between the structure, the functions, the fulfillments and the frustrations of enduring adulterous relationships on the one hand and married relationships on the other. While there are differences, to be sure—if nothing else the grudging public tolerance of the former—still the bases for attraction, the satisfactions derived, the rewards and punishments involved are remarkably parallel.

Yet adulterous relationships in this culture at this time must operate within a network of obvious threat. Even if there is tolerance as far as spouses and friends are concerned, such relationships are still illegal and, although the law is rarely invoked, no one knows when some freak of fate may force an exposure which no one intended. Then there is the risk of pregnancy which, even with present contraceptive know-how, is not completely eliminated. Persons who are quite tolerant of sexual freedom may not be tolerant with respect to reproduction outside the limits of marriage. While we found much less evidence of the double standard than we expected, one aspect showed up importantly in the adulterous relationship, namely, the feelings of "second-class" status on the part of the "other woman." Social sanctions are still more austere where women are concerned and, of course, women bear the brunt of the burden of illicit pregnancy. It is not wholly clear from our data whether this sensitivity on the part of women derives from the differential pregnancy risk and more austere social sanctions or whether it runs more deeply into female psychology, but unless she has satisfactory extrinsic gratifications in her legal and open status, it seems difficult for her to be totally satisfied by the intrinsic aspects of her clandestine relationship.

Because of the absence of institutional buttressing of the long-term adulterous relationship, it is more easily terminated, on the average, than is marriage. This may be comforting to the moralist, but the person with a concern for mental health should take little comfort from it. Other aspects of our study have documented the enormously high incidence of psychologically destructive relationships in enduring marriages and the intrusion of utilitarian motives in the establishment and perpetuation of conspicuously unfulfilling relationships in which people many times feel trapped and helpless to escape. So, while the adulterous relationships are, on the average, less enduring than the marriages, this is counter-balanced by the fact that the long-term ones are, on the average, more psychologically fulfilling than marriage. This is not because there is any strange alchemy involved in adulterous mating for any but a few romantics. Rather, it results from the fact that spousal relationships are maintained in homage to monolithic expectations, because society values mere *endurance* of marriages, even if they are psychologically unsatisfying, frustrating, and destructive. Adulterous relationships carry no such burden of expectation; when they endure, they do so for reasons intrinsic to the pair.

References

1. Cuber, John F., and Harroff, Peggy B. *The Significant Americans: A Study of Sexual Behavior among the Affluent.* New York: Appleton-Century-Crofts, Inc., 1965, (especially Chapter 8, "Other Involvements").
2. Kirkendall, Lester A. *Premarital Intercourse and Interpersonal Relationships.* New York: The Julian Press, 1961.
3. Reiss, Ira L. *Premarital Sexual Standards in America.* Glencoe, Ill.: The Free Press, 1960.
4. Wilson, J. B., with Meyers, Everett. *Wife Swapping: A Complete Eight-year Survey of Morals in North America.* New York: Counterpoint, Inc., 1965.

Gerhard Neubeck

CONCLUSIONS

What lies in the future? Much depends on the degree to which commitment to marriage and family can go hand in hand with the commitment to the executive life of spouses—the commitment of both husbands and wives to careers, whether they are meaningful or not. Spouses whose partners are more committed to their occupations than to their marriages are deprived of what they bargained for and may turn to outside interests. While it is not necessary that these interests be other persons, it is likely that their longings will find quantitative and qualitative satisfaction (perhaps in the form of a love relationship) if they look for it. Our society is wide open for it.

Value judgments as to the preferable commitment will not be made here. But it is clear that the demands of work often interfere with family demands, and, alas, something has to give. Either needs and expectations will have to be down-scaled, or arrangements will have to be made that allow third parties to enter the marital relationship. This will call for an entirely different conditioning toward marriage, where from early childhood on, mother and father are not seen and considered to be the only persons relating to each other, and where third parties are included in the life of the family as a matter of course. Adultery, of course, is illegal and has provided grounds for divorce. But mores are ahead of laws and a person who, in the legal sense, would be a correspondent, in the private sphere would become a co-relator. In a sense, solutions to the obtainment of love can be put in hierarchical order, and one might facetiously suppose that extramarital relations are higher up on the scale than incest or masturbation, that extramarital relations are the lesser of the "evils."

This family where husband and wife are not exclusive partners would be more like an extended family where members share in and interchange functions. The question remains, whether it is possible for individuals to be conditioned to this sort of life. Institutionalization will eventually follow, but what is still to come on a wholesale basis is the acceptance of a non-exclusive relationship.* (Refer to the chapter, "The Dimensions of the 'Extra' in Extramarital Relations," in which I proposed to view extramarital relations not as replacing a set of satisfactions but as in addition to or supplementing what the existing relationship offers.) Can we learn to understand that it is possible to love more than one person, to be loved by more than one person? Can we accept that? What it will mean is a reshaping of the total culture so that even the young child in the beginning of the socialization and conditioning processes can learn this idea of non-exclusive love. As a growing person, then, he will be able to see a third party other than as one providing a stab in the back, and by not reading sinister competitive notions into that kind of addition.

But I am realistic enough to see that the day of such an ideology is not just around the corner. The moment has come, however, to open up these possibilities for discussion. There is evidence (see Pomeroy's remarks above) that some people have achieved this wide open stance. Books such as *Ways of Growth* which have illustrated expanding experience seem to indicate that there is a move in the culture to experiment with forms of behaviors that have been taboo up to this point. One thing certainly can be said for these mutually agreeable couples; they are not behaving *sub rosa,* in a continuous practice of deceit, as so many couples do. Are we then headed for a society in which extramarital relationships will not occur in a clandestine fashion, but where married couples will make conscious choices, to be or not to be monogamous?

The "games-people-play" strategies and counter-strategies used to gain attention, love, and excitement, may no longer be needed. People may explore together what in quantity and quality the marital relationship can stand in regard to additional relations. Forsaking all others has never been a realistic expectation, and, based on the assumption that there always will be others, couples can explore what the possibilities for themselves and each other should be: when, where, and how the additional individuals can be incorporated into the basic and nourishing unit. They must change more overtly so that their marriages will permit them to be less exclusive. We need to learn from long term follow-up studies if such marriages do survive, and in what way. In addition to these couples, of course, we have marriages that suffer from chronic philandering. That is to be expected, as it is clear that

* Herbert A. Otto and John Mann, *Ways of Growth* (New York: Grossman Publishers, 1968).

people with essentially nonconforming personalities will always give expression to that kind of restlessness and rebelliousness.

The search for love: that is the question. As much as monogamous marriage can provide the answer for this search, there will always be an answer available outside of it. That seems to be a realistic appraisal of the situation.

INDEX

D

E

F

G